BHAGWAN SHREE RAJNEESH
HAMMER ON THE ROCK

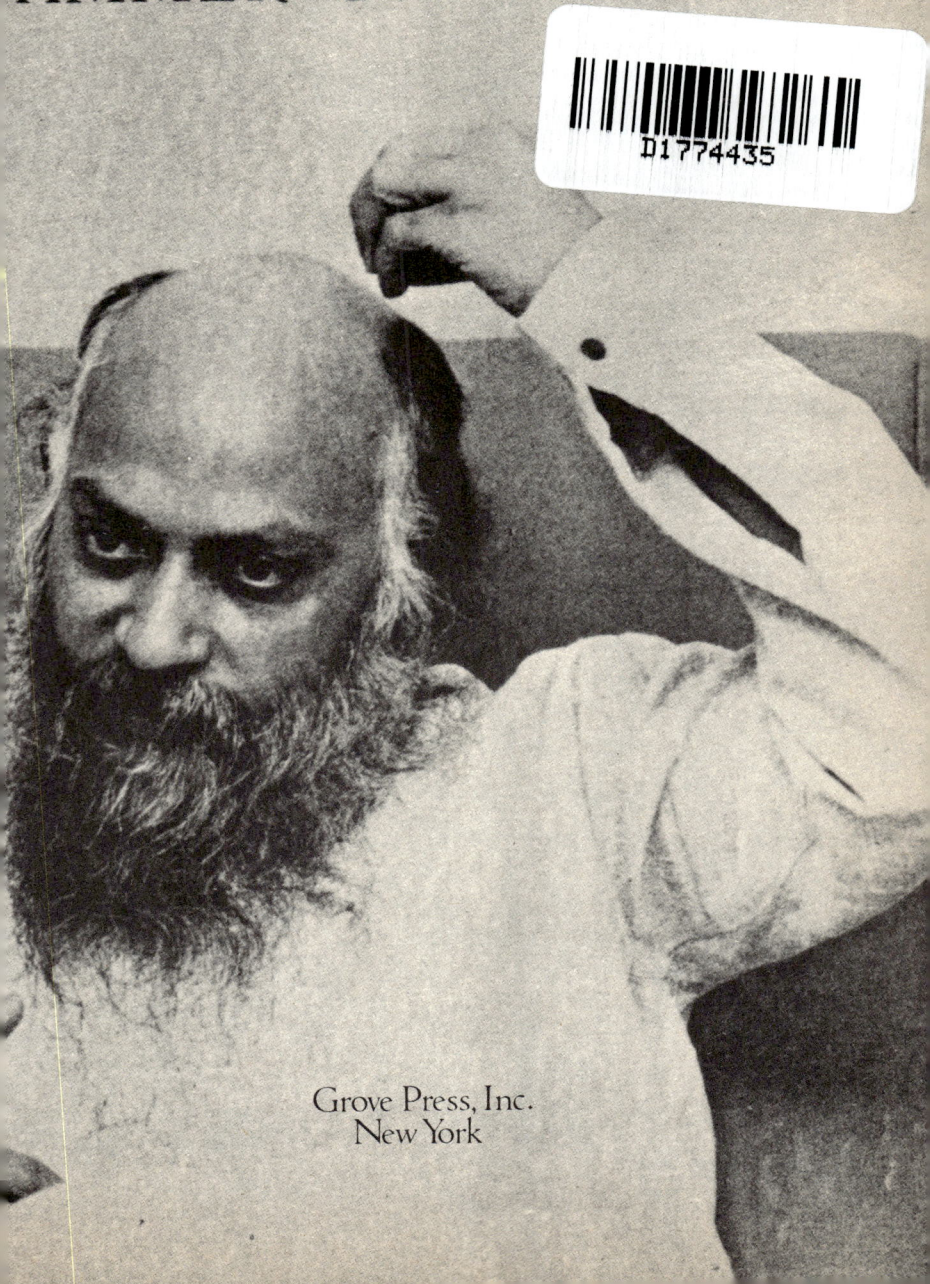

Grove Press, Inc.
New York

PHOTOGRAPHS BY SWAMI SHIVA MURTI; COMPILATION,
EDITING AND COMMENTARY BY MA PREM MANEESHA

Copyright © 1976 Rajneesh Foundation

All Rights Reserved

No part of this book may be reproduced, for any reason, by any means, including any method of photographic reproduction, without the permission of the publisher.

First Evergreen Edition 1979
First Printing 1979
ISBN: 0-394-17090-3
Grove Press ISBN: 0-8021-4260-5
Library of Congress Catalog Card Number: 79-52012

LIBRARY OF CONGRESS CATALOGING IN PUBLICATION DATA

Rajneesh, Acharya, 1931–
Hammer on the rock.

Reprint of the ed. published by Rajneesh Foundation, Poona, India.
1. Spiritual life. I. Prem Maneesha, Ma.
II. Title.
BL624.R332   1979   291.4   79-52012
ISBN 0-394-17090-3

Manufactured in the United States of America

Distributed by Random House, Inc., New York

GROVE PRESS, INC., 196 West Houston Street,
New York, N.Y. 10014

HAMMER ON THE ROCK
HAMMER ON THE ROCK
HAMMER ON THE ROCK
HAMMER ON THE ROCK
HAMMER ON THE ROCK
HAMMER ON THE ROCK
HAMMER ON THE ROCK
HAMMER ON THE ROCK
HAMMER ON THE ROCK
HAMMER ON THE ROCK
HAMMER ON THE ROCK
HAMMER ON THE ROCK
HAMMER ON THE ROCK
HAMMER ON THE ROCK
HAMMER ON THE ROCK
HAMMER ON THE ROCK
HAMMER ON THE ROCK

Also by Bhagwan Shree Rajneesh
Published by Grove Press

MY WAY: THE WAY OF THE WHITE CLOUDS

PROLOGUE

Time: Evening, on a day in December.
Setting: The porch of a large house on the outskirts of Poona, a town in India. The house looks onto a large expanse of lawn which is bordered by shrubs and trees and flowers. A bougainvillaea creeper sprawls luxuriantly over a fence — a splash of red and white, orange and purple among the green foliage.

As the curtain rises, we see on the porch of the house, a large easy chair in which a man is sitting. He is dressed completely in white. We are immediately drawn to him; he seems to radiate a grace and a serenity that is other-worldly, yet there is a sense of down-to-this-earth-ness, too. He carries a feeling of at-oneness with his surroundings, a rapport with the trees and flowers which we almost feel are standing, blossoming, shedding their leaves, and raising their flowery heads for him; are rejoicing in him, and in an inexplicable sense are protecting him, sheltering him.

His beauty has something of their world. His large soft eyes, his grey-white flowing beard, the delicate quality of his face, his slender hands in repose, are reminiscent somehow of a beautiful tree, in which strength and fragility combine.

He gazes at the garden before him, sometimes closing his eyes for several seconds. His hands are delicately folded together, a finger occasionally tapping on his hand as if in rhythm with a harmony that only he is hearing. Now and then he addresses a remark to a woman dressed in orange sitting by his side.

We move to the gate of the house which is some distance from the porch and on the other side of the building . . .

A small group of twenty or so people, orange-clad, are gathering. There are Indians and westerners of varying ages: a small girl with her mother, an indian family — grandparents, children, uncle and aunt too — an elderly couple — westerners — with a girl who appears to be their daughter, and some men and women in their twenties and thirties. They are sannyasins — disciples of a man they know as Bhagwan, Bhagwan Shree Rajneesh. They speak quietly together; but a sense of excitement surrounds them.

Among the group is a figure, dressed not in the orange of sannyas, but in blue jeans and tee-shirt. He has come to Poona in his search for a master, having already done the rounds of gurus, fakirs, pundits, yogis and magicians. Though from some he has caught a glimpse of what he seeks, still he remains discontent.

One guru, though he seemed rare, beautiful, 'high', his teachings were of the past and unrelated to the herenow of this seeker. Another was confusing, for he spoke of attaining without a master yet had a collection of ardent followers around him. Another still, spoke one thing and lived another. One said that fifteen minutes meditation was the key—yet the seeker saw no inner transformation in those with whom he meditated and talked. Another whom he had discovered almost by chance, buried deep in the Himalayas, had said that renunciation was the only way: deny love, the family, and things of this world, in favour of the other.

This man Rajneesh seems unlike any of these, from what the seeker has heard—and he has caught wind of him both in the West and in his travels throughout India. He has read some of his books, has even joined some sannyasins on a beach early one morning to do their meditation—chaotic meditation they call it. A man who can devise a meditation like this must be worth a visit.

It seems difficult to pigeon-hole him though, in spite of all he has heard. He seems to be a mixture of Zen and Tantra, Sufism and Yoga, Buddha and Zarathustra, Krishna, Christ, and Lao Tzu. His seems to be a pathless path. Certainly his ashram is unlike any other he has visited . . .

There is an air of movement here, of vitality. Sannyasins stroll in and out of the gates, someone comes careering in on his bicycle . . . a child has fallen over and is calling for its mother . . . a sannyasin passing pauses, goes to her, picks her up—her tears are forgotten. A group of sannyasins are sitting together with cups of tea, playing a guitar . . . someone sits alone, brooding . . . a couple greet each other effusively.

The seeker returns his gaze to the group with whom he is standing. This is to be his first darshan with Bhagwan Shree. He has been told that Bhagwan spends an hour or so every evening talking with his sannyasins or with visitors, answering questions concerning meditation, relationships, work—in fact almost anything related to their lives; not just a collection of interesting theories . . .

The seeker comes to with a start as his name is called among those of the others waiting. They pass through the gates and make their way slowly down the driveway, crunching pleasantly on the gravel in the stillness of the now darkening evening. Turning the corner of the driveway, they enter the porch where the man is sitting . . .

Some of the sannyasins glance quickly up at him before bending down to remove their shoes; others hurriedly shuffle out of their sandals and move towards the man, smiling—some tentatively, shyly. Others, perhaps seeing their master for the first time in many months, immediately kneel before him, then look up at him as they take their places on the floor in front of him—their faces flushed, and bodies trembling with emotion; eyes soft, love-ful, a sense of relief, of having come home, around them.

The man is smiling warmly, addresses a remark to a sannyasin, chuckles occasionally, pausing in his words of greeting to place his hand on the head of a kneeling sannyasin, in blessing. The seeker holds back a little, unsure of the etiquette of greeting this man, yet already feeling drawn to him, to his aura of total let-go. He takes his place unobtrusively behind the others.

The small girl, her arm casually resting in her mother's lap, watches the man, absorbed for a time in his face, his laughter . . . he looks like God must look.

The group bursts out in laughter from time to time as the man recounts an anecdote; now feigning a look of disbelief, now of outrage on his face, his hands moving in accompaniment. He seems to be talking to each person just for him, to where he is at. He talks of love, of total acceptance of oneself, of the beauty of spontaneity, of living life to the full, of the celebration, the festival, that life is. And not just his words speak; his very presence conveys the essence of what he is saying; he is love, he is total acceptance, spontaneity, celebration.

His words are pure poetry and yet are free of any affectation; spontaneous flowing words seem to pour from him, arranging themselves of their own accord in such a way that they shower the ear of the listener, caressing him with their beauty while penetrating him in their depth. . .

The seeker begins to relax. This man has something familiar about him. He immediately feels he can be himself with him. He is motioned forward, and suddenly, unbelievably, he is at the feet of Bhagwan Shree. He feels a curiosity, a confusion; questions of half an hour ago have fled. For the first time in his life he has nothing to say—he can find no question, yet senses this man to be the answer.

He hears himself being asked if he would like to take sannyas. His heart beats wildly—yet he feels a curious calmness as he closes his eyes and waits to receive his sannyas name. . . . He opens his eyes and gazes for a minute or two into the seemingly fathomless eyes of Bhagwan, his master.

He returns to his place, Bhagwan's words still with him—to change to orange, to use his new name . . .

'and now I will be with you. Drop the past . . . this is a new beginning . . .'

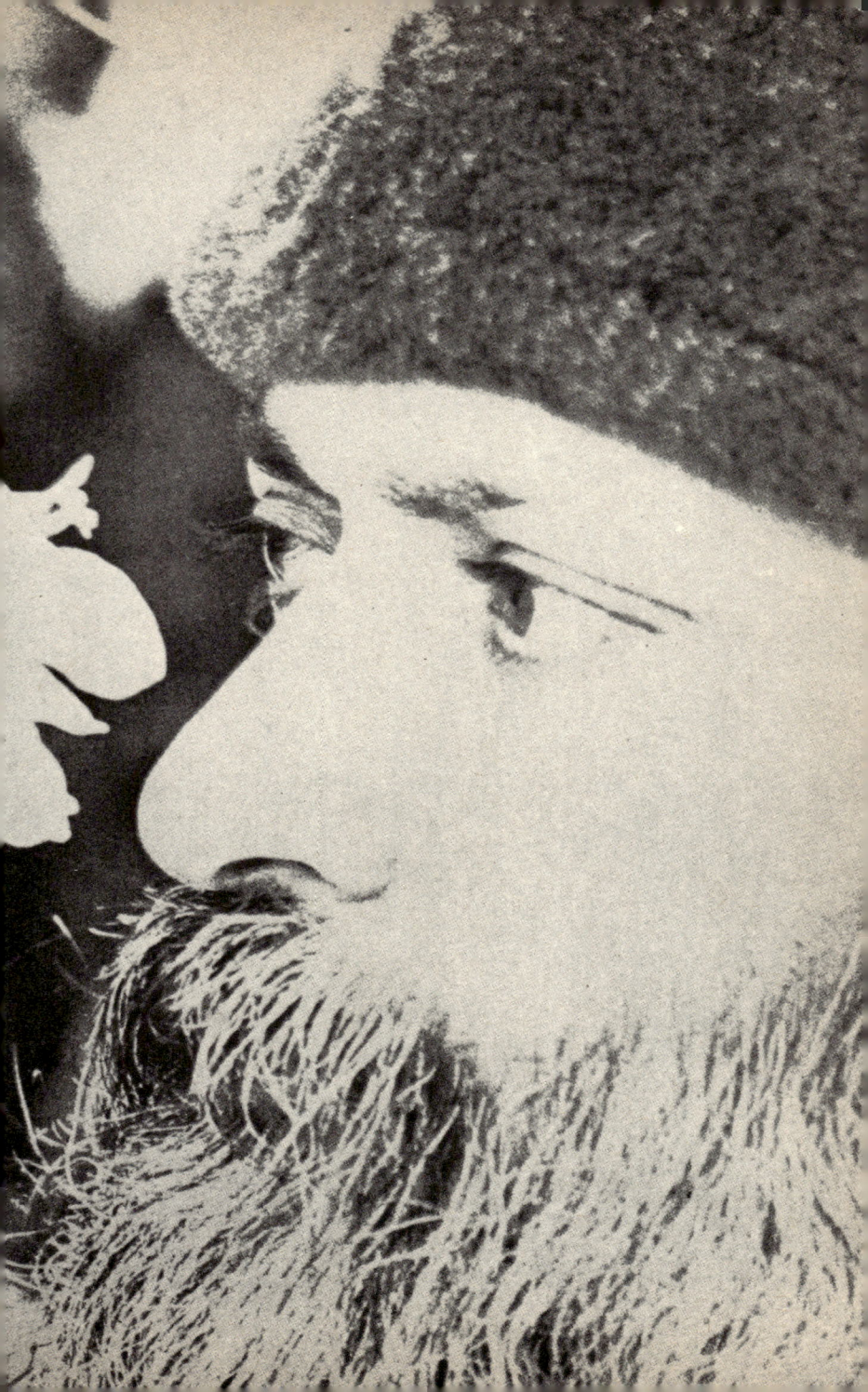

WEDNESDAY, DECEMBER 10th

    This evening, members of the Tathata group (Unconditional Acceptance Seminar), had darshan. Each of the therapy groups available in the ashram has the opportunity, once during the course of the group, to bring to Bhagwan Shree their individual and shared experiences, and to discuss insights gained and blocks encountered.
    The Tathata group aims to help individuals to learn to accept themselves and others, unconditionally, as they are. The process, the duration of which is anything from twenty-two to twenty-five hours, involves much physical and mental exertion. This brings the participants to a point of complete fatigue, in an effort to facilitate the dropping of defences and masks, so that people can face themselves and others honestly and authentically.

HAMMER ON THE ROCK

BHAGWAN (to the groupleader)   Pujari, come here. You have something special to say about the group? Then I will start talking to you.

PUJARI

> *The group was very together. It had a lot more energy, I felt, than the last group and this made it more intense. I went through a lot, as usual—not knowing what I'm doing at certain points. But again, I was satisfied with the results.*

It has to be remembered that the leader is not, in fact, a manipulator. He should not be. If you manipulate, then it is something from the mind, and that which comes from the mind cannot go deeper than the mind. So the leader has to be open to the beyond.

In the beginning the mind will be there. By and by lose it so you are possessed. That's the right word—you are possessed. Then you are no longer there. Something greater than you, something bigger than you, has taken possession. Then you do something, but you are not the doer; then something happens, but you are simply a witness to it. Then the leader is lost, and once the leader is lost, the real leader enters in. When the leader is no longer there then you become part of the group. Then those who are being led by you are not separate; no duality exists. Once the leader is possessed, the duality disappears. Then the teacher and the taught are one. The physician and the patient are one. Only then, and only then, healing is possible. And it is not only that you are healing them; you are also being healed through the process.

BE OPEN TO THE BEYOND

Until a group becomes an enrichment to the leader also, how can it be enriching to those who are being led? Unless you grow through it, how can you help others to grow? So be possessed. And that is one of the most difficult things, mm? The mind wants to manipulate, control, move on a fixed pattern. You can move on a fixed pattern, but then nothing special will ever happen. People may be helped, they may attain something through it, but the whole thing will remain on the surface, and technological. Love will be missing. And God will not be there. So allow yourself to be possessed.

You can do this: whenever you start the group, close your eyes and allow your whole group to surround you. Let them hold hands and start by a prayer. The prayer should be silent, just an opening—that God should possess you and you should not in any way be manipulating or controlling others. And you withdraw, and immediately you will see an energy entering, and there will be a tremendous change, an infinite power, inexhaustible. Allow it.

Then each group will be a new opening, a new door, a new experience. You have never been there before, it is a new space—not only for those you are leading, but for you also. There will be many surprises. And unless it happens, sooner or later the leader is bound to become dull and bored—because it is a repetition. The members will be changing; they will be new again and again. For them it may be new, but for you it becomes just the old pattern. Never make it that way. This is possible only if you become possessed and you allow the infinite energy to move. It needs trust, it needs dying of the ego.

So remember me. Each time you start the group, remember me—and leave it to me. You simply become a vehicle and the possibility is tremendous. Then you will be more able to help people because you are not there, so nobody hinders. When the leader is there, the led also feels a resistance—the ego fight enters. When you are not there, things become very simple and easy. So this has been good. But always remember—by and by you remove yourself. And then you become a worthy vessel of many many things. Good, Pujari.

PUJARI *I have a few more questions . . . one is about patience. I've always had a problem with patience and I've been impatient a lot. Sometimes I feel it is good because I get moving, sometimes I feel it hinders me being impatient.*

Be patient with your impatience. If it is there, it is there. Don't create a problem out of it, accept it. That too is an ego game—that you should not be impatient. Why? If one is, one is! Relax into it, use it. This is my understanding: that everything can be used, everything can become creative.

So it is not a question of whether impatience should be there or not. The question is how to use it if it is there, and if it is not there, then how to use the absence. Both can be used. Impatience simply shows energy—energy which is seeking pathways, energy which doesn't know what to do, energy which is so much that it is overflowing. Don't take a negative attitude about it—nothing is wrong in it. Be impatient and very patient. Allow it, use it, and soon you will see that even impatience has become a flowering.

Impatience can become an intensity, and it is if you take it rightly. It is a deep concern. When you are working on somebody and you are impatient, it simply shows that you love, that you are concerned, that you don't want to waste time and energy. . . . It shows that although you know everything is close by, this man is still missing. Jesus is impatient, very impatient, and that is the source of his tremendous attraction. Use impatience—it is energy, it is vitality.

Never label things negatively. If anger is there, use it: Be angry lovingly. And it is not a contradiction. It looks, appears, paradoxical, but it is not—in existence it isn't. In fact in existence you are only angry when you love someone. If I love you, care about you, sometimes I will have to be angry. But behind that anger there will be love. Behind the curtain, love will be hiding. Anything else?

PUJARI   *Yes. I've felt more surrendered to you since I've been here, and I feel ready just to do . . .*

Mm mm, every day you will feel it more and more, because it is a journey that starts but never ends. When you say you are surrendered to me it is just a beginning. And it is always a beginning, because more and more is possible. So infinitely more is possible than you can conceive. Every time you come you will feel more and more surrendered. The more you surrender, the more you will feel capable of surrendering.

One learns through doing—there is no other way. You go to the river and start to learn swimming. The more you swim, the more you know. Surrender is moving into the depth of consciousness, it is a swimming. The more you do, the more you know. The more you know, the more adventures will open to you, and the more challenges there will be. And I will be giving more and more challenges to you.

PUJARI *So you want me to go home at the end of these three months?*

I want you to go home, mm? I would like a few people to continuously come and go.

Whenever you feel a little tired, come back. Whenever you feel you will need a little nourishment, come back. Whenever you feel you have been missing me, come back. Feed on me — and go back. . .

FEED ON ME

(to the assistant leader) Now, you have something to say? Come here.

GOPUR

> *I thought this group was much better than the last—more intensity, more driving. That was good.*

Work as if you are almost mad. As I feel it, you still hold much, you don't go into it totally, and you remain on the periphery. You always keep a space where you can withdraw if things become too much. Whenever you move, always break the bridges that you have crossed so there is no possibility of moving back. When you have reached a height, throw the ladder. So either you have to go ahead or you have to die, but you cannot go back! Never create the situation that whenever you want, you can withdraw within yourself. No, then you will not become a real leader—and I would like you to become one.

To be an assistant is one thing, because you work like a shadow, and the responsibility is not on you. But once you become a leader, the whole responsibility is on you—and then just half/half won't help. Explode, and explode one hundred percent. Just by your explosion people will be helped. When a group sees that you are half-hearted, they will not even be half-hearted. They will only be twenty-five percent if you are fifty percent. The group will go only half the limit that the leader goes. You have to boil one hundred percent so you start evaporating. Only then will they have courage to move with you.

The whole point of all therapies, of all group processes,

is to create a situation where people can dare —
that's all. How you create that is irrelevant. You give
them an impetus and a challenge. You open an abyss
before them, and you tempt them to jump. The group is
needed because when they are alone they will never dare,
they will be much too afraid.

But when they see that one can jump and still be alive
— and not only that, but more alive than ever; when they
see that the abyss is not death but life abundant; when
they see that one who has opened has gained something,
has not lost anything, but has become richer and more
vital — then they start daring. One dares and another
follows, then somebody else, and then it becomes a
simple thing, a very simple phenomenon. But then you
have to be courageous yourself. So next group, you dare
as much as you can. And there is no excess in it. Whatsoever
you do will be always less than can be done. Good.

Bhagwan turns to another group member. . .

ASHVAGHOSHA *I've just done the group as you suggested. . . . I feel that I'm much more open now, and I feel part of what's happening around me. I've also found that my emotions are going to the extremes very often — in just a day even.*

IF YOU CANNOT WEEP, YOU CANNOT LAUGH

Allow them, because your whole life you have been suppressing them. So allow them and soon the extremities will disappear. It is as if somebody has been fasting for a few days and then you invite him for a feast. He goes on and on eating, and he eats too much—to the point where he starts vomiting. But this cannot continue every day. If he is allowed to eat, soon things will settle.

The whole of humanity exists starved, starved of a thousand and one things. Love has not been allowed; sex has not been allowed; anger has not been allowed. Laughter has not been allowed and crying has not been allowed. Man is crippled so much that it is a sheer miracle he continues to exist. Why isn't every man mad? — that is a very pertinent question. The question is not why a few people are mad, but why everybody is not mad. The whole situation is such that when you laugh for the first time after many years, or even after many lives, the laughter goes to the very extreme. Repressed so long, it explodes. If you cry and weep, then the tears go on and on, and there seems to be no end to it. But allow it and soon things will settle, because to be extreme is not the way of nature.

The way of nature is exactly the middle, the golden mean. Nature always balances. But if things are suppressed, the mind starts creating an imbalance, and to balance it you have to move to the other extreme. So for a few days, it may not be for long, for a few days, allow whatsoever happens and be in it. And don't try to think of ideals. For example, if you are crying and weeping and tears are coming, don't ask yourself what people will think. They have been telling you from the very childhood not to be a sissy, be a man; that this is okay for girls, but not for boys; be hard and a toughy.

So one becomes a toughy and then loses the tender heart. One loses the quality of crying which is tremendously beautiful. Eyes which cannot cry, cannot know what poetry is; and a heart which cannot weep, cannot know what mystery is. And if you cannot weep, you cannot laugh—they go together, as two aspects of one coin. So if you suppress crying and weeping, you will suppress laughter. At the most you smile—and that smile also seems to be painted, posed, manipulated, as if you are doing something. It is not like a flower that is coming from within and is opening. It is something forced from the outside, a head thing.

In this world you are not here to fulfill anybody's expectations. The one responsibility, and the only responsibility, is to become yourself, to realise who you are. And that is possible only if you realise all the potentialities that you carry within—unrepressed, open, floating.

Do something right now . . . close your eyes, and allow something that you have never allowed before. . . .

THINGS WILL BALANCE BY THEMSELVES

Bhagwan shone his small pencil torch on the chest of the sannyasin — who was kneeling in front of him, his head bowed. After a few seconds the sannyasin let out a short loud scream, then slowly raised his head to look at Bhagwan.

Good, mm? Very good. For three weeks be completely crazy, and after three weeks things will balance by themselves. The experience has been good. You could at least do something. (Bhagwan smiled at him warmly.) Good . . .

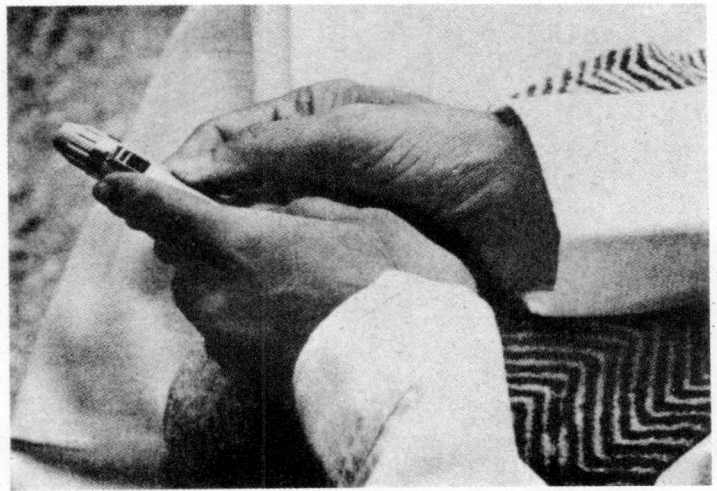

HAMMER ON THE ROCK

Rishi, how are you?

RISHI   *Pretty shaken up! I had a strong experience of the limitations I was casing myself in. I was jumping, but I was still hanging onto my parachute — but at least I was jumping more.*

(after a few seconds pause) You carry a very strong armour around you. But it is good that you are becoming aware. It is just an armour, it is not clinging to you. You are clinging to it, so when you become aware, you can simply drop it. The armour is dead. If you don't carry it, it will disappear. Not only are you carrying it, but nourishing and feeding it continuously.

But this is how civilization is—in a very neurotic state. Civilization is a neurosis, and it pays—that's why we have decided to be neurotic. But by and by as man is becoming more aware, it is becoming more and more clear that the affair is too costly. It gives something, but it takes more than it gives. It gives you many things, but it takes the inner soul. It gives you a better standard of life, but it kills you.

Every child is fluid, he has no frozen parts in him; the whole body is one organic unity. The head is not important and the feet are not unimportant. In fact, division doesn't exist; there are no demarcations. But by and by demarcations start coming up. Then the head becomes the master, the boss, and the whole body is divided into parts. A few parts are accepted by the society and a few parts are not. A few parts are dangerous for the society and have to be almost destroyed. That creates the whole problem.

So you have to watch where you feel limitations in the body. Where exactly did you become aware that there were more limitations—in the legs?

RISHI   *Yes, certainly in the legs, and around here* (indicating the neck); *a lot in the chest, also in my throat.*

Just do three things. One: walking or sitting, or whenever you are not doing anything, exhale deeply. The emphasis should be on exhalation, not on inhalation. So exhale deeply —as much air as you can throw out, throw and exhale by the mouth. But do it slowly so it takes time; the longer it takes the better, because then it goes deeper. When all the air inside the body is thrown out, then the body inhales. Don't you inhale. Exhalation should be slow and deep, inhalation should be fast. This will change the armour near the chest, and that will change your throat too.

Second thing: if you can start a little running that will be helpful. Not many miles, just one mile will do. Just visualise that a load is disappearing from the legs, as if it is falling. Legs carry the armour if your freedom has been restricted too much; if you have been told to do this and not to do that; to be this and not to be that; to go here and not to go there. So you start running, mm? And while running, also put more attention on exhalation. Once you regain your legs, and their fluidity, you will have a tremendous energy flow.

The third thing: in the night when you go to sleep, take off your clothes, and while taking them off, just imagine that you are not only taking off your clothes, you are taking off your armour too. Actually do it. Take it off and have a good deep breath — and then go to sleep as if unarmoured, with nothing on the body and no restriction. In three weeks tell me how it is going. It has been good. . . .

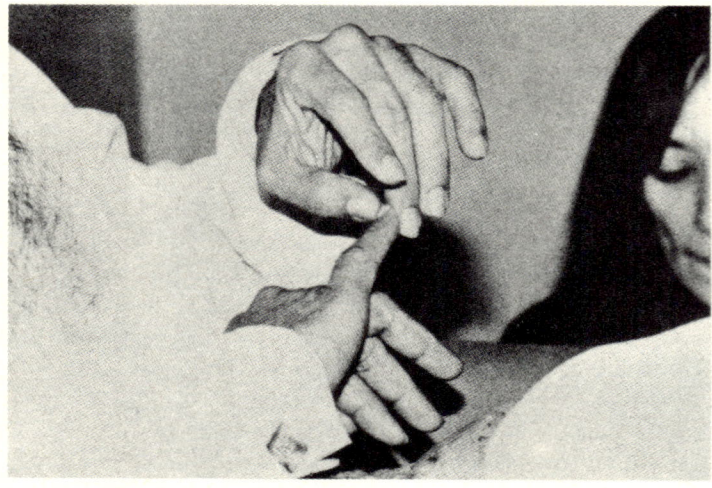

THE FLOW IS THE REAL THING

Bhagwan turned to a sannyasin who was training in Tathata and asked him how it was going.

PREM CHAITANYA — *I experienced the feeling that I could never take this group, but I think it was just me battling with the structure, because I am not structured in that sort of way.*

In fact there is no structure in it. The structure is just formal. Deep down, a very unstructured flow is the real thing. The structure is not more than a container; don't pay much attention to it, look at the content.

The structure is just to support that which is not structured. So everything that is unstructured will need a structure around it. It is just like a scaffold — it helps the building to be raised. Once the building is ready you can throw the scaffolding — there is no need for it. So once somebody has passed through an experience, and has come to know the unstructured, the unconditional, then there is no point in having a structure. He knows, he understands that the structure was just to help. Now he can burn the scriptures, now there is no discipline. But people who have attained to a state of no discipline still follow the discipline — just for those who cannot understand the undisciplined yet.

It is said about Bodhidharma, who introduced Zen into Japan and China, that when he became enlightened he continued meditating. Some of his disciples asked, 'Why do you meditate? You have attained.'

He said, 'Because of you. Unless I meditate, you will think, "What is the point of meditating? The

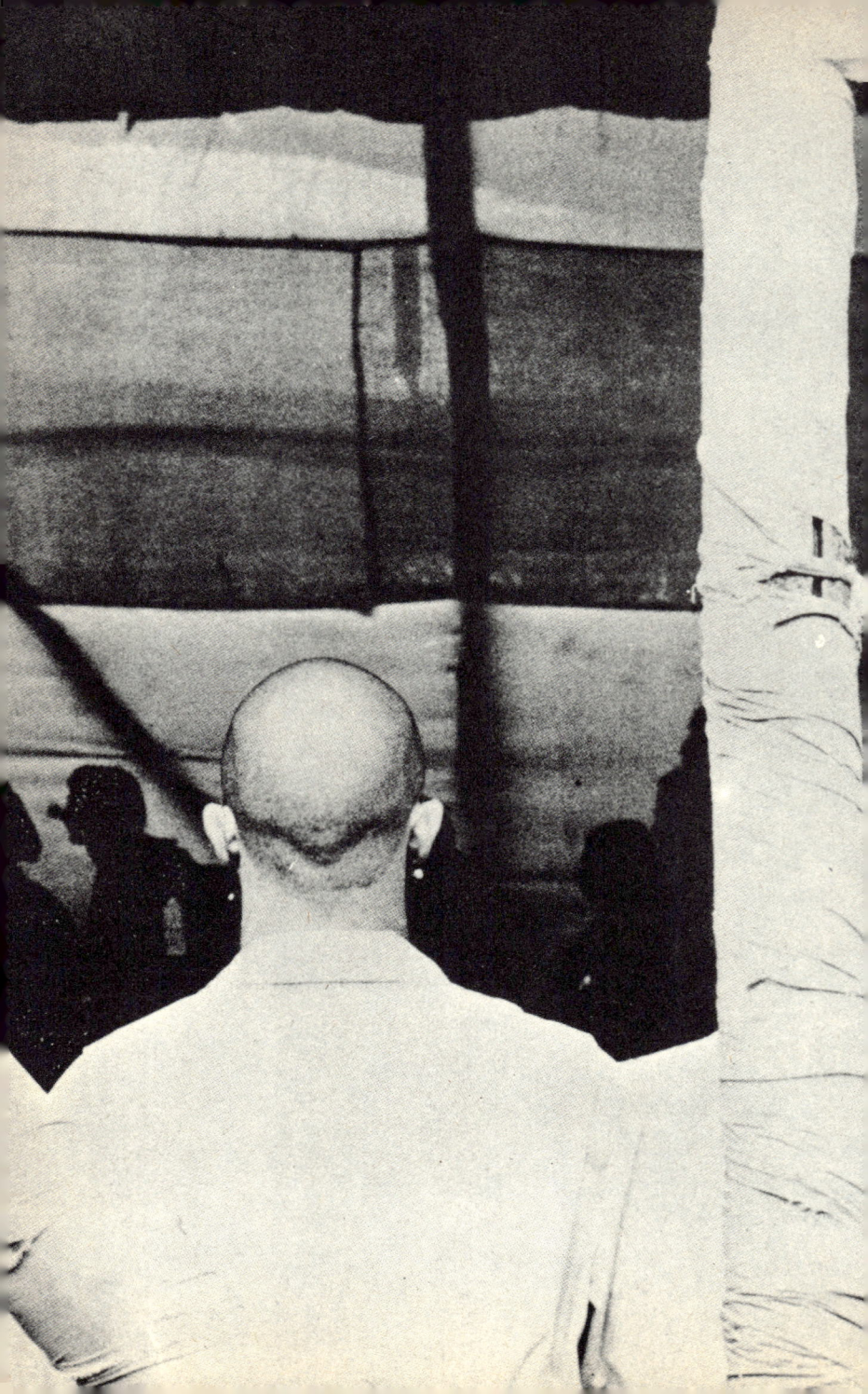

master is not meditating, so we can leave it." But it will be dangerous for you. For me there is no point now; I simply sit so that I can help you to sit.'

Buddha said to his disciples, 'When you become enlightened, don't throw the discipline away, because there are many foolish people around thinking that discipline is not needed. They will never enter discipline and they will be destroyed.'

All I am doing here, or allowing to be done here, is basically unstructured, but the structure is needed. It is just a superficial need. Good, this has been a good understanding.

Sariputta, what about you?

SARIPUTTA *. . .I can't really tell what's happening. I don't really know I know that something is going on. . . .*

In fact, whenever it is so, whenever something is going on, it is very difficult to say; it is very elusive. It is not a particular thing, it is more like a climate that surrounds, a milieu. It is like a fragrance that you recognise, and yet you don't recognise. There are moments when clarity comes, and there are moments when there are again clouds and all clarity is gone. In the moments of clarity, you think you can say what is happening, but when those moments are gone you cannot recapture it. And the thing is so big that you can cry, or laugh, or dance — but you cannot say.

That's why in Zen, when the master gives a koan to meditate upon, he waits for the disciple to someday come and act what he has experienced. If he keeps on coming and talking, whatsoever he says is rejected. Sometimes he has not said anything and the master says, 'Don't say it; it is wrong' — and he had not said anything! The master waits for the moment when the disciple will show it, not say it.

So whenever something real happens, you can show it, but you cannot say it. The next time when you feel, you can come and dance, or you can sing a song, or anything. Or you can just sit silently, not saying anything. I will understand. Just trying to find the words is always difficult: the word is so small, the experience so big. It cannot be confined to words.

But good. When something happens which you cannot say, very good. Good, Sariputta; you are opening.

I CRIED REALLY DEEPLY

The next sannyasin appeared before Bhagwan, grinning a little shyly, flute in hand — as if to illustrate what Bhagwan had just said! Laughter. . . .

Good!

ANANDMURTI   *I do have something to say! The group was very good for me. Things from my past that I still carry around with me were stirred up, because it was so heavy. . . I cried really deeply. I rejected at first that the past was still part of me, then I realised that it was, and I began feeling better. It has given me a lot of energy — more than I know what to do with.*

HAMMER ON THE ROCK

Much energy is wasted in fighting with oneself; in rejecting, in condemning. Much energy is wasted. If you start accepting yourself, you become a reservoir of energy because then the conflict ceases; then there is no civil war; then you are one piece. Much energy is preserved, and that overflowing energy is creativity. A person who is in conflict with himself can never be creative. He is destructive, he is destroying himself, and through himself he will destroy others also. All his relationships will be poisoned.

The most basic and the most fundamental commandment is to love oneself. I don't say only accept, because that word is not enough — you can accept and you may not love. You may accept, because what can be done? — you are in a deep helplessness, but that is not acceptance. Unless you accept yourself as a blessing, unless you accept and welcome yourself, unless you accept yourself in deep gratitude, unless you love yourself, you will never become an overflowing energy. Then the energy can flow in song, in dance, in painting. A thousand and one ways of creativity can be found; or it can simply flow in deep silence. And whomsoever comes in contact with that deep silence will be transformed and will hear for the first time the music which is celestial. So not only accept, but accept with deep gratitude. Be thankful that God has made you *you*, and not anybody else.

Everybody has a unique function to fulfill, that's why he exists. And when I say everybody, I mean everybody. A Judas is as much needed as a Jesus. Without Judas, Jesus will be poorer; something will be missing in the story. So Jesus has to be thankful to Judas also. Not only accept yourself, but accept everybody else as he is. God knows better.

I have heard a story about Byazid, a sufi mystic. He was passing on a road with his disciples and he saw a very beautiful red stone by the side of the path. He took it up, brooded for a moment, then replaced it. The disciples

THE MOST BASIC COMMANDMENT: LOVE YOURSELF

asked, 'What are you doing? You took a rock and then you replaced it.'

He said, 'God must have had some function for it, that's why it is there. Who am I to change it, to change its place? I was just going to commit a sin. The beauty of the stone tempted me, but just in time I remembered God. It must be there, it must be needed there.'

When you accept yourself, suddenly you accept everybody. A person who rejects himself rejects the whole world. A person who rejects himself cannot accept God. How can you accept God who made you? The moment you accept yourself, everything is accepted. Then everything is as it should be. Then there is no difference between should be and is. Then the should is 'is'. And suddenly a celebration arises. So accept it. Now play a note on your flute!

Anand, looking somehow just as a flute player should, curly-headed and bright-eyes, picked up his flute, grinned mischievously at Bhagwan, and piped out a compelling sprightly tune which ended rather abruptly, leaving Anand looking somewhat surprised at himself!

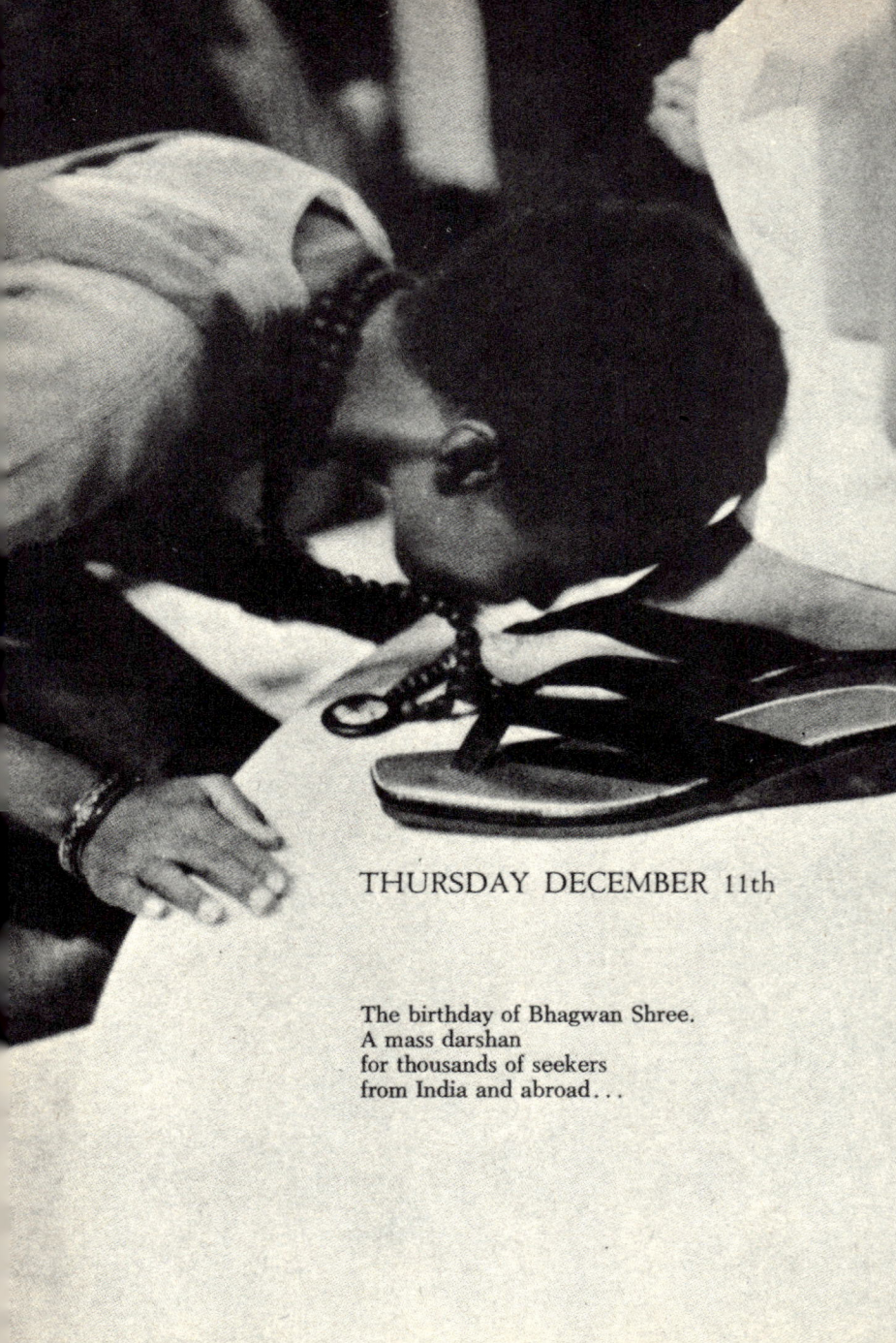

THURSDAY DECEMBER 11th

The birthday of Bhagwan Shree.
A mass darshan
for thousands of seekers
from India and abroad...

FRIDAY DECEMBER 12th

Members from the Enlightenment Intensive group were present at darshan tonight. The aim of this group is to provide a situation in which one can gain a glimpse into what goes on behind the mind, and directly encounter one's consciousness. The method used is a synthesis of the East and West: the Zen method of using a koan (concentration and meditation on a question), is combined with western communication technique. The basic question asked is, 'Who am I?'

The group, which is residential, runs for eighteen hours each day for three days. Apart from the asking and answering of the koans, physical movement, simple labour, and a walking meditation are also part of the process.

BHAGWAN (first addressing a sannyasin who had just learnt that her father died)
. . . how are you feeling? Your father had been ill at all?

SANNYASIN (looking subdued, but quite together) *No, but he was seventy-three. He lived a full life, so I don't feel sad. And I feel it was good he died on your birthday.* (a quick smile)

Yes, that was good. . . . Death should never be a cause to be sad. If one has lived, and lived well, loved, and loved well, then there is no cause to be sad about it. A death can be as beautiful as life can be beautiful. All lives are not beautiful and all deaths are not ugly. And the death depends basically on the life. It is the culmination, the crescendo, the total life in a sense. But that is not the point.

When somebody dies, you don't cry and weep for him — you cry and weep for yourself. Every death reminds you of your own death. And in every death a part of you dies — and particularly the death of a father, a mother, a wife, a husband, a friend — someone with whom you have been closely related, with whom you have been involved.

The sannyasin began to show some response to Bhagwan's words. . . . Colour came to her face and her eyes began to fill with tears.

When they disappear, something within you disappears — an emptiness is left. That emptiness has to be lived. So if you feel like crying, cry; if you feel like weeping, weep. Don't suppress it in any way, and

BE A SMALL CHILD

don't avoid it in any way, mm? Don't rationalise, because we always rationalise. If you rationalise and you avoid the fact, then something like a wound will remain with you. So cry and weep and let tears come. And if you want to, talk to your father; say the things you always wanted to say and couldn't. Be a small child and allow the emotion to possess you.

This is one of the problems for the modern mind. We rationalise everything, and by rationalising we suppress things. And that can be very dangerous because it poisons the whole system. That's why I called you.

You just close your eyes . . . and let death happen. . . .

The sannyasin closed her eyes. Bhagwan shone his torch in the direction of her third eye, leaning from his armchair closer and closer. The face of the sannyasin seemed to blanch. She swallowed several times as if to push down something that she did not want to feel. She then began slowly swaying backwards and forwards, her face turned upwards. Bhagwan slowly lowered his eyelids and sat silently with his eyes closed as if to feel what was passing through the sannyasin sitting before him.

To gaze upon the face of Bhagwan when his eyes are closed is a moving experience. One feels a mixture of awe and affection, sadness, serenity, and joy — almost all at the same time.

After a few seconds Bhagwan opened his eyes, addressing the sannyasin. . . .

Good, Champa. And tonight, before you go to sleep, just sit on the bed and allow it. It will be coming; it is there. Allow it to take possession — it has to be lived. If you cannot live it right now, then later on it will become a problem — it will always be there. This is how we go on accumulating unlived experiences.

Each moment has to be lived so totally that you are
finished with it. It may be love, it may be death, it
may be anything else — but live it totally, mm? And
don't be wise about it. Don't let the head have its
say; rather, listen to the heart.

This night, curl up in bed, cry and weep, and
don't let the head interfere. And by the morning you
will be so fresh. You will have learnt something
from death.

This is a precious moment — when the father or
the mother dies. It is a sacred moment and you can be
enriched through it. You can attain much through it;
it can become a great insight. So don't waste it, mm?
This night you try. (softly) And I am going to help. . . .
Good, Champa.

(to a group member) You were in the group?
Come here. . . . How was the group?

ANALYSIS IS A WAY OF AVOIDING LIFE

NIRAKAR   *Well, I went straight from the camp to Tathata, then the Primal, and straight into the Intensive!*

Very good! (laughter)

NIRAKAR   *Yes ... it was too much to think about. I can't analyse it.*

No, there is no need.

NIRAKAR   *No, I know. I just feel great.*

No, there is no need for analysis. That's why I wanted you to go so fast — so there is no gap for thinking to come in. Analysis is not needed; it is not going to help. Analysis is a way to avoid life — then you don't live it, you think about it. You think you love a woman, but you don't love her — you think about loving her. You think that you love her and the whole thing becomes false. You can deceive others, but you will be wasting your energy. Analysis is a disease of the mind; it will give you false ideas. If you analyse love, you will reduce it to something ridiculous. If you analyse life, then you will have chemicals and nothing else. If you analyse a beautiful flower, the beauty will disappear and only matter will be left in the hand. All that is true, all that is beautiful, all that is good, escapes analysis.

That's why Freud goes on analysing. He starts thinking about love and only sex is left — love disappears. Analyse a poem and prose will be left, because there are things which simply escape analysis. So don't do that. That's why I wanted you to do one thing after another — so fast that there would be no interval and you couldn't think. That's why you are feeling great. (a chuckle) Feel great — and don't try to analyse it!

Good, it has been good!

Something to say?

BUDDHAGHOSHA (coming forth with a spring) *A wonderful and exhilarating feeling during the group at one point. At several points. A very sudden change.*

You look as if it has been very good. You still carry the climate of it. I received your letter . . . very good.

Much more is possible now. And always remember, the journey starts but it never ends. Deeper and deeper satoris will be happening. And never think that this is the end, because deeper is always possible if you are waiting for it. Only that happens for which you wait. If you are not waiting for it then it will not

happen, because you are not looking for it. And this
is the point to be understood at this moment: don't
desire, but wait. If you desire it will not happen,
because the desiring mind is so excited, so tense, and
so intrigued, it is already in the future.

So don't desire — just wait as if something is
going to happen. You don't know what it is — nobody
knows. It has been a misfortune that people have
given names to it — God, Enlightenment, Nirvana, Satori —
it has been a misfortune. Simply wait with no idea and
doors beyond doors open.

This has been very good.

BUDDHAGHOSHA (rather hesitantly) *I have
been thinking for a while — I
think I have changed my mind
about it though — the feeling of
being alone was such a delicious
one I felt that I almost wanted
to accentuate it — like going
away for a short time to be
alone. But I think I would rather
stay here.*

No, you wait. Right now to go away won't be
helpful. There are right moments to be alone. Otherwise
one can fall back into the old habits of the mind.
Rather, you start feeling alone here and now. Even
with so many people around you, start feeling alone.

Aloneness has nothing to do with crowd or no crowd;
it is a quality. You can be alone in the crowd, and
you can be in the crowd when you are alone. So it has
nothing to do with loneliness. Aloneness is just an
attitude.

So first try to be alone here. If you succeed in it — and you will succeed, there is no problem about it — then you can go in a retreat for a few days. If you can be alone here, you will be alone there. If it is difficult here, it will be more difficult there — because when we are in the society, with people, we are in our element. It is natural to be that way. The fish is in the sea, and when it is thrown out of the sea, on the bank, in the sand, it is out of its element — and there is going to be much trouble. So first learn to be alone in the natural environment of the society, and then go. Then in a lonely retreat much is possible.

But my emphasis is always that one should learn to be alone in society. In India we have experimented, and the experiment failed tremendously. We helped many people in the past to go into lonely retreats. Then they became afraid of coming back. They became so habituated to it that rather than becoming masters of themselves, they became slaves. So they renounced the world. India suffered much because of this. The great minds were the first ones to renounce — those who could have been an Einstein, a Bertrand Russell, or a Freud, escaped immediately. That door was always open. And those who escaped didn't become masters — because mastery needs the opposite. They became, in a way, poor.

Once you know the convenience and comfort of being lonely and secluded, out of the society, the mind tends to remain in it. It is not like life, it is more like vegetating. So, as you are doing so well now, don't disturb it. Just continue here and leave it to me. If I feel that you have earned it I will send you. . . . And everything is good.

I'M STARTING TO LIKE IT HERE

You were in the group? Come here. What about your false problems?

Much laughter from those present. Last darshan, when the sannyasin had come as a member of the Encounter group, Bhagwan had told him he had absolutely no blocks; that he was simply imagining them.

PREM DHAN (laughingly) *I think I've started to create new ones....*

(chuckling) New ones? That's very good! (More laughter!) Tell me what.

PREM DHAN *I'm worried about going home. I'm worrying whether I could have been the right one to work in the ministry.* (bashfully) *I'm starting to like it here....*

But I am sending you back.

PREM DHAN (grinning) *Mm, it feels good that you say that!*

I am sending you back because something is going to happen there. Something has happened, but the situation was so new, it was easy. I would like to try it in the old situation back home. So you simply go as a new man. You are new.

PREM DHAN Yes, I feel new.

You simply go as a new man. You start doing the work and everything as a new man. Let the situation be as the old—you be the new. So in the contrast you will feel for yourself what has happened.

It is a constant observation that when people are here they attain much, but not until they go home do they become aware that they have gained a tremendous experience. It is the contrast, mm? There is the temptation to fall back into the old trap. That too helps one to become aware.

So you have to go back. Next time you come, then we will see. If you want to be here, you be here, mm? So that is your meditation now, back home: that you feel new, that you be new, and that you don't get into the old pattern. People will try to force you into the old pattern: your family, your friends, office people—they will all try. You just have to remember that you don't have any problem.

It sometimes happens that a person is brought to me and they say he is mad. He meditates and he is perfectly okay; nothing is wrong. Then he goes back home and the family again expects the madness from him. Then he starts falling into the old trap again. He has to play the role.

This is one of the most significant things to understand: almost ninety percent of the people who are in madhouses

I FEEL NEW

are not mad. They are just playing a role because people have forced that role on them, and they accepted it. They find it comfortable and convenient, and once they accepted it, it doesn't look good to destroy people's expectations. This is my understanding: if you say to a hundred mad people that they are not mad, ninety can come out immediately — if they are allowed to come out, and if they are made to understand that they are just playing a game. And it is a foolish game, because they are the losers.

So you just drop all that nonsense that you had. Go with a good laugh. Whenever you go, come and see me first.

PREM DHAN (smiling)   Oh I will!

And I am going to hit your head! (a loving chuckle)

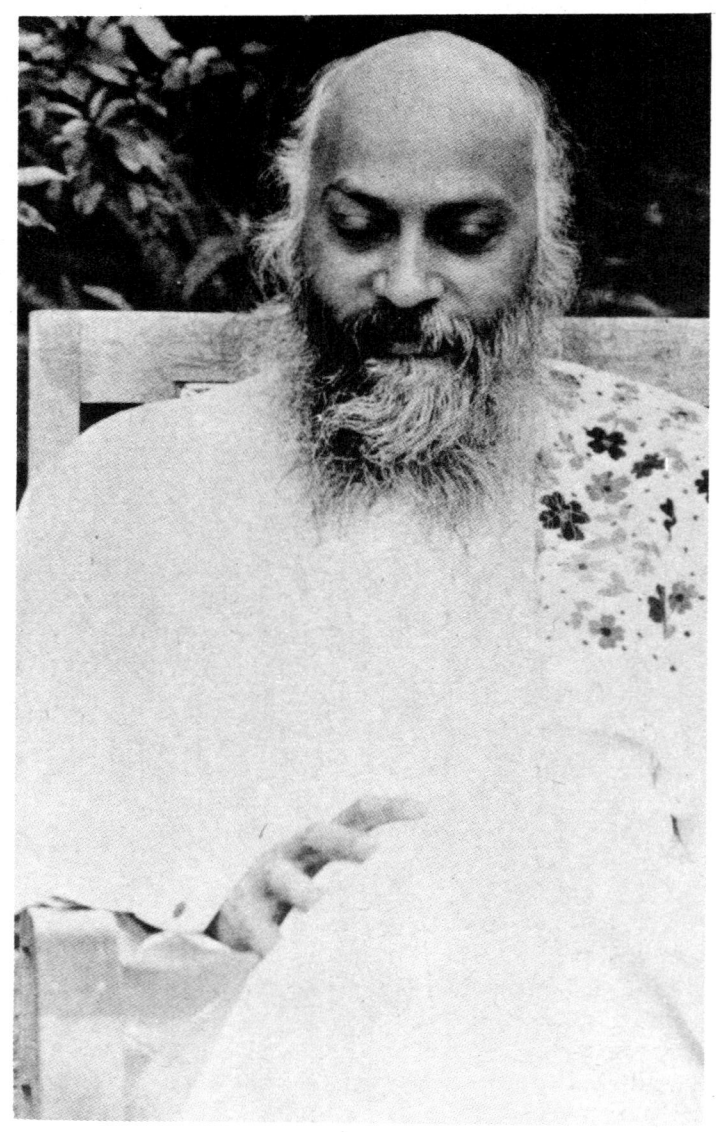

SATURDAY DECEMBER 13th

The first sannyasin Bhagwan addressed had sent him a letter earlier saying that she was in a deep loving relationship with her husband, but at the same time she felt attracted to someone else.

BHAGWAN Two things to remember. The first: love grows only in deep intimacy and trust. If you change persons, from A to B, from B to C, it is as if you are transplanting your being from one place to another. You will never grow roots. And the tree will grow fragile and weak. To gain strength, deep roots are needed; and to gain roots, time is needed. And for love even eternity is not enough. Even eternity is not enough, remember, because love can grow and grow and grow — and there is no end to it. There is a beginning, but there is no end.

So don't take love as a superficial thing. It is not just a relationship. Through love, your whole being has to be discovered. It is sacred, but in the West it has become very profane; it has almost lost the meaning. It has become more and more sexual and bodily, very superficial and casual. In fact I am afraid that the West may lose the very dimension of love. People may completely forget that there was a possibility of inner endless growth in it.

If it is a question of excitement, then it is good to change partners. Then you are more excited and your partner is something to discover. With an old partner everything is known and settled; the whole territory is known. One starts feeling a little fed up, a little bored. This is natural. But if you love the person, you love even the boredom. If you love the person, you also love even his old habits, the old ways, the old territory. Old things have a charm of their own, mm? Just the old armchair you sit on—it has something that no other chair can give, it fits perfectly. Not only that you know it, it also knows you.

LOVE IS A LIFE COMMITMENT

There is a familiarity in the old room in which you have lived, the old house. There is a certain affinity, a certain tuning, so that by and by you are not two separate things. You have melted into each other and have become one, and the boundaries have become blurred. With new things, boundaries are very shy and the separation is very clear. Old things have their charm, but one has to discover it.

Only children are interested in new things. The more grown up you are, the more interested you are in the old things, and the less one is bored. Then you go on finding that these are just levels, layers, that when you love a person one layer has been known—but don't conclude that that is all. A deeper layer is waiting to be provoked and challenged—and there is no end to it. In fact the person himself is not aware how many layers of being he has. If a lover challenges his being, not only the lover will know, the person himself will come to know his being—and only through love. We come to know each other when we challenge each other, and go on provoking each other.

So try to find out new ways with the old person — and you will never be at a loss. Once you know the key of how to always discover a new layer, then the old person is never old. Or, he is old and yet new. Then you are not bored or fed up. Then by and by roots grow.

A point comes in deep love where the lover and the beloved almost become one. I say almost, because the bodies remain separate; but they come to feel a harmony. Now even new research shows that if two persons have loved each other very long, they need not say anything to each other. If a thought arises in one person, it is immediately transferred to the other. Old lovers don't say much but they understand. By and by lovers become twins, mm?

So love is a great adventure, it is not a casual thing. It is a life commitment — and if you can understand, it is a commitment for lives, not only for one life.

Because of Christianity and Judaism and Mohammedanism — and these three religions have become very important in the West — the concept of rebirth has been lost. But if you love a person very deeply in this life, you will find him in the next life again. There are recorded phenomena about the same couple being born again and again for many lives, going on discovering each other.

So let love be your meditation. Make it a sacred thing, not a casual phenomenon. Let it be a challenge. Each challenge is painful because each growth is painful. So for six months you have to make love your meditation. Forget that anybody else exists except your lover. And see what happens in these six months.

If someday some idea arises about somebody — because mind goes on thinking; it is a betrayal of the inner spirit, it is a renegade, a Judas — don't repress it, because repression is not going to help. Each night, whenever you have any desire, any erotic desire arising, for half an

A LITTLE FOOLISHNESS IS GOOD

hour close the eyes and let that desire have full play in fantasy. Whatsoever you want to do, do in fantasy. Don't condemn it; it is natural, just human. Devote that half hour completely to it so that it is finished with.

Soon you will start seeing the whole game of the mind, and within six months all ideas of other persons will disappear from the mind. And when that happens, for the first time you will know what love is. Up to now you have only heard the word, mm? So six months. And then every month you go on reporting how things are going. Good, Anupama.

The sannyasin next to Anupama, after she had moved to sit before Bhagwan, said that she was feeling like becoming part of the ashram.

Bhagwan said that it would happen soon and that she should wait a little longer . . . .

RADHA (sitting hunched up and rather pale of face) *I'm feeling terribly tense and — searching, you know. . . .*

Tell me what the tension is.

RADHA *It is . . . like greed—greed for God. And I cannot accept my stupidity. I feel stupid but I cannot accept my stupid parts. I don't know what to do with them.*

Nothing is to be done. They are needed, they are fun! If you are not stupid at all and you become completely wise, life will be too burdened. A little foolishness is good so that one can enjoy also. And every great man . . . it is not that he has dropped foolishness, he has used it. He has transformed it into his wisdom.

Nothing has to be dropped and nothing has to be cut away, otherwise you will always remain a fragment, you will never be whole. That stupid part is also you. And who is condemning it? It is the ego. In fact the stupid part is more natural than this ego which goes on condemning and saying that this part is stupid and to drop it.

Don't be serious — there is no need, no need. And whether you accept yourself or not, you are you. Your rejection doesn't make any change. It only makes you miserable, that's all. If you accept, you can dance and be happy and celebrating. If you don't accept, you become serious and tense. So the real question is not whether to accept or not, but whether you want to be happy or unhappy.

Once Diogenes, who had become a hundred years old, was asked by somebody why he was always happy and what was his secret. He said, 'Every morning when I get up I have two alternatives — to be happy or not to be happy. I always choose to be happy!'

What is the point in being miserable! And this is the most important thing: if you are happy you start changing. Happiness is the only alchemy in the world. It is the only secret of transformation; there is no other. Unhappy people never change, and because they don't change they become more unhappy.

Happy people continuously change, and because they change they become more and more happy; and then more and more change is possible. Why do I say that happiness is the only alchemy? It is because in happiness you are flowing, your energy is not frozen; it is not blocked. You have an inner dance of energy, a dynamic energy, that is needed for transformation. When you are unhappy you are dull, solid, rock-like; nothing is flowing, everything is frozen. How can you change?

BE MADLY IN LOVE WITH LIFE

So don't be serious! This is one of the pitfalls for people who are searching for God. People who are searching for God are almost always serious people. Non-serious people don't get interested in God—and they are the right persons to find Him! They are so much involved in life, in love, in enjoying small things—'eat, drink, be merry'—they are moving in the world, mm? They don't go to the temple or to church—it seems too serious and seems to belong to death and not to life.

And they are the right people, the festive people, who can attain to God. But this is the misfortune—that they never become interested. The people who become interested are always depressed, sad, blocked. They are people who have missed their lives somehow: egoists, moralists, puritans, all sorts of ill people. They get into the church, and because of them God cannot enter the church. I can understand God's difficulty, because what can you do with serious people—they will kill you!

God is where life is, where the dance is still happening and the flowers blossoming, the rivers flowing, and the world of stars. He is there—in life. God is life. You can forget the word 'god' and nothing will be lost—'life' is enough. And when I say 'life' I don't mean life with a capital 'L', no; just a lower case 'l' will do. Just a simple life, not even with a capital L. That life is God.

So this is a problem, and this is the problem I have to face every day. I would like you to be happy and merry and cheerful. I would like you to be madly in love with life, because that is the only way one knows what God is. When you are lost in love and life, you have found Him. When you are too serious in the mind, and after Him too much, you can go on chasing Him but you will never find Him—because you are not the right person. He will not want to meet you. (Radha laughs) Your company will be too serious.

God has always been avoiding the saints, and He has

done well to avoid them. So don't be a saint! Even if you
are a sinner it is okay. But be happy, because a happy
man cannot sin. By and by the happiness transforms. You
may be a saint, but if you are unhappy you are already
committing the greatest sin that one can commit—the sin
of being unhappy. A person who is unhappy will tend to
make others unhappy. You can give to others only that
which you have.

So drop all this nonsense! If you want to be religious,
drop all religion. And if you want some day to know what
God is, forget all about Him—life is enough. Be more
festive, mm? And there is nothing to it—just a simple
understanding. So start being happy from this very
moment, right?   (Radha smiled tentatively)

And that is why I am not allowing you into the ashram
yet. When I see that you are really dancing and happy I
will allow you, otherwise you will have to wait outside the
gate a little longer, mm? You know that is the barrier—
because I am afraid of serious people. (Bhagwan laughed
with the group.) They can come and destroy the whole
thing that I am trying to create.

I don't think that you are naturally a serious person.
There are people who are born ill, who are born serious.
It is very difficult for them to drop it. But for you, I don't
see any problem. You can simply get out of it as one
gets out of the clothes, that's all. You be yourself, and don't
bother with seriousness. Good, Radha. From this very
moment, mm?

A sannyasin asked Bhagwan about the nature of epilepsy, from
which she had been suffering for several years. She only had
attacks — and only of two minutes duration — when she was asleep.

She added that the fits left her feeling rather strange and
empty. . . .

. . .don't be worried; it will disappear by and by. There is nothing wrong in it. Try and make it a meditation. Just do one thing: every night when you go to sleep, just repeat three times that whenever it is going to happen, it will be tremendously peaceful and silent and blissful. That's all. And next time when it happens, something of meditation will have entered into it and there will be a change. Epileptic fits and estatic fits are similar: the mechanism is the same, only the quality is different.

Ramkrishna used to have fits. Doctors diagnosed that they were epileptic and that he was going insane. Had he been in the West he would have immediately been given electric shocks and been put into a mental asylum. You have the fit for only two minutes. He used to sometimes have a fit for six hours, and once he remained unconscious for eighteen hours.

In India we know that the symptom is the same as in epilepsy, but that the person is only unconscious in the body — deep inside the consciousness is there and he is perfectly peaceful.

Next time it happens you will have a very ecstatic and blissful experience — deep silence and calm. And those two minutes will give you a tremendous insight into your being.

But use the same words every night and in the same order, so the mind doesn't get confused. Next time it will be beautiful, it will not be a disease anymore, mm?

ARVIND   Bhagwan, I have some questions, a few problems.

Come here.

ARVIND   *One is my hair.* (He boasts a long, thick head of curly hair!) *When people ask me why I don't cut my hair, I always say because you don't want us to. But this time when Poonam* (a sannyasin who runs a London centre) *asked me in England. . .then I got into trouble!* (laughter from the group)

Mm, don't cut it.

ARVIND   *Okay. Then that problem is gone!* (more mirth) *Another problem: when I work in the centre, I often feel difficulties both working and meditating. I would like some guideline. . . .*

TRY TO REACH BEYOND YOUR GRASP

Don't you have some helpers there?

ARVIND *Yes, I have, but I work much.*

No, you work much. Working is never bad, and one can never work too much, never. We never work too much.

ARVIND *Oh, that was my last question, so now you have answered them all!* (Bhagwan and the group laughed at his delight)

We never work as much as we can, we never work to the maximum potential. In fact, at the most, people work fifteen percent of their potential — and those are the very hard workers.

As I see it, you are not working more than seven or eight percent. The more you work, the more you are capable of working. The less you work, the less you become capable of working. Life has its own logic.

Jesus says, 'If you have, more will be given to you. If you don't have, even that which you have will be taken away from you.' If you work hard you will get more energy. If you don't work hard, if you don't work at all and you avoid it, even the energy that you have will disappear. So whatsoever you want to do, do it, and do it to the optimum. And soon you will see that more and more doors are opening, and more energy becomes available.

Always try to reach more than you can grasp; always try to reach beyond your grasp. That is how one grows. If you always try that which you can do, you will always fall flat on the earth — you will not be growing. Try the impossible and it becomes possible. And if you don't try the possible, even that will become impossible.

There is a time to work, a certain age limit where you can work hard. If you have worked hard at that age, in your remaining life the glow of work remains with you. If you miss that time, then you miss the glow. Then you simply repent that you missed the time when you could have worked hard. People who have been really working have a different type of energy in their old age — a glow, something, as if a light is burning inside. They may not be working then, but you know that they have earned a rest and now they can relax. Relaxation has to be earned.

So do whatsoever you can do right now, because right now you have energy, mm?

ARVIND

I find it difficult to work and meditate each day. I find it easier to work a lot, then spend some time meditating.

You don't understand the mechanism. In fact, one should continuously change, because the brain has many centres.

For example, if you do mathematics, then a certain part of the brain functions and the other parts rest. Then you read poetry: then that part that was functioning in mathematics rests and another part starts functioning.

That's why in universities and schools we change periods — forty minutes, forty-five minutes — because each centre of the brain has a capacity to function for forty minutes. Then it feels tired and needs a rest, and the best rest is to change the work — so that some other centre starts working and one relaxes. So continuous change is very very good; it enriches you.

CHANGE ENRICHES YOU

I understand the difficulty. . . . You do a thing and the mind becomes obsessed, you go mad after it. But that's bad; one should not become so possessed. While doing it, become absorbed, but always remain a master; otherwise you will become a slave. And slavery is not good. Even slavery to God, to meditation, is not good. If you can't stop doing a certain thing, or you only stop very reluctantly, that simply shows that you don't know how to change gears in the mind.

So do one thing: whenever you are doing something... for example, you are meditating and now you want to do something else. Then after you stop meditating, for five minutes simply exhale deeply, as deeply as possible. Then let the body inhale, don't you inhale. Have a feeling that you are throwing out everything that was in the mind and in the body and in the system. Just five minutes, then start doing some other work, and immediately you will feel you have changed.

HAMMER ON THE ROCK

You need the neutral gear for five minutes, mm? If you change gear in a car, the gear has to first move to neutral — even if just for a single moment, but it has to move. The more efficient the driver, the faster he can move from neutral. So give five minutes to the neutral gear. You are not working at anything — just breathing, just being. Then by and by you go on dropping: after one month, four minutes; after two months, three minutes.

Then by and by there will come a point where just one exhalation is enough and you are finished with the work — closed, a full stop — and then you start other work. You try this, and next time you come you will be perfectly okay.

SUNDAY, DECEMBER 14th

A sannyasin, pale-faced and tense, was sitting with Bhagwan Shree as we entered the darshan porch. After Bhagwan had greeted us and we were all seated, he continued to talk to her.

He shone the torch he always has at hand onto her face, first telling her to close her eyes and allow the energy to move as it wanted. After a few moments she started to sob, her whole body shaking with emotion. Bhagwan instructed her to allow it. After a few moments her weeping subsided. . . .

BHAGWAN Good, mm? Good. Now come back, come back. . . .

Now a few things have to be understood, mm? No relationship can be secure. It is not the nature of relationships to be secure. And if any relationship is secure, it will lose all attraction.

So this is a problem for the mind. If you want to enjoy a relationship, it has to be insecure. If you make it completely secure, absolutely secure, then you cannot enjoy it — it loses all charm, all attraction. The mind cannot be satisfied either with this or with that, so it is always in conflict and chaos. It wants a relationship which is alive and secure. This is impossible, because an alive person or an alive relationship or anything which is alive, has to be unpredictable. What is going to happen in the next moment cannot be forecast. And because it is unpredictable, this moment becomes intense.

You have to live this moment as totally as possible because the next moment may not come ever. You may not be there, the other may not be there. Or you may both be there, but the relationship is not. All possibilities remain open. The future remains always open. The past is always closed, the future is always open. And in between the two is the present, a single moment of present, always trembling, shaking.

But this is how life is. The shaking and the trembling are part of being alive — the hesitation, the cloudiness, the vagueness. The past is closed. Everything has happened and now nothing can be changed, so everything is absolutely closed. The future is absolutely open, nothing can be predicted. And between the two is the present, with one step in the past, one in the future. So the mind always remains in a dichotomy, in a divided state. It is always split, it is always schizophrenic.

The understanding that is needed is that this is how things are and nothing can be done about it. If you want to have a very secure relationship, then you will have to love a dead man; but then you will not enjoy it. That's what happens to a lover when he becomes a husband: a husband is a dead lover, a wife is a dead lover. The past has become all, and now the past decides the future.

In fact if you are a wife you don't have a future; only the past will go on repeating itself, all the doors are closed. If you are a husband then you don't have a future; then you are confined, in an imprisonment.

So security is sought continuously but when you find it, you get fed up with it. Look at the faces of husbands and wives. . . . They have found the security — the much-sought-after security — and now everything is in their bank balance, and the law and the court and the constable are all there to make everything secure. But now the whole charm, the whole poetry, is lost; romance is no longer there. Now they are dead people, they are simply repeating the past; they live in memories.

Listen to wives and husbands talking. The wife goes on saying that the husband doesn't love her as he used to; and they go on talking about past moments, their honeymoon and other things. What nonsense! You are still alive. This moment can be a honeymoon! This moment can be lived, but you are talking of the past, trying to repeat it.

Security never satisfies, and in insecurity there is fear — fear that the relationship can be lost. But that is part of being alive. Everything can be lost, nothing is certain — and that's why everything is so beautiful. And that's why you need not postpone for a single moment. If you want to love a person, love him herenow. Love him, because nobody knows what is going to happen in the next moment. The next moment there may be no possibility for love, and then you will repent for the whole of your life. You could have loved, you could have lived. Then remorse surrounds a person; repentance and a deep guilt is felt — as if you have been committing suicide.

Life is uncertain. No one can make it certain, there is no way to make it certain. And it is good that nobody can make it certain, otherwise it would be dead. Life is fragile, delicate, always moving into the unknown — that's its beauty. One needs to be courageous, adventurous. One needs to be a gambler to move with life — so be a gambler.

Live this moment, and live it totally. When the next moment comes, we will see — you will be there to tackle it. As you have been able to tackle the past, you will be able to tackle the future also. And you will be more capable because you will be more experienced.

So it is not a question of whether Veeresh (her boyfriend) is going to be there the next moment. The question is that if he is available to you in this moment, love him. Don't waste this moment in thinking and worrying about the future, because this is suicidal. Don't pay a single thought to the future — because nothing can be done about it, so it is a sheer wastage of energy.

Love this man and be loved by him. This is my understanding: that if you live this moment totally, there is every possibility that in the next moment the person may be still available. I say maybe. I can't promise you — maybe. But the possibility is more because the next moment is going to come out of this one. If you have loved the man and the man feels blessed, and the relationship has been a beautiful experience, an ecstasy, then why should he leave you?

In fact if you go on worrying, you are making him, forcing him, to leave you. And if you have wasted this moment, the next moment will come out of this wastage; it is going to be rotten.

And that is how one becomes self-predictable. You go on fulfilling your own prophecies. The next moment you say, 'Yes, I was saying from the very beginning that this relationship was not going to last. Now it is proven.' Then you feel very good in a way; you feel you have been very clever and wise. In fact you have been foolish, because it is not that you predicted anything. You forced this event to happen because you wasted the time that was given to you, the opportunity. So love him and forget about the future. Just drop the whole nonsense of thinking about it.

If you can love, love. If you cannot love, forget this man, find somebody else — but don't waste time. The question is not of this lover or that lover — the question is of love. Love fulfills, people are just excuses. But the whole thing depends on you, because whatsoever you are doing with Veeresh, you will go on doing with another if you change lovers. So why not try with Veeresh? He is as perfect a man as you can find; a beautiful person with much understanding, and mature in many ways.

So love him and make him so happy that the happiness itself creates the possibility of him staying. If you make a person happy why should he leave you? But if you make him unhappy then why shouldn't he leave you? If you make him unhappy then I will help him to leave you. But if you make him happy nobody can help him to leave you! Then there is no point; he will fight the whole world for you!

So become more happy, mm? Use the time that one has, and there is no need to think about the future. The present is enough. From this very moment, try to live this moment. If he leaves, that's okay. I will find a better man — forget him! But use this moment not in worrying, but in living. Small things can become so beautiful. A little caring, a little sharing — that's all life is.

So for one month this is going to be your meditation: live the moment, and bring yourself again and again to the present. Whenever you escape into the future or the past, catch hold, bring yourself back. And for one month, with no worry, not seeking security — just live. And everything will be okay. Everything is always okay. Mm? Good, Asha, good.

Nartan, come here.

NARTAN

> ...it always used to happen that my dealings with people were through words, a lot of verbal communication. And now that's not happening so much for me. Words just aren't coming. I feel very choked up inside. It's like ... I want them

NOTHING IS MISSING

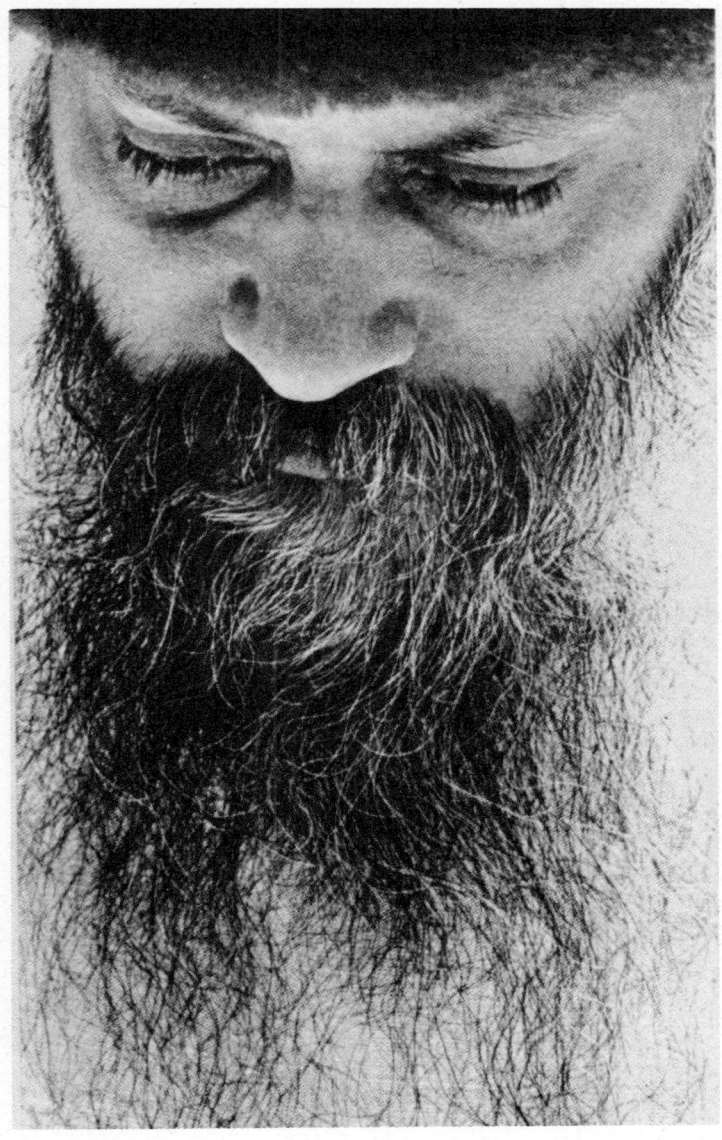

> *to be there. I feel a real void, and it feels like something is missing. I feel frustrated.*
>
> *It doesn't happen with everybody. With people I am not very close to, it's easy to make conversation. But with people I'm closer to there's nothing to say.* (a little laugh) *And I don't feel very comfortable with it. It is as though something is missing.*

No, nothing is missing, nothing at all. It is just that you are growing, and for the first time you are feeling close to people.

You have never felt that closeness. You have always remained just casually related. When you are formally related to someone you can go on chattering about a thousand and one nonsensical things, because nothing matters — it is just a pastime.

But when you start feeling closer to someone and an intimacy arises, then even a single word that you utter matters. Then you cannot play so easily with words, because now everything is meaningful. So there will be gaps of silence. One feels awkward in the beginning because one is not accustomed to silence. One thinks something must be said, otherwise what will the other think? But whenever you grow close, whenever there is some sort of love, silence comes and there is nothing to say. In fact, there is nothing to say.

(with a laugh) *Ever?*

WHERE LOVE IS, THERE IS NOTHING TO SAY

Mm? There is nothing. With a stranger there is much to say. With friends, nothing to say.

And the silence becomes heavy because you are not accustomed to it. You don't know what the music of silence is. You know only one way of communicating and that is verbal, through the mind. You don't know how to communicate through the heart, heart to heart, in silence. You don't know how to communicate by just being there, through your presence.

You are growing and the old pattern of communication is falling short of you. You will have to grow new patterns of communication — non-verbal. The more mature one becomes, the more non-verbal communication is needed. Language is needed because we don't know how to communicate. When we know how to, by and by language is not needed. Language is just a very primary medium. The real medium is of silence. So don't take a wrong attitude, otherwise you will stop growing.

Nothing is missing; this is a wrong idea. Something new has come into being and the old pattern is not enough to contain it. You are growing and your dresses are becoming short. Not that something is missing; something is being added to you every day.

The more you meditate, the more you will love and the more you will relate. And finally one comes to a moment when only silence helps.

So next time when you are with somebody and you are not communicating with words and you are feeling very uneasy, feel happy. Become silent and allow that silence to communicate.

Language is needed to relate to people with whom you have no love relationship. Non-language is needed for people with whom you have a love relationship. One has to become innocent again like a child, and silent. Gestures will be there: sometimes you will smile and hold hands, or sometimes you will just remain silent, looking into each other's eyes — not doing anything, just being. The presences meet and merge, and something happens which only you will know — only you to whom it has happened. No one else will become aware; it happens in such depth.

So feel happy next time, feel thankful that you are growing. Enjoy that silence; feel and taste and savour it. Soon you will see that it has its own communication; that it is greater and higher and deeper and more profound. And that communication is sacred, it has a purity about it.

It is a good sign. I am happy.

NARTAN *Me too!* (a cheerful grin and a laugh)

Alok, something to say? Tell me.

ALOK *Well, ten years ago I was a Christian minister and I was in the business of making myself and others feel like sinners, and then offering them salvation. I'm still doing that to some extent.*

Right now I want to tell you that I still experience a lot of fear and doubt, and I don't feel at ease in my relationship with my woman, or with other women. I don't feel sure of myself sexually. And my mind is doubting a lot. But then at other times I just feel that there's nothing wrong.

THERE IS NOTHING WRONG

There is nothing wrong, but the Christian training must have poisoned you.

ALOK   *Very much.*

It poisons. You have to unlearn it. It has to be dropped, otherwise you can miss your whole life.

Once you start hating yourself, or even part of your being, you will never be at ease with yourself, never be at home. There will be some sort of split and a continuous conflict.

Christianity has done one of the greatest harms, and that is that it has made people feel guilty about any and everything. Particularly whenever you feel happy, suddenly by the side you feel guilt arising. Christianity has made that conditioned so deeply — that all enjoyment and all happiness is sin. So when you are sad, everything is good. When you look like a martyr, you are a saint. But when you look happy, laughing, dancing, then you are a sinner. Happiness is a sin.

Just the contrary is the case. To be happy is to be religious, because only a happy person can be grateful towards God.

And the body is beautiful. It is the temple. Take care of it and be grateful to it. It provides a great opportunity, because it is only through the body that you have come to know what life is, what love is, what light is. It is through the body that you have seen, you have heard, you have touched; that you have loved and been loved. It is through the body that you have become aware. Be thankful towards the body and never take an antagonistic attitude towards it.

But if the training has been there, you have to consciously drop it, because it goes deep and it goes on functioning without you knowing. You will never be able to love a woman deeply, mm? That Christian will be standing there looking at you and saying, 'What are you doing? Sinning again? You will be thrown into hell!'

And suddenly you shrink and the fear takes over — and love disappears. Love is so delicate, and the fear is so strong — it can destroy it.

So watch, and don't allow the Christian in your bed-chamber. Otherwise you will always find between you and your woman, the Christian standing. The whole church will be there, and it can destroy all happiness. Drop it! Never feel guilty. Always feel grateful.

Happiness has to be enjoyed as much as possible. The happier you become, the closer you come to God. So I teach delight in life, and I teach a dancing god. And unless a god dances, he is no god at all.

So drop it consciously. You will have to struggle a little, mm? Because once the mind is wrongly conditioned, you will have to uncondition it — but it can be unconditioned. Whatsoever can be conditioned, can be unconditioned.

ALOK

> *I've worked on myself to drop it for many years now. There is a very beautiful magic child in me that loves to be in the present, that delights. . . .*

THE WORLD IS SUCH A DELIGHT

Mm mm, I can see it there. And it is growing, and it will go on growing. There is not much of a problem, but you just have to remain alert, mm?

The conditioning goes deep. It becomes almost part of you and you don't know it. When you look, it is there like a layer of ice. When you touch, it is there like a layer surrounding your hand and your skin. You touch a woman with love, but there is something that shrinks in, withdraws.

The whole world is such an affluence of celebration. It is an overflow of energy; so many flowers, so many birds singing, so many stars — an infinity of stars, galaxies upon galaxies. The world is such a delight, the whole universe is such happiness and such a great harmony. Jump into it!

Become a star or become a flower, but don't be a Christian! Right? And the child is growing, it will come....

Bhagwan turned next to address a sannyasin who, usually bubbling over with energy and joie de vivre, was looking rather tense and a little rebellious!...

What about you?

SAROJ *It has been two very very heavy days. They were the days of my period, and I always go really mad during it. Yesterday I broke some things in the house because I was very*

> *upset, and sometimes, just . . . like . . . things coming up from the inside. And it doesn't make a problem for me, I can enjoy them. Somehow I feel a little guilty about feeling that way. I feel more and more wild and I enjoy that, but also I feel that . . . what will happen to me if I become that way?*

You broke something yesterday?

SAROJ (trying to look contrite) *Yes.*

(trying to look stern) What?

SAROJ A pot. (It was later revealed that two broken tape recorders were also rescued from the deluge of Saroj's wrath!)

To feel wild is not bad, but to break anything is not good, mm? Whenever you feel wild, dance a wild dance — but never destroy anything.

LEARN FROM EVERY EXPERIENCE

It may not be a problem — you can destroy a pot — but the very idea of destruction is bad. It gives you a destructive attitude towards life. And the pot is just an excuse. You would really like to destroy more valuable things — even valuable relationships, people, mm?
But you cannot destroy that much, you cannot bear it, so you break a poor pot — and he has not done anything!
(a little laugh of belated compassion from Saroj)

For many women the days of the period are a little destructive, and the reason is very biological. You have to understand and become a little alert and aware so that you can rise a little higher than your biology; otherwise you are in the grip of it.

If you are pregnant, the period stops because the same energy that has been released in the period starts being creative: it creates the child. When you are not pregnant, every month the energy accumulates and if it cannot be creative then it becomes destructive. So when a woman is having her period, for those four or five days she has a very destructive attitude, because she does not know what to do with the energy. And the energy vibrates, it haunts the innermost core of your being, and you cannot give any creativity to it.

All creative energy can become destructive and all destructive energy could have become creative. For example, Hitler. He wanted to be a painter in the very beginning, but he was not allowed. He could not manage to pass the examination and enter into the art school. The man who could have been a painter became one of the most destructive men in the world. With the same energy he may have become a Picasso. And one thing is certain — he had energy. The same energy could have been infinitely creative.

Ordinarily, women are not destructive. In the past they were never destructive because they were continuously pregnant. One child is born, then they are again pregnant;

again another child is born and then again they are pregnant. For their whole life they used their energy.

Now, for the first time in the world a new danger is arising, and that is the destructiveness of women. Because now there is no need for them to be pregnant continuously. In fact pregnancy is almost out of date. But the energy is there.

I see a deep connection between birth control methods and the Women's Liberation Movement. Women are becoming destructive and they are destroying family life, their relationships. They may be trying to rationalise it in many ways, but they are trying to be liberated from the slavery. In fact it is a destructive phase. They have the energy and they don't know what to do with it. The birth control methods have stopped their creative channelization. Now if some channels are not opened to them they will become very destructive.

In the West the family life is almost gone. There is continual conflict, continual fighting, quarreling and being nasty to each other. And the reason is — and nobody understands what the reason is — a biological problem.

So whenever you feel that the period is coming, be more alert, and before it starts, do wild dancing. The Ethiopian dance will be helpful.

Saroj is a member of the ashram's Ethiopian Dance group. This group, which formed about two months ago under the instruction of an Ethiopian sannyasin, Niraj, demonstrated at darshan recently what they had learnt.

The dance form is primitive and erotic — but in a very dignified and beautiful way. Niraj, in dance, is the epitome of the proud, compelling male, strutting like a peacock displaying his virility and beauty. Saroj, who partnered him, danced a wild Carmen Jones — beautifully spontaneous and abandoned.

GO BEYOND NATURE

You can go beyond nature because you have a higher nature also. One can go beyond biology, and one has to otherwise one is a slave to hormones! So whenever you feel destructive, start dancing.

What I am saying is that dancing will absorb your energy. You are doing the opposite. You say you like to rest and not do anything during these days, but do something — anything, go for a long walk — because the energy needs release. Once you catch the point, once you know that the dance relaxes you completely, those four days of your period will become the most beautiful because you will never have so much energy as then. Mm? You try. . . .

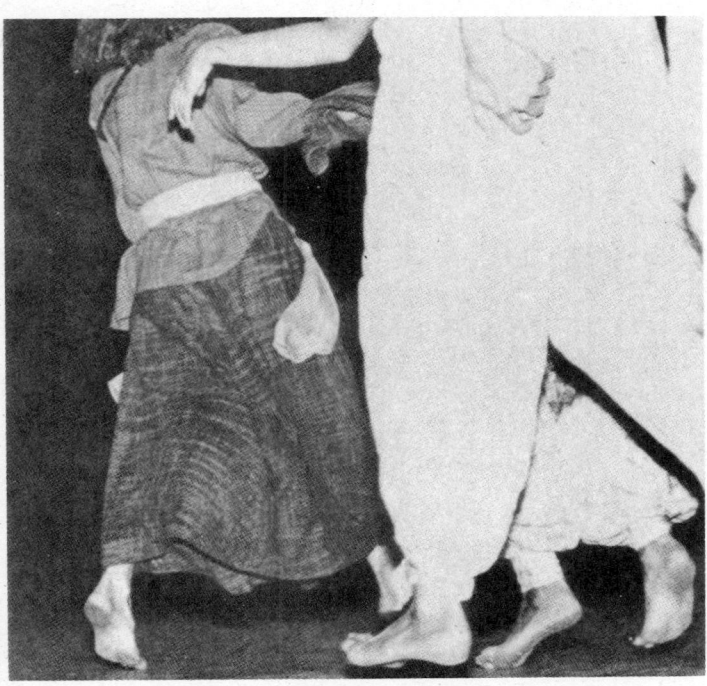

MONDAY DECEMBER 15th

Bhagwan said recently that soon there will be many hundreds of people from the West coming to him, and that those of us with him now should use the opportunity of being so close to him before the deluge starts!

Over the past two weeks or so, many of the resident sannyasins expressed feelings of wonder at the sudden influx of visitors and meditators. It seems the flood gates have been released!

There are so many people pouring in — literally — by day, taking sannyas by night. And with each new arrival one can feel the change in the energy: a subtle movement, a something that defies definition, that seems to be changing the whole gestalt continuously.

Bhagwan turned first to speak to an elderly woman, the mother of a sannyasin who was also present.

BHAGWAN   When did you arrive?

WOMAN   *A week ago. I can't believe I'm here. I turned my back on religion many years ago, so I've been saying no for a very long time.*

That's very good! I was talking about you this morning!
(Bhagwan had talked about yea-sayers and no-sayers that morning in the discourse.)

The religion to which you were saying no is not religion at all, and it is good to say no to it. Only religious people will say no to it.

WOMAN *I've been calling myself a humanitarian.*

Yes, that is a new name for it, but not as good as 'religion'. (a little chuckle) Because unless the human mind tries to reach beyond itself, it cannot grow. All growth comes to you only when you try to reach higher than your best. When you try for the impossible, then only the possible happens. Humanitarianism is good, but then only humanity becomes the goal and that is not enough. Good, but not enough.

WOMAN *Well, I feel I've been chattering out of the top of my head for many years and I've been locked up inside.*

That will open, that will open.
And God does not mean anything else: just an effort to bring your humanity to its total functioning. God is just a function of the total human being — a quality. When you are functioning at your optimum, at your omega point, then you are God. It has been good that you remained a skeptic, that you said no. Now your yes can be total.
Close your eyes, and if something starts happening in the energy, allow it. . . .

GOD IS A QUALITY

The woman sits looking down at her feet, motionless. As Bhagwan places the mala around her neck she begins to cry, then looks lovingly at Bhagwan as he explains her name to her.

Good. Now I will be with you. You were getting ready for me!

The new sannyasin, Garima, returns to her place in the circle beside her daughter. They kiss and the daughter looks very moved. Mother and daughter sit holding hands, gazing at each other for several minutes.

Two days later, at the morning discourse, Bhagwan mentioned Garima when he was talking of the commandment to love one's neighbour as oneself', saying:

A few days before, a beautiful woman, a rare person, came to see me. She has been a humanist for her whole life — not believing in God, a no-sayer.

She told me that she was surprised that she was here. Her surprise is natural. She has never been to any temple, church, or to so-called religious people — and now she has come here. And not only that, she wanted to be initiated into sannyas.

SAY NO TO GOD,
BUT NEVER SAY NO TO HUMAN BEINGS

She herself could not believe what was happening! But I could look into her. She has been able to come to me because she has loved human beings. She has taken the first step towards the temple. She may not have gone to any temple, that is not needed. She may never have thought about God — that is not needed — but she has taken an authentic step. She has loved human beings.

She has been a no-sayer, but that is the base to say yes. She has earned her sannyas. She has arrived, her whole life has been a preparation for it. She said no; to say yes to human beings she denied God. Perfectly good, as it should be. Say no to God, but never say no to human beings, because if you say no to human beings . . . then you will never be able to reach God!

What about you . . . something to say?

SANNYASIN *I wanted to ask you why you gave me the name Asanga.*

Mm mm, it is one of the most beautiful names. Asanga was a Buddhist mystic. Literally the word means unattached, non-attached, or one who is alone; one who doesn't need the other, mm? But the name belongs to a Buddhist mystic, and something in you is going to fit with it.

Two words have to be understood: one is loneliness, the other is aloneness. Loneliness is a negative state, aloneness is very positive. In the dictionary their meanings are the same, but not in life, not in existence.

You feel lonely when you miss the other. You feel alone when you have yourself. You feel lonely when you are bored with yourself. You feel alone when you are delighted in your being.

Asanga means alone. So alone, like a Himalayan peak. So absolutely alone that the other is not needed. That doesn't mean that you will not love. In fact only a person who does not need the other can be loving. When the need disappears then love arises. If you need the other, you use him. Then all your love is a sort of manipulation, a deep exploitation, because you are using the other as a means. Because you cannot be alone and you need somebody to fill your loneliness, you talk about love, but it is not really love. You are using the other, and love can never use the other. For love, the other is the end and can never be reduced to a means. This is the highest morality there is: when the other is the end and not a means.

Only a person who is absolutely alone, who is capable of aloneness, can be capable of love—because it is not a need. On the contrary, love is an overflow. It is not a relationship; it becomes a state of being. You may be sitting alone in a room but love goes on flowing. There may be nobody to share it, but it goes on flowing. It is just like a flower that blooms on a path where nobody passes, but still it goes on sending its fragrance to the air, to the winds. Or a star at night—nobody is looking at it but it goes on shining. Whether you are with somebody or alone makes no difference then. It is a state of being.

I have given you the name Asanga for all these reasons. You have to learn to be alone. I am not saying that you have to escape from the other, no. I am saying that you have to realise yourself. Don't escape from yourself to the other.

That is going to be your life work: to attain to a purity of aloneness where love can become a state and not a relationship.

That is freedom — what we in India have been calling moksha, nirvana, the last word in freedom — where you don't need the other; where love is not a need but has become an overflowing of energies. So keep it in mind. Good. . . .

Garima's daughter came to sit at the feet of Bhagwan, all signs of the happiness shared a little time before with her mother replaced by seriousness and concern.

BHASHA *I want you to share some burdens.* (a heavy sigh)

Mm, tell me.

BHASHA *I feel like I'm getting so narrow. I feel that all my behaviour and all my thinking is always the same. All day, all the time, I hear myself saying the same thing over and over again. I'm just — desperate.*

Mm mm. Accept it. Accept it, because mind is a mechanism. Mind is repetitive and it can never invent a single original thought, never. That is not the capacity of the mind, so you are asking something that is not possible. And because you go on asking, you become more and more frustrated about it. Mind can only repeat that which it knows.

It is as if you feed a computer and then you expect that that computer is going to give you something that you have not fed into it. It cannot. The mind is a bio-computer: you feed it with something, it goes on repeating it. It is a parrot.

So the first thing to understand is that this is the nature of the mind. It is not something peculiar happening to you. Once you understand this — that the mind is repetitive — you drop the effort, and suddenly you see that you are separate from the mind. You are not the mind. So the real thing is to accept the mind and grow into a deep unconcern.

Who is it that is aware that the mind goes on repeating, that asks that it should stop? Just become aware of that. You are that.

So first accept the limitations of the mind. You accept the body limitations; you know that you cannot fly — but nobody tries. But the mind is invisible. You don't know what is happening to Mukta's mind, what is happening to Teertha's mind. (two sannyasins sitting close by) You are confined to your mind, Mukta to hers, and Teertha to his — and nobody knows what is happening to the other.

In fact everybody needs a small window in the head so people can look in! (the group laughs) Then they will not be worried about such things because it is happening to everybody. Then you simply accept that this is just natural. The blood goes on moving in the body, the breathing goes on moving in and out; blood

THE DOGS OF THE MIND GO ON BARKING

circulates, breathing circulates, thinking circulates — nothing is wrong in it!

So second thing: become unconcerned. Soon you will see it is just like the barking of the dogs there. (the local dogs were arguing heatedly somewhere in the background as Bhagwan was speaking) Far away in the night the dogs of the mind go on barking and you are unconcerned. And the more unconcerned you are, the bigger the distance becomes. One day you come to realise that the distance between you and your mind is greater than the distance between you and the farthest away galaxy. Because the galaxy is still at a certain distance from you, it can be measured. But from the consciousness, the thought is so far away that it cannot be measured. Even in light years it cannot be measured, because the difference is not of distance; it is of different planes.

It is just as the difference between you and other human beings is not very much, but between you and a tree it is very much; and then between you and a rock it is tremendous.

Mind and consciousness are diametrically opposite poles, but this has to be realised by and by. The first step is to accept the limitations of the mind, don't expect the impossible; and secondly, become unconcerned, forget about it.

And feel blessed that the mind is still making noise, the clock is still tick-tocking. There is nothing to worry about, just a distance has to be felt — and it is there. It is only a question of feeling it. You understand me? Try it!

Bhagwan turned to a sannyasin who was leaving Poona to return home to America. He told him to help the centre near where he would be living, and gave him a little black box. The little black boxes hold a secret that cannot be disclosed. You have to wait until you can discover it for yourself. And when you do, make sure you don't tell anybody else!

Bhagwan asked what work the sannyasin did.

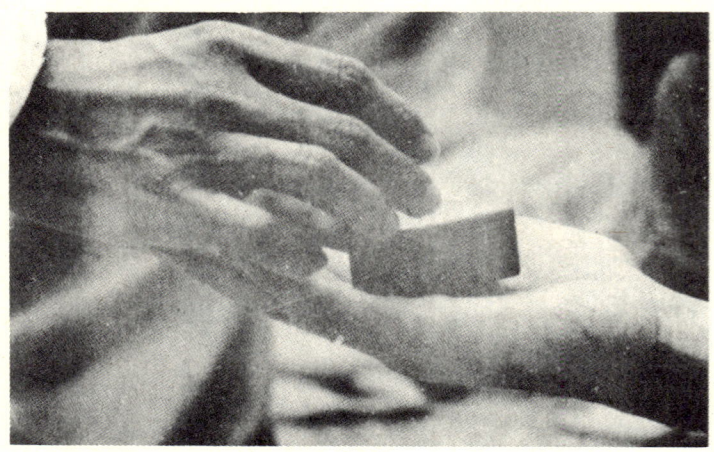

PREM NIRVAN   *Psychology, mental health counselling, working in hospitals. I am thinking also of trying to do a little work privately.*

Mm mm, start working privately, and you can be more helpful. By and by introduce meditation wherever you are and whatsoever you do. Many mental patients

MADNESS IS A HIDING PLACE

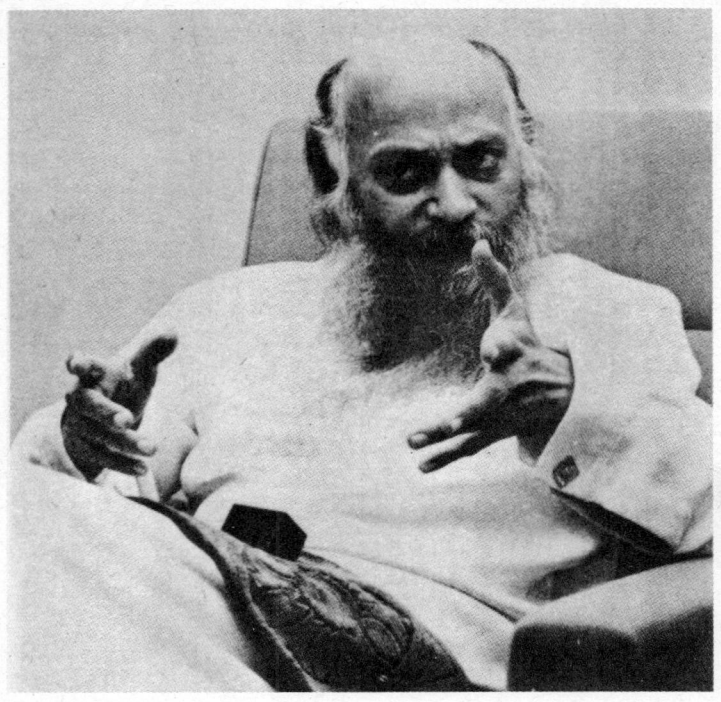

can be helped through meditation. In fact western psychology has not proved of much help. So with psychiatry, side by side start helping patients to meditate.

If a mental patient thinks he can do something about his illness himself, that very idea helps tremendously. If he feels that he cannot do anything—that he just has to remain helplessly dependent on others, on drugs, on psychiatrists, psychoanalysts, treatments, electric shock and a thousand and one things—by and by he loses confidence. But you can tell him that he can do something and can come out of his misery, and that it is not in fact a disease, but, rather, an attitude.

Now western psychology is discovering that madness is not always a disease; rather, it is a hiding place. Life had become too much for the person and he could not find anywhere to hide. So madness becomes a hiding place, a defence.

NIRVAN   *That's good! The problem is that most people will still want to hide.*

No, not once he knows that it is not a disease. That hiding is not conscious, it is absolutely unconscious. He has come to feel the convenience of it, but it has never been a conscious decision.

For example, you are burdened too much with financial difficulties; too many family responsibilities, and a thousand and one problems. You can't sleep well, you feel depressed, and by and by you see that if people start thinking that you have gone out of your mind, then suddenly they don't make you responsible. On the contrary, you become their responsibility; then they have to help you. And once the unconscious gets the hint, it relaxes.

But this is unconscious. Consciously no one would like to be mad. At such a great cost, no one would like to. But once it happens it becomes a comfortable thing. The government takes care of you, everybody sympathises, the children cannot demand, the wife cannot quarrel with you—you are not in your senses. And then, too, one does not want to come out, and that too is unconscious.

So help them to see the fact: that just for small comforts they are destroying their whole life, missing a great opportunity in which much was possible and still is possible. Tell them that they can do something about it if they decide to come out of it.

It happened once that I stayed in a friend's house.

LIFE IS A GREAT OPPORTUNITY

His father was mad and he had always been so. But I suspected something because the man looked very clever.

So when there was nobody there and I was sitting with this madman, I told him, 'I suspect you cannot be mad. You look too clever!'

He looked surprised. Then he said, 'How did you come to know?'

Bhagwan laughed delightedly. His laughter is so total, so spontaneous and flowing. His eyes really do dance and his face really has a glow of joy about it. He continued amid the laughter from the group. . . .

Then he told me the whole story: that his father was a very hard taskmaster and he had learnt a trick—by and by he proved himself mad. It was very comfortable and convenient, with nothing to worry about. The father worked till the day he died, and this boy never had to do anything! Then his children started working—because their father was mad!

'So,' he said, 'it was such a convenient thing. First my father worked and now my children work, and I have lived at ease! But, please don't tell anybody!'

NIRVAN *Yes, I've found a few of those myself!* (laughter from the group)

Mm, there are!

TUESDAY DECEMBER 16th

BHAGWAN   Sushila, leaving tomorrow? Come here. How are you feeling?

SUSHILA   *Well, feeling a little bit anxious about leaving. Umm... feeling I'm beginning to work on myself and just beginning to... with the relationship going deep, and now leaving. And I know everything is alright, but it's just coming up....*

Bhagwan pauses, looking down at his lap for some time before answering.

Mm mm... just relax and don't become anxious about it because anxiety disturbs everything. It doesn't help in any way; it creates only more and more hindrances. If you love and anxiety comes in, it creates a distance and then the relationship becomes a burden. If you meditate and anxiety comes in, then meditation becomes impossible.
   Whatsoever you do, do it without anxiety. Anxiety is just a habit. Try to find out why it arises. It is not because of a certain situation; it is just an old habit.

If you want to perform something, to show something, if you worry about what others are going to think, then anxiety arises. It is part of the ego, part of selfconsciousness. If you are unselfconscious, anxiety is impossible. It is just a shadow.

For example, you go on talking and you talk beautifully. Then suddenly you are on the stage and you have to talk to a thousand people, and then the anxiety arises. You have been talking your whole life, and the same is to be done; you are not going to do anything new! And it has never been a problem. You may have talked to each of these thousand people separately, but why does anxiety suddenly arise?

Now, facing a thousand people, you suddenly feel you are being judged; you feel that they will form an opinion about you—how you act, how you speak, how you perform. Once the idea of performance enters then the natural flow is lost and anxiety arises. So whenever you feel it coming, just seek deep down and you will find it is a selfconsciousness—whether it is a relationship, or work on oneself, or anything else.

And there is no need for the anxiety because there is nobody who can judge you; nobody has the authority to judge anybody and you need not depend on anybody's opinion. In fact this should be the criterion of inner growth. If you can be happy absolutely alone, and you don't need others to make you happy; if you can be flowing, silent, beautiful, alone, and you don't need others to make you whatsoever you think you are; if others are not needed to prop you, or for any sort of approval, then you are grown-up. Only children ask for others' approval—what daddy thinks, what mum thinks. When you are grown-up you are on your own; you need not bother what others think.

So drop all anxieties. And they can only be dropped if you accept that you are whatsoever you are. You are not expected to be anybody else and you cannot be. So simply be yourself and relax, and don't ask for anybody's approval, anybody's opinion—and then suddenly there is no anxiety.

And growth takes care of itself. It comes of its own accord; it is not that you have to grow. You have to accept whatsoever you are and the growth follows. Seek it and you will miss. Allow it and it is always there, available. Nothing is needed; you are accepted as you are and God doesn't ask for any proof. In the very first place He has accepted you, that's why you are; otherwise you would not have been.

And to look at existence in such a way that you feel at ease and at home is all that religion is about. So you go without anxiety. . . . Good.

What about you?

LEELA   *It's good to see you again!*
                              (a shy smile)

(chuckling) Very good!

LEELA   *You told me to do the camp and tell you what was taking me deep . . . .*

Mm mm, you tell me.

                              Well. to me they are all the same (the meditations). *They are all like playing games, but I like them. But the only thing I think is taking me deep is you.*

(smiling) Right, that too is right. Good. Very few people find all the meditations are good. But if you really understand then all the meditations are the same. They are different doors to the same temple, mm?

And that second understanding is also true; that's very good. So play and enjoy. Don't be serious, just take them as fun—the less serious the better. When you are just playing, many more things happen to you.

I have heard about one musician who was very sad and was just sitting by his piano playing idly. Suddenly he struck the chord for which he had been waiting his whole life. It was tremendously beautiful; he was transformed to another world.

Then he tried again and again but the same chord wouldn't come back, he couldn't create the same harmony. He tried for months and almost became mad, but he went on missing. Then he dropped all effort, and one day after a few months, once again he was sitting and playing in a not very serious mood—and again it was there!

Then he knew the secret: that that which is beyond comes to you only when you are not trying to grab it, not trying to manipulate it. Because it is so vast it is uncontrollable. It comes only as a surprise.

So play and take everything as fun. The whole point is to delight in it, mm? Then many things happen. It has been good, mm? I am happy!

LEELA   *I'm happy too!*

GO AS DEEP AS POSSIBLE

Something to say?

BHADRA *You asked me last week to tell you about the meditations. They are all powerful. I have been depressed sometimes, and very happy other times, and it goes on and on....*

Meditation stirs many things. It stirs your happiness and your sadness too. Sometimes you are thrown in a valley of darkness—sad and depressed. Sometimes you are raised to the clouds. It is good, allow it, and whatsoever happens accept it.

When you feel depressed, don't try to escape from it. In fact go as deep in it as possible. Drown yourself in your sadness, become really sad, so that you can touch the very bottom of it. Once you can touch the bottom of sadness, you will suddenly realise that it is the same as the bottom of happiness. The difference is only on the surface; as you go deeper, the differences are lost and the bottom is one.

So next time you are sad, be really sad, drown in it. Don't make any effort to save yourself: don't cry, don't move from the sadness to something else so you can become occupied and can forget it. No, remain with it. It is difficult, arduous, heavy—but it is worth trying. Once you touch the rock bottom of it, suddenly you are smiling.

Then you can never be sad again, because once you have touched the rock bottom of any feeling, you go beyond it. Very good. You continue....

A sannyasin told Bhagwan that she had discovered that she had healing powers and she wondered whether it would be good for her to develop this power. Bhagwan asked when she first became aware of it.

PREMDASI

> *Just about a year ago. I first became aware of it when I put my hands on someone I was giving a massage to, and my hands started vibrating, and the man said, 'What are you doing?'*
> *I said, 'I don't know. My hands are vibrating.' He said it was like an electric current through him. I just wondered what it was about. Then it happened at other times and I found that if I placed my hands over a place that hurt—not on it, just over it—then again the person would feel this current and the pain would go away.*

Just raise both your hands and close your eyes. If something happens, allow it.

Premdasi raised both her hands above her shoulders, palms facing towards Bhagwan. The right hand immediately started trembling, then vibrating quite vigorously; the left hand remained unmoving. Bhagwan shone his torch on both her hands. Premdasi began to breathe deeply, her head and body jerking spasmodically, her mouth falling open.

Bhagwan indicated to a sannyasin, a woman who was sitting in the group, to come forward and gently touch the right hand of Premdasi. The girl did so and said she could feel nothing. A boy was then beckoned forward to do likewise. He said he could feel a lot of warmth from her hand.

Premdasi gradually stopped trembling and opened her eyes. Her body continued to give little jerks for the following few minutes as she sat listening to Bhagwan. . . .

I WILL BE HELPING

Good, you can come back now. . . . You have the capacity, but there are two or three things. Whenever you want to heal somebody, do the humming for at least three minutes. Never do it without it.

Bhagwan was referring to the humming meditation, the Nadabrahma meditation, where one adopts any sitting position that is comfortable, and with eyes closed begins to hum. You do it loud enough so that people around you can hear it, and so that your whole being is vibrating with the resonance.

You have the energy, but more subtle vibrations are needed. The more subtle they become, the more helpful — and they will not exhaust you as much as gross vibrations. So three minutes of humming before you do it, mm? So you are almost vibrating all over the body. Cooperate with it; you were not cooperating — the hand was moving on its own, you were not cooperating. Help it to move so that the whole body is vibrating; it is not just a local thing.

And the second thing: if you want to heal a woman, it will be difficult. Your vibrations will be very helpful to a man, but for a woman it will be difficult. So for one year don't try on a woman, because if you fail a few times then a wrong auto-suggestion goes into your being that nothing is happening and that you don't have the capacity.

So for one year only try on men, not on women, so that one year will give you such a deep trust in your energy that then you can start working on women. And you will succeed on women too, then. Very good! And I will be helping! . . .

Bhagwan has said that we owe our parents a debt, for it is they who have given us life. And, he said, the greatest thing we can give them in return is meditation.

With the increasing number of young seekers coming to Bhagwan, there are also many older ones, among them parents of sannyasins.

Bhagwan—whose own father took sannyas recently—pointed out that for a parent to follow the example, to follow in the footsteps of his own child, is a tremendous happening.

Another mother took the plunge into sannyas this evening....

Having first been initiated into sannyas by Bhagwan, Prabhudasi, through the help of our resident Italian/English translator, said that she felt a Christian with Christians, a pagan with pagans, and a sannyasin with sannyasins.

Bhagwan replied that this could be very good if you were centred, but very dangerous if you were not. He continued, saying:

If you are centred, wherever you go you are at ease, at home with whomsoever you move. But this is only a possibility if you are centred, if you know who you are, otherwise you will get confused. One day you are a Christian, another you are a Hindu, the next a Mohammedan, and then the whole thing will create confusion.

Prabhudasi said that she felt it was the religious feeling that linked everything together.

That is what I am saying. If you know what religion is, if you have attained to that link, then it is perfectly good. But I don't see that link at all. I don't see that centredness in you at all. I don't see that this is going to help you.

Prabhudasi said that she knew she had not reached this point and looked humbly up to Bhagwan.

PATHS ARE DIFFERENT, THE GOAL ONE

The whole thing is not to go on accumulating impressions from everywhere, because all the paths are different. The goal is one, but the paths are different.

So at the end it is perfectly beautiful to say that everything is one, but in the beginning it is very dangerous. And no one can travel on many paths simultaneously. You have to travel on one path only, and you will reach the same goal as others who were travelling on different paths.

So don't be against anybody — Hindu, Christian, Mohammedan — but be for something. Choose something for which you can say, 'I am for it.' Followers of many paths simply become confused, fragmented. They become a crowd: one hand going to the north, another to the south, one leg to the east, another to the west. They are torn apart.

So what you are saying is good if you have reached. It is good for me, but it is not good for you!

So we will see. You start meditating....

A young attractive-looking German woman shyly came forward to Bhagwan's feet, her little child holding onto her hand.

The child sat down near Bhagwan in a self-possessed and centred manner, looking without shyness or fear at Bhagwan's face. She did not give one the feeling of precocity or sophistication, but rather a feeling that she was at ease with herself and the world around her.

Her mother said that the child wanted to take sannyas.

(To the child) Very good! Ready?
(To the mother) And you have not taken sannyas yet?
(an apprehensive little laugh from the mother) This is very good!

The group laughed. It is really beautiful to watch Bhagwan with children....

Come here! This is very good; you are more courageous — come here! Close your eyes, close your eyes....

The little girl before Bhagwan sat, as children do, with her head bent back and her small face upturned, completely exposed and vulnerable.

She looked like a little flower, her golden hair falling in curls around her shoulders, that special glow that only children have on her face, her child's hands resting in her lap, waiting....

Her profile was in direct line with that of Bhagwan. They looked so absolutely perfect together, a harmony. There was none of the feeling that surrounds adults when they are confronting Bhagwan, where one can sense many things: an internal struggle-of-will, of fear, love arising. With this meeting there was just a feeling of rightness, of friends reunited.

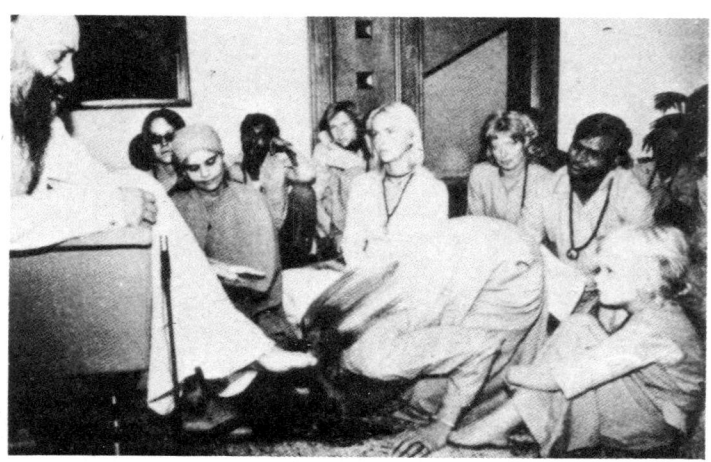

YOU MAY BECOME THE BRIDGE

Good! You can open your little eyes!

He places the mala over her head and tells her mother to retain her old name—Tanya: Ma Prem Tanya. Bhagwan said that Tanya should be helped to meditate, as much could be done with one so young; 'a rare child' he added.

Tanya got up and returned to her place in the group. For several seconds Bhagwan continued to stare unblinkingly at the ground in front of him where she had been sitting. . . .

The mother then took the jump too, following her daughter into sannyas. Then her husband came forward saying that he too would like to become a sannyasin.

He said he was studying with a Buddhist, whom he loved very much, in Germany. He asked that if he became a sannyasin would Bhagwan still be with him if he went back to his teacher.

I will be. I will be working with him also, so don't be worried.

All buddhist methods are good, tremendously good, and they have nothing to do with religion. They are simply scientific. You need not call them buddhist, you need not call them anything—they are simple methods. Buddhism is not a religion, it is just a psychology. It is not like Christianity, it is not like Hinduism. It is pure science—and pure science belongs to nobody.

So you can continue to work with the man, and soon you may become the bridge for him to come to me! Now close your eyes. . . .

The family circle, married through sannyas, fathered by Bhagwan, was completed.

A couple, newly arrived in Poona, said that they were finding that their relationship had changed since being here. The girl said she did not feel like love-making so often; her boy-friend said he was feeling attracted to other women.

Bhagwan suggested that they make love just once a week, but to have such a total experience that they were completely satisfied.

When you make love, make it really wild so that it is not just a local release, but your whole being throbs with it. You have to scream and jump so that it becomes a meditation. When you make love, the whole world should know! Then it will satisfy you so completely that for one week you won't think about it. That mind goes on looking at other women because you are not satisfied.

In the East we have been enquiring into the sexual energy; the West is only enquiring on the periphery. We have come to see that it is not a question of this woman or that; it is a question of female and male energy. If they can meet, really meet, there is such an orgasmic experience that the ego disperses for a few minutes and you are not there. You have disappeared and the whole universe dies with you. Your nature has exploded, all civilization gone. You are wild animals—innocent, vibrant, possessed.

But this is only possible, it can only be a deep orgasmic happening, if you are celibate—then you gather the accumulated energy. It becomes a reservoir and then you explode. Otherwise, if you make love an everyday habit, it becomes just like taking tea or smoking a cigarette —nothing much. Then it is no more than a release, just like a sneeze. So don't make sex a sneeze, otherwise you will miss the whole mystery of it.

So decide the day that you will make love, and make that day sacred and a day of deep meditation. Once a week —let it be Sunday, the religious day. And let it be a very sacred phenomenon. Prepare that day from the very morning. Be as loving to each other, as careful, as possible; no conflict and no anger—because that distracts the energy.

The whole day you are to feel that the moment is coming when you are to make love. You have waited for six days, and now prayerfully, meditatively, move into it. Before making love both meditate together. Pray to God to be with you, to envelop you so that you both dissolve into Him.

Let sex be as divine as possible. It is divine because it is the creative force, the creative energy. Nothing is more divine than sex.

So make it so satisfying that soon you will say that one week's celibacy is not enough, that you need three weeks of celibacy, or four. Because it is so satisfying, the glow, the after-glow, continues for weeks—you are bathed in it. So start it this way, mm?

A sannyasin said that she had come in contact with a lot of mistrust and fear in the meditations, at the point where she felt that her body was taking over.

Bhagwan said that the fear had to be transcended, otherwise she could never go into the meditations, could never grow. He compared it to a seed, saying that whenever the plant starts growing, the seed becomes afraid because it has to die if the plant is to be born. Whenever you come near the death point, where the ego, the egg, the shell, has to drop and a new being is coming, the fear will take possession of you. But you have to go on in spite of the fear. He reminded her that he would be with her. . . .

The sannyasin said she had been leading groups in Germany and did not feel the need to do groups here as Bhagwan had suggested. Bhagwan said that the role of groupleader could be a protection, adding:

This has been my experience — I see groupleaders are not grown at all, because when you are leading others you remain outside; you are not involved.

You become very wise intellectually, but existentially you don't grow. If you are led, the groups are totally different. And here they are totally different because you have to work together with meditations, and they help.

If you have been a groupleader, you have to pass through the groups as a must. To be a leader is a very ego-fulfilling phenomenon — and the ego is the problem! By and by almost all of the groupleaders of the world are going to come. They have to, because they have become leaders and they have not grown up; they are like little children.

I WILL HAVE TO DESTROY YOU...
ONLY THEN CAN YOU BE REBORN

Once you become a leader it is very very difficult to grow, because then your whole prestige is at stake.

I will have to destroy you; only then you can be reborn. I will have to be hard. I will have to be like a hammer on your rock, mm? Good.

Much of what is communicated at darshan has to go unrecorded, because much of what happens—in touches, glances, smiles and laughter, and in silences—cannot be interpreted into verbal dialogue; that would seem much too gross, and totally inadequate besides.

Unexpected things can happen to one in the presence of Bhagwan. People, usually self-possessed and articulate, suddenly find that any prepared speech they might have had has simply disappeared, dissolved. Words fail, and they are left with themselves and Bhagwan—and nothing in between. Bhagwan has said that his very presence gives a shock to the mechanism of the mind; that this is good and one should allow it.

Sometimes a sannyasin will say, 'I had many questions an hour ago but suddenly they have disappeared!' Or that a problem that had been bothering him for weeks now seemed no longer a worry. Being at Bhagwan's feet, you feel that you have left one world behind and entered a new one; a feeling of being in a new dimension almost, where time no longer exists.

Bhagwan said recently that with him, to use words was useless; that words could in fact act as a means of avoiding communicating.

Only in deep silence there is a merger and a meeting, and the boundaries dissolve. Something of me enters you and something of you enters me.

So many sit quietly without talking in darshan, simply content to be in his presence: watching him, drinking him, imbibing his fragrance—taking their fill of him.

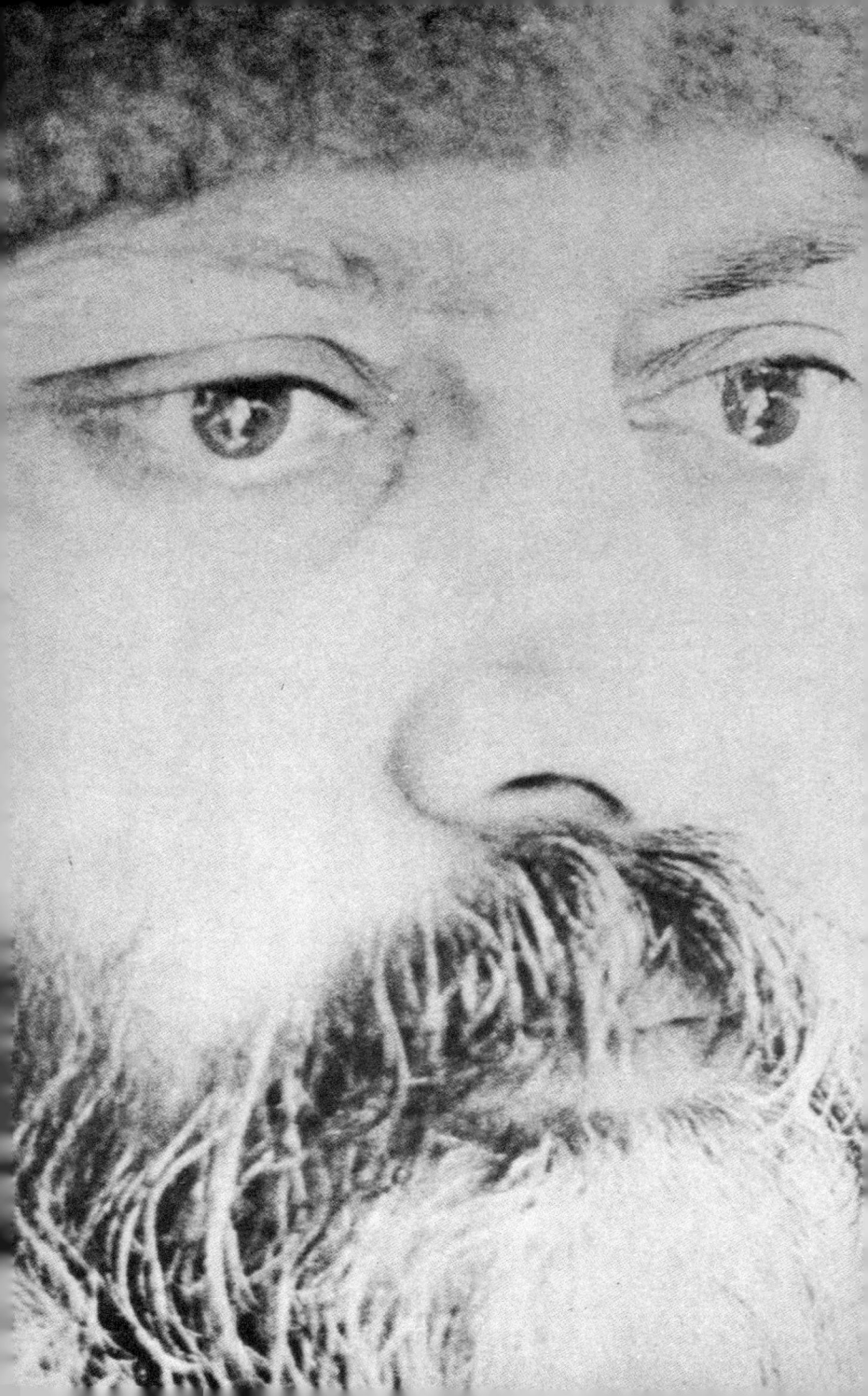

Be quiet, still, silent, waiting; be feminine. . . .

THURSDAY DECEMBER 19th

BHAGWAN (to a new sannyasin) . . . this will be your new name: Ma Deva Rikta. Rikta means emptiness, deva means divine — divine emptiness.

That is how you, by and by, have to imbibe the spirit of emptiness in you. Inside there is just emptiness, mm? That is how I feel your seed is. The more empty you feel, the more empty you can become. And you can feel it easily, it will not be difficult; it will just come naturally.

Emptiness has never been part of western religion, but in the East, emptiness has been the deepest-going meditation. In the West, emptiness is felt to be somehow negative, as if an empty mind is the devil's workshop. It is not. In fact an empty mind is God's workshop. If the mind is empty the devil cannot enter. The devil can enter only through thinking, through some occupation. If the mind is empty, then only can God enter.

Rikta means emptiness. So you try this: walking, just feel emptiness walking; when you are talking, just feel emptiness talking; loving, just feel emptiness loving. Continuously remember that inside there is nothing. And that is the nature of man, that nothingness. It is not an absence, it is a presence, it is fullness. When the emptiness is total, it is fullness.

So try it, and I will start working on you from this moment, mm?

I WILL NOT BE COMING AGAIN

A sannyasin had earlier sent a letter to Bhagwan, as she found it a little difficult to express herself in English, asking the following question, which Bhagwan read out:

> 'This morning (at the morning discourse) *I did not quite understand your saying that the fulfilled, enlightened spirit going back home doesn't have to come back to earth for another life. This may be my western-trained mind, but what is happening to this fulfilled enlightenment, this attaining, this evaporation? How do you explain having come if you will not be again?*'

You come only if something is still missing, something is still imperfect. So the last life is the life of enlightenment.

I have come because something was still missing. But now it is not missing and I will not be coming again.

That doesn't mean that you become non-existential, no. That simply means that you become so absolutely existential that the body cannot contain you. The body becomes small and you become so big for the body that you cannot be contained in it. You become so infinite that the finite mind cannot contain you. But one has to come again and again, even if something is missing, to learn it.

The world is a school, it is a learning, a discipline, a training. Once you have learnt, you are not sent back, because there is no need, no point.

So an enlightened person can help people only in his last life. Then after that the help is impossible, then he evaporates. So only for a few years the possibility remains open and available. If you are not enlightened, you cannot help people. If you are enlightened, you can help only for a few years, because this is going to be your last. . . .

A sannyasin said to Bhagwan that since she had written to him yesterday, her feeling of having all those troubles had changed to one of peace. Bhagwan chuckled.

This seems to happen often. Just the very act of sitting down to write to Bhagwan about a problem that is troubling you, or a dilemma you are experiencing, seems to change the whole situation. The problem dissolves, or suddenly another side of it appears — and the answer is there.

Similarly, in verbalising a problem to him in fantasy, perhaps addressing his picture, an answer can come in his words, with his expressions, inflections. . . .

Perhaps it is nothing more than the fact that things have been clarified by giving utterance to the problem. Perhaps it is just that the unconscious has supplied the answer, but I wonder. . . .

Prem Savita continued, saying that she was just beginning to feel that she had many things to work on and wondered if Bhagwan could suggest something to help her.

Everybody has much work to do because nobody comes perfect, and once you do become perfect, then you cannot come back. Much work has to be done and it is difficult, but not impossible. Sometimes you may feel it is so difficult that you begin feeling hopeless. Those are the moments to remember that the project is very difficult — Project Man is very difficult — but not impossible.

And it is good that it is difficult. If it were not, then it wouldn't be worthwhile. If inner growth is easily available, cheap; if you don't have to work for it, earn it, or become worthy of it, then it will be worthless. The more

THE LONGER THE JOURNEY..
THE DEEPER THE REST

difficult it is, the more worth it has. The longer the journey, the deeper the rest. And when you reach the goal, the longer the waiting has been, the more fulfillment you will find.

That's why all shortcuts are false—and dangerous. They can only delude you. There is no shortcut for inner growth because the very way, and the very difficulty of it, is part of the growth. If you avoid the difficulty, you avoid the growth also.

But many things are going to happen, mm? You just have to remain available. Start meditating, and while meditating bring your total energy to it. Don't go on withholding anything, don't be clever.

That is one of the troubles, because the mind is very clever. It always goes halfway and keeps one step ready to withdraw if things go beyond control and you cannot manipulate. But if you are ready to withdraw you cannot go in, because one has to go with both legs, not only with one; and one can go only totally, not partially.

So remember one thing: that meditation has to be done as totally as possible, and every day more and more totality will become available. You will find every day that more and more is coming up, and you will see that you are still holding—and by and by the ice melts. So go totally into it!

Many times one reaches near the goal and loses the track. Many times you are almost, almost there, and again you are very far away. These are the glimpses; these are the glimpses that in Japan they call satori. Just a small glimpse, but the glimpse gives you courage that yes, it exists, the truth exists; that you are not groping hopelessly. Hope is there. And sometimes thousands of satoris are possible, but each satori becomes more and more definite, more and more solid. And each satori brings you nearer and nearer the goal. And when suddenly you are there at the goal, you are not, only the goal is. Then we call it samadhi.

That is the goal of all human effort, the very peak of all consciousness. But one has to work hard — so start working!

A seeker, not yet a sannyasin, said to Bhagwan that he often talked about the significance of having a master, yet he had heard that Bhagwan himself had attained without a master. How, he asked, was this possible, and did one who became enlightened without a master enter a higher level of enlightenment than one who had had a master?

No, enlightenment has no higher or lower grades. How you enter does not make any difference: from the front door or the back, like a master or a thief, makes no difference. Once you enter, all differences are lost.

There is a possibility of entering enlightenment without a master, but then you should be ready for more struggle, more risk; have more patience and courage.

One day it is going to happen, even if you are not taking anybody's help. If you go on groping and groping and groping, though it may take many lives, one day you are going to find the door. That's how many have found it. But once you have found it you can make it a little easier for others. It may have been difficult for you, but for others it can be made a little easier. You can give some indication, some keys, some hints. You can guide.

This has to be understood: that a master in fact does not lead you to truth. He simply helps you to avoid untruth. Truth cannot be indicated. It is not something existing out there. It is something that will come into existence through your effort. Your truth will have to be born in you. A master can help you to grope better so that many pitfalls can be avoided. He cannot indicate the truth but he can indicate what is not truth — and there are a thousand and one untrue doors. He can show you that these are untrue doors: avoid this, avoid that. That's what they call in the Upanishads 'neti-neti' — this is not, that is not. The master goes on negating, and only that which is, is left.

That's how a master can help. A few people struggle on their own but that is very rare. And you are not that type of person, because if you were, you would not have come to me. I never went to anybody even to ask this, because even this is taking help. Even if you go to that type of person to give him the truth, he will close his ears. He will say, 'I don't want it. I will find it myself.'

This type may look in the beginning to be very egoistic, but he is not. That's the way he is; he wants to seek his own truth, he does not want to borrow it from anybody. Not that he is arrogant; he is humble. And he is not afraid of wasting time. He is not afraid of waiting for lives. He is not in a hurry; his patience is infinite. But he may look like an arrogant person. It is not that he is incapable of surrendering, no. He is surrendered, but this is his way, this fits him.

Then there are people to whom it cannot suit at all. They need someone to whom to surrender; they need someone to help them. Not that they are weak, remember; not that they are in some way inferior — they are not. It is just that natures differ, types differ, and these are the two types.

So this much I will say: that you are not the type who can work without a master, otherwise you would not have come. So don't waste time. If you can find somebody with whom you feel attuned, then surrender, and allow him to help you. Think about it, mm? Good.

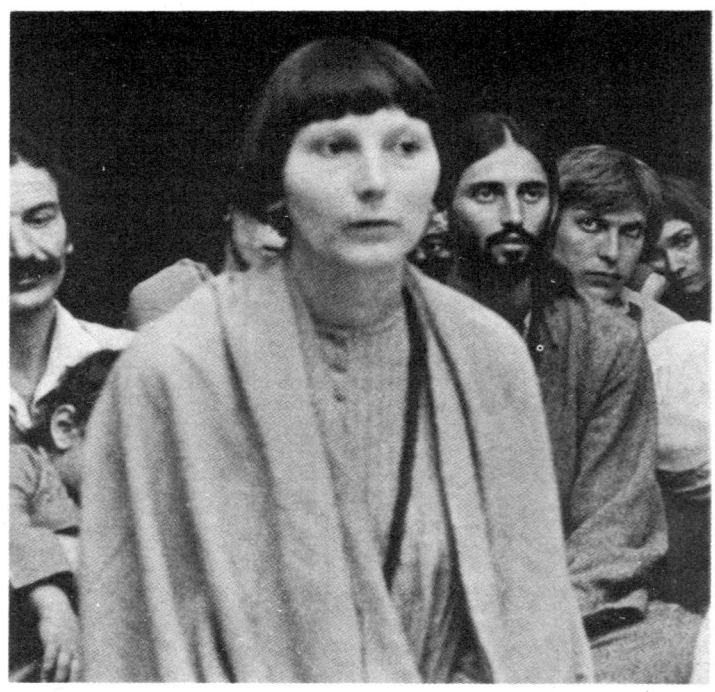

A sannyasin said that her lover was very closed to her lately. Since the celebration of Bhagwan's birthday, on December 11th, she said he had changed, becoming closer to Bhagwan but more distant from her, and she felt excluded.

She expressed confusion as to whether she wanted to continue the relationship or not. . . .

It always happens that when people are alone they become fed up with their aloneness. They are sad, but calm and quiet; not excited about life. So they seek somebody, some relationship, and then the excitement comes, but with it come many problems — anger, fight, jealousy, and a thousand and one other things.

Sadness disappears, but anger comes because it is the same energy. Sadness is anger suppressed, because alone you have no one to express the anger to, so you carry it. And anger is sadness suppressed. These two cases have to be understood.

Unless you can be calm and quiet in love, love is not going to solve anything. It has to be understood that love in itself, or just by having a relationship with someone, is not going to give you happiness, unless you bring happiness with you. And if you don't have happiness, it is better to be alone.

And this always happens: unhappy people seek a relationship, thinking they are unhappy because they are alone. That is not the real thing. They are unhappy — whether they are alone or in a relationship makes no difference. And when you are together your unhappiness will become more intense; it cannot disappear just by being together. You have to drop it.

Always remember that when someone is with you, he is with you to be happy. Everybody is seeking his own happiness. But whenever someone is in love, you start having the illusion that he is seeking your happiness. Why should he be?

If you both bring happiness, the relationship can be beautiful; otherwise it is going to be on the rocks any day. So whenever a relationship starts it is good, because both are deceiving each other unknowingly. Only the beautiful face is there, and only when things settle does the ugly face come up. Then reality erupts and things go wrong.

If you feel that you have to cathart, then close the room and cathart on a pillow. Why destroy a relationship for it? Everyone is seeking his own happiness and there is nothing wrong in it. That's the only way to seek happiness. If you are together, help each other. If you feel it is harmful, separate. But remember, it is not only with this relationship; it is always going to be so. So face it, talk to him.

One should learn from every experience. Nothing is bad because everything can become a learning. Good, Prafulla. . . .

(to a young, pleasant-looking sannyasin) What about you?

ANAND
I was wondering if it is okay for me to go to Scotland? I was thinking of going back, just to get things arranged so that I can come back as soon as possible. It should take two or three months.

Finish them and come back!

ANAND
Also, I was going to say that my parents were missionaries in India for twenty-five years and I was wondering how to tell them that Christ is here. . . .

Bhagwan chuckled modestly and said he would find a way, and that he would be with him in Scotland.

In August of this year, Bhagwan Shree said that he envisaged that one day we would have here something like a university where all types of therapies — Encounter Groups, Primal Therapy, Enlightenment Intensives, massage, Arica Training, Unconditional Acceptance Seminars — along with Aikido, Tai Chi, Karate and

Acupuncture, would be available.

He said that people should be prepared to stay for at least three months, in which time they could experience as many groups as considered necessary for their growth. All existing therapies from the West, combined with those of the East, would be available. So if one could not be helped here, one could not be helped anywhere.

In September, therapies — Primal Therapy being the first — were introduced to the ashram. At the time of writing, ten different types of groups and courses are underway. All groups are led by sannyasins who have had extensive experience in their particular field. Bhagwan said that leaders could, in time, become masters in their own right and world-renowned, with people coming here specially to be helped by them.

The therapies, plus the meditations and the presence of Bhagwan, both invisible and materialised, provide a unique, an absolutely unique, experience for seekers. Bhagwan said that with his presence, groups here would be a different experience for both the leaders and the led. It is certainly so — sannyasins who have done groups both in the West and here say that they feel in more of a let-go knowing that Bhagwan is here. They also felt the therapist to be simply a channel for Bhagwan's energy. Some said they had never experienced Bhagwan so strongly as when in the group. Others commented that what had happened for them in the group became just part of an ongoing process, as they continued to interact and move with the same people. Many people mentioned that they felt part of a family, a community, since doing groups here.

Continuing regular meditations while taking part in various groups helped to intensify whatever was happening and to bring up material that had not come up through group work. It also allowed the process to continue further, as the energy was kept moving.

When camps are not in progress, groups are operating in the ashram and subsequently the energy level is kept high. This creates a very dynamic atmosphere and gives one a feeling of vitality and movement.

Not only that, but to see the participants of the various groups before, during, and after their courses, is tremendously exciting: seeing bodies actually being transformed — shoulders straightened, faces cleared, pseudo smiles replaced by genuine responses, energy really flowing. There are real tangible changes that make one aware that we are part of a birth process here with Bhagwan.

The Arica programme is shortly to be introduced into the ashram for the first time. The course lasts three days and the format includes gymnastic exercises (psychocalesthenics), mantrams, music meditations, African dance and body awareness.

The eight sannyasins, who have all trained in the West in Arica, came to darshan tonight. Bhagwan talked about Arica and suggested that the trainers bear in mind several things when taking the groups.

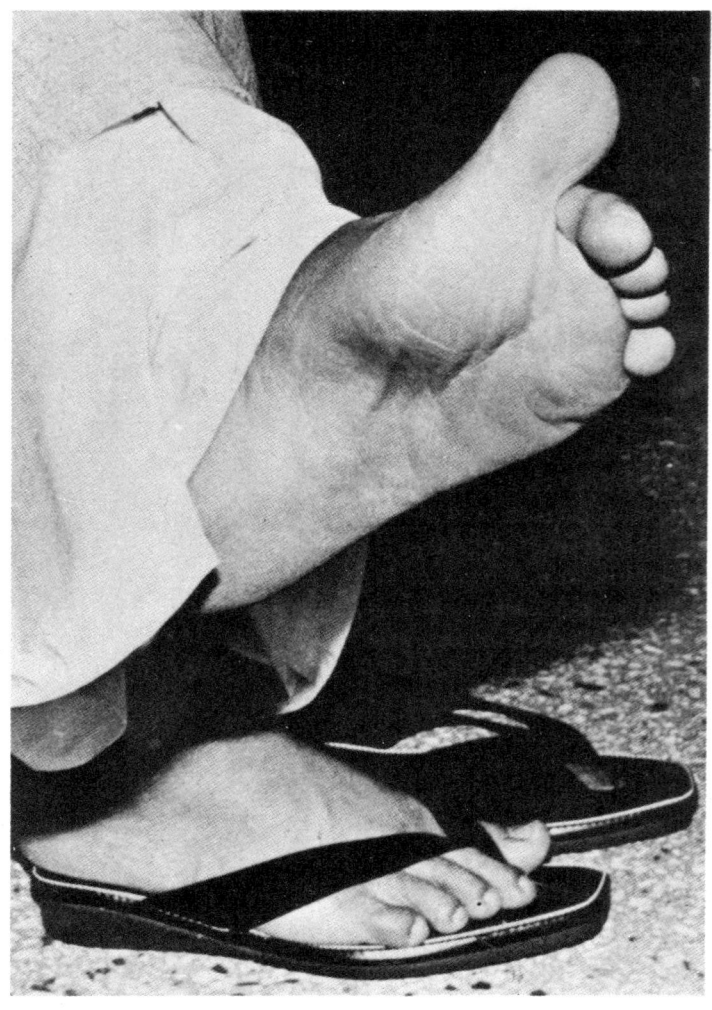

LOVE—THE GREATEST TECHNIQUE

There are just two or three things I would like to say before you start your work.

One is: bring more love into it. The techniques are beautiful, but love is lacking. Whenever you just become technique-oriented, then by and by you forget that love is the greatest technique. All else is secondary—can be helpful, but cannot replace love.

So don't be just technical, otherwise you will help a little but not enough, and you will not be able to help to the very end. Sooner or later a technique comes to an end, but love never does. Each technique should become a vehicle of love, so that when the technique ends, love takes over. And one never comes to the point where one can say that now the journey is finished and there is nothing left.

When you work on people, don't work on them as if they are means. Each individual is an end. The technique exists for the individual—the sabbath is for man, not man for the sabbath. Always remember this, because the mind tends to forget. It is very technical and does not believe in love.

So help people, but remain alert to give them as much care and love as possible. You will see that the same methods used in the West—which work up to a certain limit and then stop—don't stop anywhere; they go on and on. So make it a very loving process. You follow me?

And the second thing: always start with a prayer and always end with a prayer. In the beginning you pray with the idea of asking for help. In the end it is a thank you. Always ask for divine help, because man is helpless; and if you remember this, you will never condemn one who fails. Whenever you work with techniques, the fallacy is possible that you start thinking that man is enough. You forget God, you forget the Whole.

In Yoga they simply dropped the concept of God. Only once in Patanjali's sutras is God mentioned—and

that too as a technique: that if you surrender to God —
not that God exists, no; He is just an excuse for surrender —
it will be helpful. Yoga is completely godless. The word
yoga means technique, and technique always feels that
man is sufficient unto himself and that there is no need to
ask for help from beyond.

So make it a point that you start with a prayer together,
the teacher and the taught both. The teacher should
never feel that he is special. He should always feel that
both are part of an ongoing process of growth; that he is
also going to learn much, not only teach. Don't become
teachers, just remain helpers, fellow travellers; don't
become 'holier than thou' — and then you will be very very
deeply helpful. All Upanishads in India start by a prayer
which is done by the teacher and the taught together.
They pray that they should not go astray; they, the teacher
and the taught, the master and the disciple, should not go
astray.

And the third thing: always try to see that if some
technique is not working on someone, then don't go on
forcing it, because all techniques are not for everybody.
So give them a try, and if one is not working, then there is
no need to create the feeling that the person is lacking; just
say that this technique does not suit you, but there is
nothing wrong in that.

Never create the feeling of failure, remember, because
by and by the person can start becoming a failure. He
begins to feel that nothing is going to happen; that this is
not for him, it is only for very special and rare people, and
he is an ordinary person. Once this happens, a great rock
has fallen on his being. And many of the teachers in the
world go on doing that. Rather than helping people, they
hinder. So don't condemn anybody, otherwise you will be
closing their whole possibility of growth.

If in your three days' work you can give only this much
to a person — that he comes out more confident: more

confident about himself, more certain of his step, his growth, more confident that it is going to happen—you have given him something beautiful, a treasure; you have succeeded.

But always remember that if he leaves the group feeling he has been a failure, then you have betrayed that person, you have harmed him and put him back. These three things. . . .

A sannyasin, appropriately called Sadhana, asked Bhagwan how she could use what she had been experiencing here with him and through meditations, in her work of producing films.

You can bring newness to your work only by you yourself being new, because the work is nothing but your outer expression. It is always lesser than you, it can never be more. Whatsoever you are is reflected in it, and you cannot

deceive. If you deceive, it means that you have a deceptive being that is reflected in your work.

When I say to bring a new dimension to your work, I mean bring a new dimension to yourself. Unless it comes into your being, it can never come into the work that you are doing. Many people go on trying to bring something new into their work, but the whole process is frustrating if you just go on working on your work. A man can write poetry and can try to bring something new into it, but he almost always just goes on repeating himself. Maybe there is a new word, maybe the form is changed a little here and there, maybe a little modification, but nothing original.

BE COURAGEOUS ENOUGH TO BE A FOOL

When I say original, I don't mean that you have to do something that nobody has ever done. I mean something that surprises you. Only when it is completed do you see that something new has happened. You become aware that you have given birth to something new.

When something new comes into your being, automatically, of its own accord, it starts flowing into your work. You say something which you have never said before; you sing something which is simply not of you. This new element which has come into your being is going to be

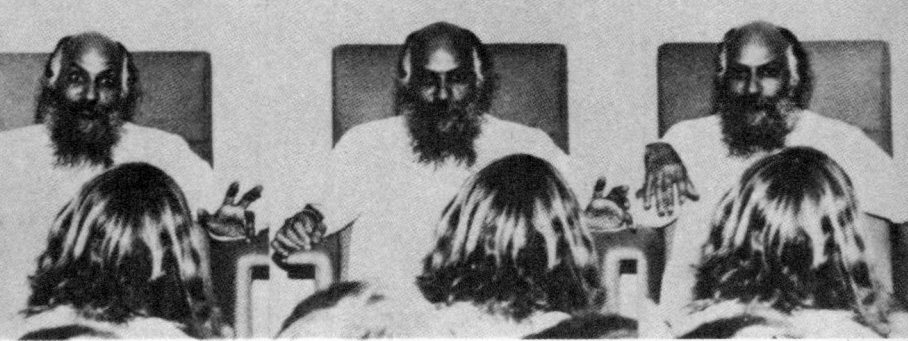

reflected, and every man has millions of dimensions and aspects to his being.

Man is not limited, but almost always he is focused. In one direction or another he becomes so efficient that he only flows through that direction, and he becomes afraid of other directions because they are new. He may not be so capable and so efficient in them — and that is the fear that destroys creativity.

A creative person has to overcome the fear of being in error, of being laughed at, of public opinion. One who wants to be creative has to be courageous enough to be a fool, because all daring in the beginning is foolish, and whatsoever you do in the beginning is always laughed at. By and by the recognition comes, but by that time, that dimension is already boring. By the time people start applauding, the creative person is no longer interested, because people only applaud when they see something they recognise. So it means it is already old, already repeated.

Now he has to start again, and he always has to start from A B C. That is why a creative person always remains like a child, fresh. A creative person is eternally amateurish; eternally, I say. The moment he feels that now

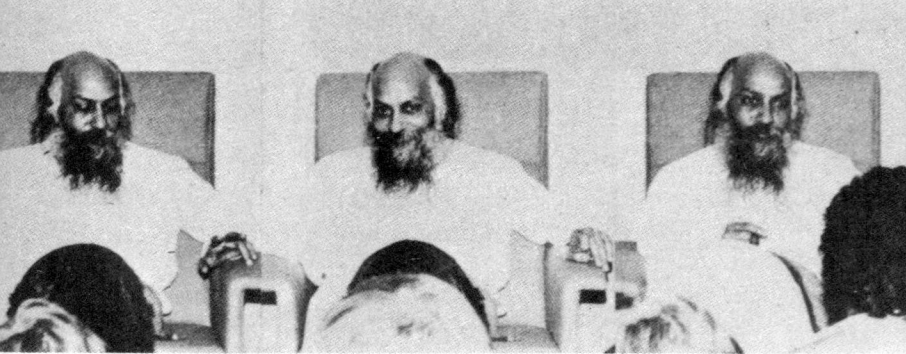

he has become an expert, he becomes alert and has to change.

An expert is one who is already dead, whose being has a fixed mode. He has a character, a pattern, and is predictable. If you are creative you are always flowing; you have no mode, no fixed pattern, no character.

The richest man has no character. He is fluid, he goes on moving in different dimensions. He seeks and searches from every direction. He is always a child with wondering eyes; always in awe, always searching and running after butterflies and collecting pebbles. He never feels he has arrived, never. His whole life is one of arriving and departing, but he never comes to the point where he can say

THOSE WHO HAVE ARRIVED ARE DEAD

that now he has arrived. Those who say that they have arrived are dead; they are corpses, carrying their tombs around with them.

So remember this, and bring something new into yourself. Meditations are going to help. Try to extend your visit a little longer. One month is not long enough at all. To be with me, even one life is not enough. But one month is certainly not enough!

GANGA

In the meditations I am aware of my body and the two sides feel very different — sometimes it disturbs me. I can't accept it all the time. It gives me a feeling of being torn apart.

Everyone's body is different. Everyone's left and right sides are different, because everyone has two brains, not one. Both the brains function separately, but a few people have a slightly bigger gap. Yours may have a slightly bigger gap, but there is nothing to worry about. Continue meditation and that gap will be bridged.

It will be good if you do some groups, particularly the Enlightenment Intensive. They will help you to bridge this gap. The gap is not in the body, it is in the brain.
Sometimes it happens that the bridge can be cut, or sometimes somebody falls and the bridge is broken, and the person becomes two different people.

Then your left hand can do something and your right hand will not know. You can kill somebody with your left hand and your right hand cannot be a witness to it. So when your one mind is functioning, you can promise something, and then when the other brain is functioning, you completely forget you made a promise — you never knew that you had made it really. So it is not a question of the body, but the brain.

That's why meditation can help, because it can bring the brain closer and closer. So don't worry and don't be afraid, mm?. . .

A sannyasin asked Bhagwan if it would be good for him to join the recently formed drama group.

Acting can be very helpful if you remain both conscious and involved. That is the whole art of acting — that you remain yourself, and yet you become someone else.
If you are playing a Judas, you remain yourself, you never become Judas, yet you pretend and play a lie. And you play the lie so beautifully and so sincerely that it appears like a truth.

That's what a successful actor is. He plays the lie so beautifully that it looks like the truth, but deep down he is aware that he is just a watcher, totally separate.

LIFE IS A CONSTANT DRAMA

If this realisation goes deep, then allow it to be continued in your ordinary life too, because there also a constant drama is going on. Somewhere you are a husband, somewhere a son or father, a friend or foe, beggar or king, rich or poor; these are all roles. The drama is so big, the stage vast and the players infinite, but still, it is a drama.

If you can keep on watching, you will attain to the witnessing self; what we call in India 'sakshi', the one who only witnesses, the one who is never a doer.

All doing is acting, and beyond the acting is the watcher—that is your being. That is the whole point, mm? If you learn that, then drama is perfectly beautiful. Be in it! Good.

A young American boy came to Bhagwan's feet next and began talking about himself and the feeling of confusion he was experiencing. He said he planned to go back to the West, yet he knew the West had nothing for him, and he was curious about what was happening here.

He had overcome his initial reaction against orange people, and even had some sannyasin friends now! He spoke in a rather rambling way, his thoughts rather elusively scattered through his words.

The seduction began. . . .

I think leaving is not going to be of help right now. You can go after a month, because this month will settle many things in you, mm?

Right now you are just becoming something. Something in your consciousness is settling, and if you give it a little time you will become centred. Then you can go, and nothing can destroy you—not even the West. Because once you are centred, once you know a little of yourself, then nothing can deceive you, and worldly things cannot become the goal. You can have them, you can enjoy them, but you are never worried about them. If you have them, good. If you don't have them, that too is good.

But right now you will be just escaping from an opportunity. It happens to many people. Whenever they start growing they have a certain restlessness, because it seems that if they remain a little longer they may change. And the mind is always afraid of change. It always wants the old, the convenient, the trodden path where you have always been moving. The new always makes it afraid, but the new is life, and through the new you reach to newer sources of life, new happiness.

I cannot say to you to be here, because you are still not a sannyasin. If you were a sannyasin then I would start ordering! When you are still an outsider I cannot. If you take sannyas first, then I will not suggest that you be here —I will simply tell you!

BILL
It doesn't matter...sannyas. I feel I am with you anyway, Bhagwan.

No, it matters; it matters because it is a gesture. You materialise your gesture into a certain thing.

For example, if you love somebody, you would like to hold their hand, to kiss or embrace them. Those are just the gestures to show something that you feel within. It cannot be shown in any other way.

Sannyas is nothing but a gesture that you have fallen in love with me. And then I can decide for you, mm?—

because then I have a responsibility. Right now I can only suggest that it would be good if you were here for a month, and you can do a few groups.

Once you are settled I will send you back, because I am not in favour of renouncing anything. Everybody has to go back to the world, to his world, wherever it is, to work it out. But before you enter into the world you must be centred, otherwise the world is too much.

So if you can be here it will be good . . . and if you are ready, I can give you sannyas right now. . . .

Bill looked at Bhagwan for only a second or two, and then with no more ado. . . .

BILL Yes, I'm ready. I'm ready for sannyas! I'm ready to be your lover, Bhagwan!

Good, close your eyes! (a chuckle) Close your eyes and I will find a name for you.

With a wave of Bhagwan's magic pen, Bill was transformed into Swami Anand Murti.

Now I will be with you! Anand means bliss; murti, image—image of bliss . . . and become one!

A sannyasin said to Bhagwan that he became very sad when he saw that there was so much suffering around him. He said he was able to help people suffering from bodily pain by the laying on of his hands, but not pains from 'inside'.

Bhagwan told him that before touching people to help them, he should first pray and become just a vehicle for the divine to work through him. He gave him a box and said that it would be useful if he could not feel the energy. He should close his eyes, feel collected and open, and then start to work with the person in pain. Bhagwan reassured him that he would be able to help with inner pain as well. . . .

Chit Vilas continued breathlessly:

> *I feel sometimes that you are speaking through me. I feel sometimes my voice changes . . . . I feel . . . you . . . me . . . .*

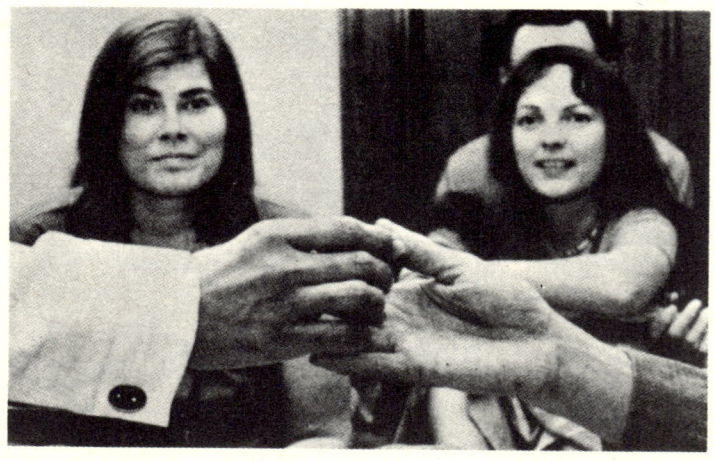

I DON'T WANT MISSIONARIES...
BUT PEOPLE WHO ARE THE MESSAGE THEMSELVES

He gave up trying to verbalise what he was wanting to express, throwing up his hands and making a movement between Bhagwan and him.

(laughing kindly) Yes, I know! Good!

What about you? Something to say?

PREM DEVIKA

> I really find it hard to talk whenever I see you at darshan or after the lecture. I get . . . I don't know what. . . . I don't know . . . . (laughter from those in the group who were sympathetic) . . . I get . . . I can't even describe it, a light feeling. . . . I'm very happy, I can't even get depressed anymore. And like, like now I'm shaking. . . .

Bhagwan encouraged her to allow the shaking. Her body shook, swaying backwards and forwards. After a few minutes she slowly lowered her head to the ground; the shaking ceased.

Bhagwan said that her energy was flowing perfectly, that whenever she felt like shaking she should allow it; that to make contact with the earth as she had just done then would give her a feeling of centredness.

Devika asked what she could do for Bhagwan, for herself.

Your only problem is that you are not feeling any problem! (Devika joined in the laughter of the group.)

Because you are not feeling depressed, unhappy, it becomes a problem, because one has always remained

with those things, and now suddenly they have disappeared.
One feels empty, lost, because the old pattern is
disappearing. One loses one's identity.

But that is what I am here for—to help you to lose
your identity. So whatever is happening is perfectly
beautiful. Be happy in it. If you cannot be unhappy,
don't become unhappy about it!

Just let it be so, mm? And soon the new will arise.
The old has gone and the new is getting ready, and
there is a gap. The gap is always like this: you cannot
describe it, you cannot say what it is. You can feel,
but that feeling is also vague, surrounded by mist—but
it is beautiful.

You just remain happy, flowing, and don't create
any problem. This is the way—if you remain flowing
—then you help me. If you remain flowing, whatsoever
happens in that flow will help my work, mm? This is
the way my work is going to be helped. If everybody
becomes flowing and happy, just enjoying the moment,
then my work is done!

I don't want to create missionaries. I just want
real people, authentic people. They don't carry any
mission—they are the mission, they are the message
themselves. So wherever they go, their very presence
creates a climate. You will become . . . mm?

IF GOD WERE PERSONIFIED...

Yes, unexpected things do happen when you are in the presence of Bhagwan Shree....

When they first come to Bhagwan, many people experience a powerful energy. This energy tends to be unfamiliar and rather overwhelming, so the first, maybe the unconscious response, is to channel this energy into a familiar source—which for most Westerners is sexual.

Some women may feel simultaneously repelled and attracted as the force is so strong. One usually becomes acclimatised after a time and the sexual connotation drops.

Paradoxically, the closer one comes to Bhagwan, the further away he seems; the more he appears not to be there. He is like a horizon. Drawn by its beauty you move closer and closer until it appears to be almost within your reach. You move to touch it—but it is no longer there. In fact it is further away than ever.

Sitting a little distance away from him is beautiful. But when you are actually at his feet, everything disappears from your mind—there exists only you and him. Then you are no longer there, and he is no longer the person you thought you were seeing.

His face has become vast, blurred. Then that too is gone, and there is just an oceanic feeling, as if a vast expanse of sea is before you. If you can let go into it, merge, be drowned, something falls away, something is added. Millions of years later you emerge, but you are a little less you and a little more something else....

Apart from the energy he emits, Bhagwan is an extraordinarily beautiful person to look upon. It is difficult not to fall in love with him immediately. Photographs may catch a glimpse of some of the many subtle nuances of expression that play over his face: his quick bursts of laughter, the sadness and humour in his eyes, the grace with which his hands move, the dignity of his walk. Trees cannot walk, but if they did they would carry something of the dignity of Bhagwan with them.

A story comes to mind of a zen disciple whose master died. The other disciples and villagers were gathered around the body in silence, but this one disciple, who was himself enlightened, was weeping unashamedly.

Several of the other disciples hastened to him saying that it would not do for him to be seen weeping. Did he himself not say that the soul was deathless? He, enlightened, and crying? What would people think!

The disciple answered, saying, yes, he knew the soul was deathless, but still the tears were coming of their own accord. And though the soul was eternal, the body of his master was gone for-

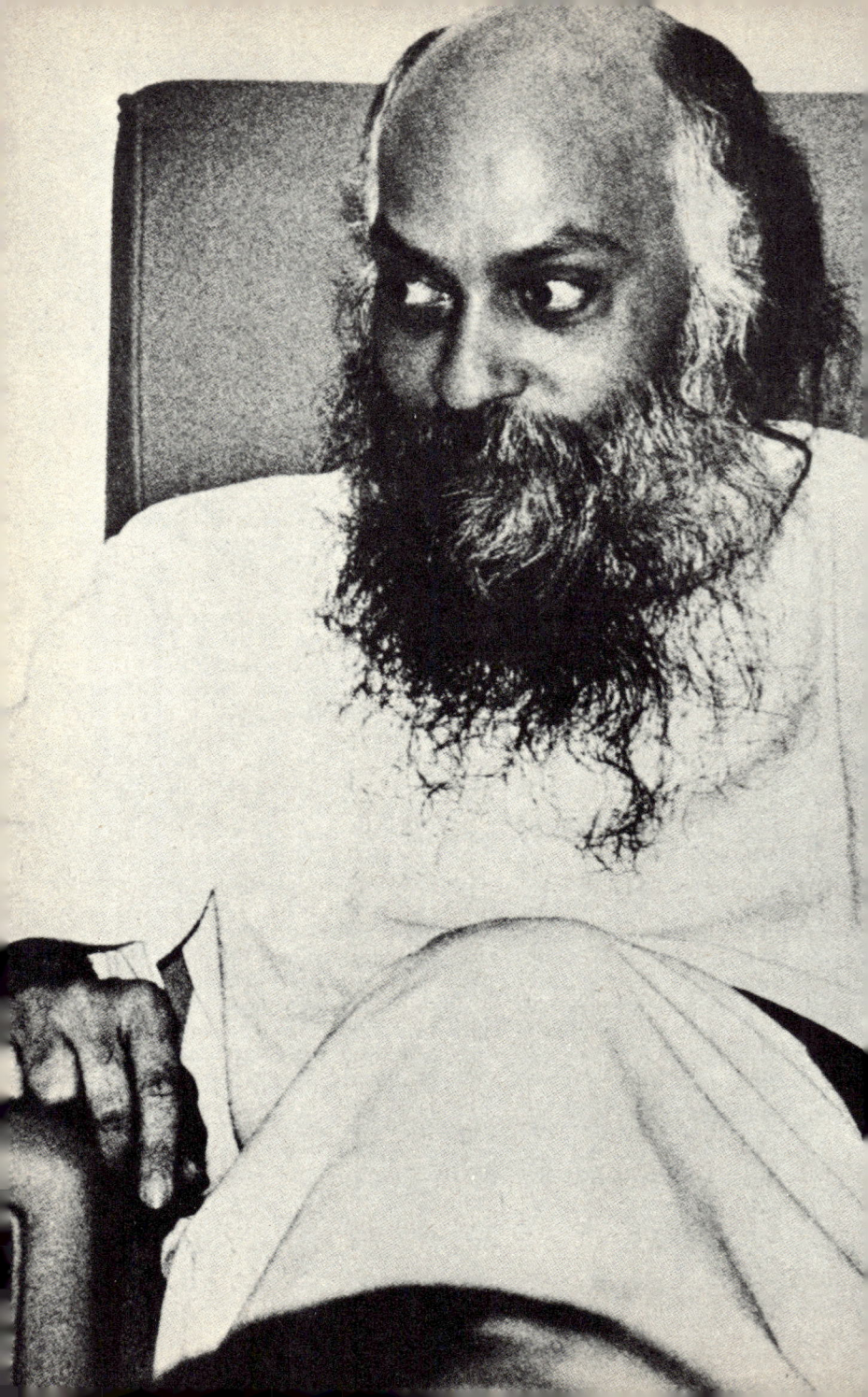

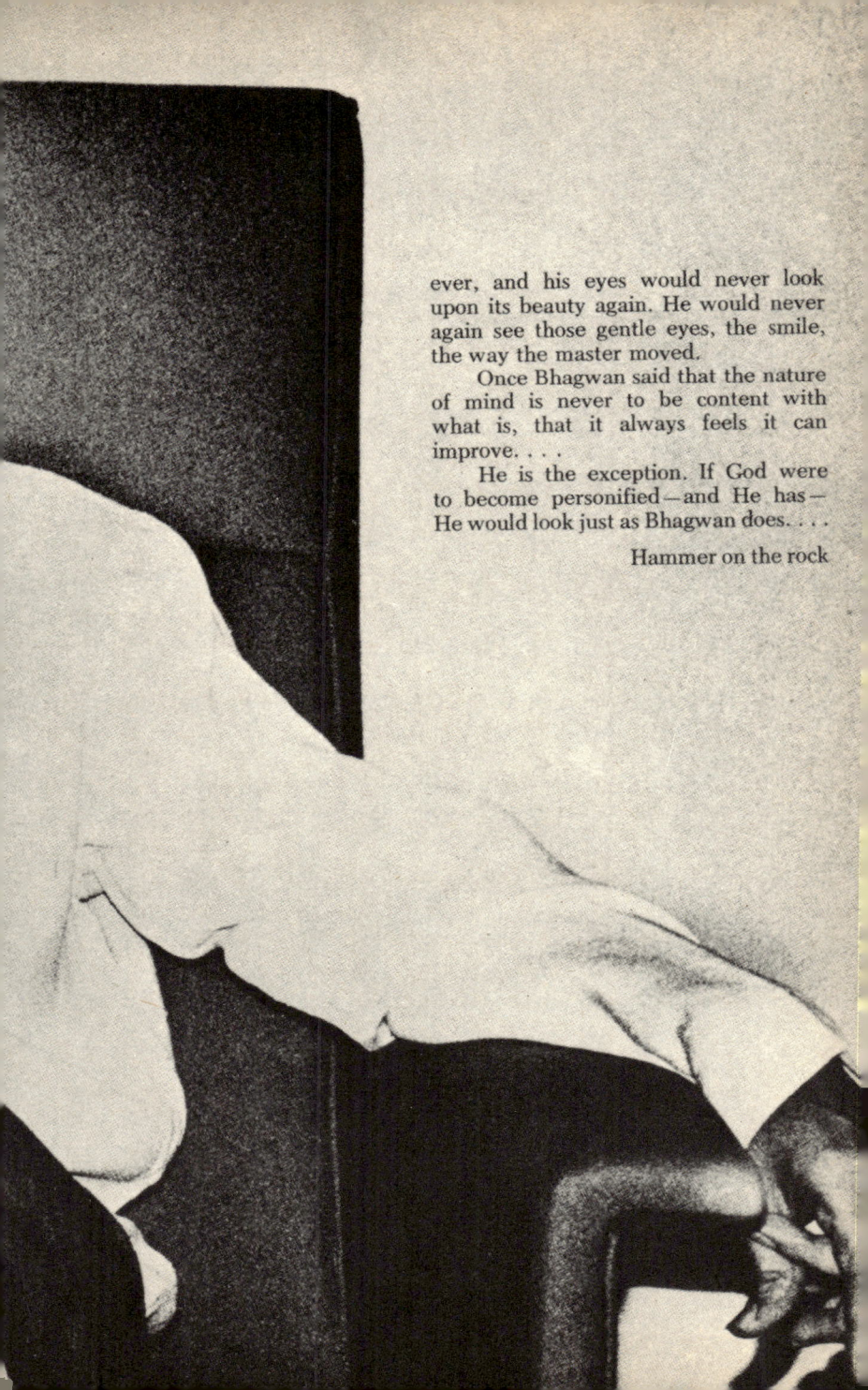

ever, and his eyes would never look upon its beauty again. He would never again see those gentle eyes, the smile, the way the master moved.

Once Bhagwan said that the nature of mind is never to be content with what is, that it always feels it can improve....

He is the exception. If God were to become personified—and He has—He would look just as Bhagwan does....

Hammer on the rock

SUNDAY DECEMBER 21st

A visitor—not a sannyasin—asked through a translator if Bhagwan could explain to her the meaning of an experience she had had two years ago.

She described the experience as one in which she felt like an empty box, nothing was there. It reached a point where she couldn't remember her name, or who she was. She could not function, couldn't talk or answer people when they asked her what was happening. It was a very beautiful experience.

To Bhagwan's enquiry as to how it started, she replied that she did not know; it just happened.

BHAGWAN Mm mm. . . . Close your eyes and just remember the experience.

The girl, a pretty, serene-looking girl of about twenty-five, closed her eyes and sat motionless while Bhagwan shone a torch on her. After a few moments Bhagwan continued:

It has been very significant. It always happens that whenever you suddenly fall into a vacuum you cannot function.

For a few days, a few hours, you have to tell people around you not to disturb you, if it happens again. You should be taken care of. Simply relax: close the room, lie down on the bed, and in deep darkness relax inside; fall into that empty box, allow yourself to be pulled in.

That could have become a great realisation. It will happen again—it is not predictable when—but it can happen again any moment.

BECOME A SANNYASIN!

The girl asked what the experience was.

It is a glimpse of satori. Do you understand what satori is? It is a glimpse of one's real nature.

One's real nature is empty, it is just like non-being. It is like sky, empty space. Whenever that glimpse happens, you lose your identity, you don't know who you are. And your name is just arbitrary, artificial—your form also.

Within this body you carry emptiness—that emptiness is your real nature. So you had a glimpse of it. And people can go mad if they don't understand it. If you can understand it, the real sanity arises.

It has been a blessing, mm? It has been good, feel thankful for it. Meditate more and it will happen again some day. It may look like death, but don't be afraid—it is not. It is really life. Be happy about it!

Bhagwan then asked the boy who had translated for her if he wanted to say something about himself.

NIMROD
I've been here for seven days doing the meditations, and I feel now like going and then coming back. But knowing myself, I know that once I go it will be hard to come back. . . . I just need something to make a stronger pull.

Become a sannyasin! That will help, mm? Close your eyes, and if something happens, allow it.

After writing down his new name and placing the mala over the boy's head, Bhagwan told him to change into orange—that would be a remembrance. He continued:

One needs some day to have a complete break with the past. Then habits and old patterns change automatically.

This will be your new name: Swami Anand Prabhat. Prabhat means morning and anand means bliss — a blissful morning. Morning is going to be your meditation time, so wherever you are, never miss the sunrise.

Just fifteen minutes before the sun rises, when the sky is becoming a little lighter, just wait and watch as one waits for a beloved: so tense, so deeply awaiting, so hopeful and excited, and yet silent. And just let the sun rise and go on watching. No need to stare; you can blink your eyes. Have the feeling that simultaneously inside, something is also rising.

When the sun comes on the horizon, start feeling that it is just near the navel. It comes up over there, and here, inside the navel, it comes up, comes up, comes up, slowly. The sun is rising there, and here an inner point of light is rising. Just ten minutes will do. Then close your eyes. When you first see the sun with open eyes it creates a negative, so when you close your eyes, you can see the sun dazzling inside.

And this is going to change you tremendously. And you will be coming back... I will pull you!

Another seeker came forward to Bhagwan's feet. Although he was already dressed in orange he wondered whether he was ready for sannyas, saying that doubts were still there, everpresent.

They are always there. One has to take the step in spite of them. If you wait for doubts to go and then think you will take the step, then you will never take it, because they never go.

In fact just the contrary happens: when you take the step, then they go. And doubts are human; they should be there. How can it be so easy to have trust? But one takes courage and moves. That's how the whole life has to move. When you fall in love with a woman, are you totally in love? Isn't there a doubt? In spite of that you move, because if you wait for all doubts to clear then you will have to wait for eternity and love will become impossible.

And this is a kind of love. So take the jump in spite. . . .

Having become Anand Prakash, the boy asked which meditation he should do as he liked the Nataraj (dancing) meditation best; in fact that was the only one he felt comfortable with. He felt that he had had too many expectations to begin with. . . .

Sometimes it happens that the meditation you feel most uncomfortable with maybe is the one that is going to help. The discomfort may be because it fights against certain of your habits and deep-rooted things. This is my observation: that the meditation you like is not always the best, and the one you dislike most is not necessarily the worst, because you like something that fits with your mind.

Your mind means the past, and you are trying to change that mind. So you are almost creating a situation where change will be impossible. In fact something that will create a certain conflict inside you, a discomfort, a struggle, friction, is going to help. So don't bother whether you like it or not. Continue Kundalini and Dynamic meditation in the ashram, and do the humming at home, and whatsoever groups are available.

To expect too much always creates a barrier, so never expect. If you really want something to happen, then just go open, in a playful mood, not very serious. When you are serious you become closed. And anything that is going to happen will happen when you are in a mood of fun, relaxed and floating, because then you are like a child—innocent. So when you do these groups and meditate, be joyful; don't be religious about them! You simply enjoy. Good!

It is beautiful to be at darshan when someone is taking sannyas, however many times you have been witness to it. It is like waiting for a child to be born. . . .

There is a certain tension, a sense of excitement. Is the time ripe? Will it be a painful or traumatic passage? Is the child really ready? Will he want to come?

Some come only with much coaxing and assurance. Their shelter has been cosy and secure. True, they had begun to feel confined and further growth was difficult, but who knew what lay ahead? Only darkness and a void—seemingly never-ending; an abyss, a world they couldn't begin to comprehend. At least this womb, though prison-like now, is familiar, known . . . can those large and gentle midwife's hands be trusted?

For other people, taking sannyas is like the baby who comes out a little unconventionally—perhaps leg, or even arm first. The passage is a little tricky, there is a little bruising, but at least they have come through!

Others can hardly wait for Bhagwan's invitation to become sannyasins. They are like the babies who come out almost bouncing, scarcely able to contain themselves before leaping into the waiting arms of the midwife. Flushed, glowing, alive and kicking!

An elderly sannyasin said to Bhagwan that she felt very much in contact with the universe when she was surrounded by nature. But, she added, she had some problems she needed help with. . . .

PREM

> When I am taken by surprise and am in a state of unawareness, if someone provokes me I get into terrible anger. I see that it is absolutely stupid and ridiculous, but I can't get out of it!

Don't try to get out of it. . .

PREM

> But then I'll get more and more angry!

Be! One has to live everything that happens. You are creating a duality within you. One part of you wants to be angry, another part is trying to top-dog it, to manipulate it, so you create a conflict...

PREM *A terrible conflict!*

...and that conflict is a sheer wastage of energy, and it is never going to help you. Both parts are you, so a victory is impossible. That's not the way. The way is to be one, unitary.

So when you feel angry, there is no need to be angry against someone; just be angry. Let it be a meditation. Close the room, sit by yourself, and let the anger come up as much as it can. If you feel like beating, beat a pillow....

PREM *That isn't sufficient for me. I'm much more angry than that —to be helped by hitting a pillow.*

So do whatsoever you want to do; the pillow will never object. If you want to kill the pillow, have a knife and kill it. It helps, it helps tremendously. One can never imagine how helpful a pillow can be. Just beat it, bite it, throw it. If

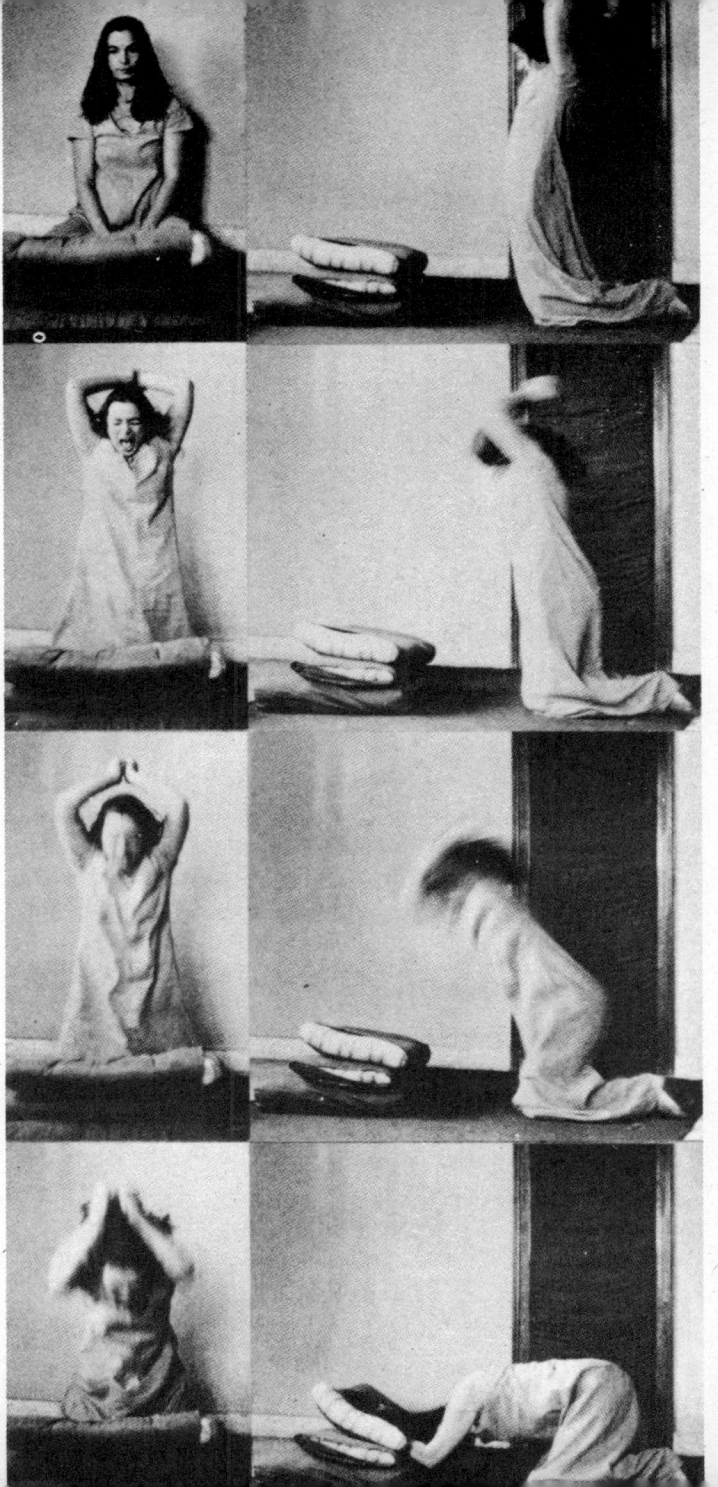

you are against somebody in particular, write their name on the pillow or stick a picture on it.

You will feel ridiculous, foolish, but anger is ridiculous; you cannot do anything about it. So let it be and enjoy it like an energy phenomenon. It is an energy phenomenon. If you are not hurting anybody there is nothing wrong in it.

PREM *But when you are with somebody, you want to hurt them.*

When you try this you will see that the idea of hurting somebody by and by disappears. You make it a daily practice — just twenty minutes every morning.

Then watch the whole day. You will be calmer, because the energy that becomes anger has been thrown out; the energy that becomes poison is thrown out of the system. You do this for at least two weeks, and after one week you will be surprised to find that whatsoever the situation, anger is not coming up. Just give it a try.

And nature is good, get more and more in tune with it. Whenever you are in nature become more like a child. Talk to the trees. . . .

First do this experiment with anger; then next, if you are sitting beside a tree or a plant, just talk loudly, a dialogue. That too will be ridiculous in the beginning. . . .

PREM *That I don't feel to be ridiculous.*

COMPARISON IS OF THE MIND

That's very good. (to Shiva, a sannyasin near him) Bring a small pot!

A small pot plant is put in front of the sannyasin. Bhagwan continues:

Have a little dialogue with the plant. Forget everybody. Only this being is here, so whatsoever you feel, talk to it. You can even answer from his side. You just go into it.

Bhagwan sits back, closing his eyes.

PREM   (avoiding the plant and addressing Bhagwan) *Oh, but I'm always with nature and plants, and they help me when I'm troubled.*

Bhagwan remains with eyes closed. She turns her eyes to the plant in front of her, saying hesitantly:

You and I are nature, and we are the same. I have seen more beautiful plants . . . but that's the way you are. . . .

(looking down at her from under his eyelids, in his 'stern voice') Now! From his side say something! Just get in tune with him, because he has to answer you.

She looks at the plant for a second or two, then. . .

> *I think you have much to learn . . . (a pause) . . . but I hope it will come one day.*

She looks at Bhagwan and then around the group as they laugh their approval. Looking somewhat relieved, she joins in the laughter too.

(still chuckling) Right, very good. And he answered you well! Mm! He answered you well. That's exactly what he wanted to say. And the thing that you have to learn is not to compare. That's what he wanted to say — that you don't say, 'I have seen more beautiful plants than you,' because that is hurtful.

And comparison is meaningless because everything is unique. Comparison is of the mind: when the thought enters and the feeling is lost. That's what the plant told you immediately, and it told you through your unconscious because your unconscious can also feel it — that you have brought comparison in and it is ugly.

PREM

> *You have to accept everything.*

Yes. Not only accept, you have to love.

GOD IS IN EVERYTHING

PREM
> *There I have difficulty. You see, you say 'love God', but I think God is so extremely above me that I couldn't feel like loving. It is just like a symphony of Bach: there is no love in it . . . but it is purity.*

I understand, and your question is relevant.

It depends on how you conceive of God. If He is purity, then He is very far away. If He is taken as an abstract concept, you cannot touch it, feel it, comprehend it — and you cannot love Him. If you conceive God as manifest in everything, in this plant also, then there is no problem — then you can love. And when you have touched this plant, you have touched God.

That's what I meant this morning (at the discourse) not the god of philosophers, but the god of Abraham, the god of Jesus, of simple people; not thinkers, very ordinary but sincere people.

In India you have the real God. Somewhere just a tree — nothing else — but they worship the tree as God. Somewhere else a stone — not even a statue — they colour red, and it has become God. It has an authenticity. And India has not worried about what God is. It has been simply taken for granted that He is; it is not a question to be decided. He is, so now something has to be done about it.

So you continue talking to plants and trees and much is going to happen out of it. Do the anger meditation, and later I will give you something for love . . . and it will come!

MONDAY DECEMBER 22nd

Two sannyasins, who were returning to England and wanting to start a centre, asked Bhagwan if they should approach the local mental hospital to introduce the meditations to the patients.

YOU NEED A LITTLE LAUGHTER

BHAGWAN Yes, you can help them to do some dynamic types of meditations. That will help very much because mad people need nothing else but catharsis. It is the only treatment, and it is because people have been so suppressed that they are in such a bad space. If everything is allowed, if they are allowed to be mad, then madness will disappear.

The whole world is mad because nobody is allowed to be mad. We must make it a point that everyone has a certain space reserved where he can simply be mad, where there is no need to be worried about anybody else. If a person can be mad each day for half an hour, then for the remaining twenty-three and a half hours he will experience only tremendous sanity.

Madness is also part of humanity; it is a deep balance. When you become too serious you need a little laughter to bring you down to earth. When you become too tense you need something to help you to relax. In fact, there are many socially accepted ways in which we allow people to be mad.

For example, in a football match or a volley-ball

match the spectators almost go mad. But it is accepted, and they feel very relaxed. Even watching it on TV they go mad — they jump and become very excited. But it is an accepted thing.

If somebody from Mars was watching for the first time, he would not be able to believe what is happening, because there seems to be no need to be so excited. Mm? — just a few people throwing a ball from here to there, and others are returning it — and millions of people are so excited! They don't know that this is a socially accepted avenue of release, a device. And each country has its own, creates its own device.

War is also a device that is needed continually so that people can go mad, can hate and destroy. And they can hate and destroy for a great cause, so there is no condemnation! So you destroy and you feel good, you feel happy, and there is no guilt — and you are simply becoming mad. War will continue until and unless we allow everybody a certain amount of madness to enjoy.

So you go and do the meditations and let the mad people watch. They will enjoy it tremendously, and they will say that there is not much difference between us and you! Then they will participate and you will be able to help them.

A madman doesn't need a doctor, he needs a friend. A doctor is too impersonal, too far away, too technical. And a doctor always looks at a madman as if he is an object to be treated. In his very look there is condemnation: something is wrong and has to be put right. A madman needs someone who loves, who cares and is friendly; someone who does not make him an objective thing, and accepts his individuality. And not only that, but also accepts his madness, because he accepts deep down that each man has a sane part and an insane part.

Insanity is the night part of man. It is natural, there is nothing wrong in it. When you can say to a madman

DEATH IS NEEDED FOR REBIRTH

that not only are you mad but I am too, immediately a bridge is made. And then he is available, and it is possible to help him.

So go, that will be helpful . . . and I am going with you!

Members of the Tathata group had darshan tonight. One person had discovered that though he had booked himself up for all the available groups, he did not want to change; another, that though she knew growth was good, and pain an intrinsic part of it, she still felt a resistance to it.

To the first Bhagwan said:

You want to change, and that is why you joined the group, but when things start happening you become afraid.

Growth is difficult. It hurts because something has to be dropped; because only then something new grows. Something has to be destroyed and only then something is created. A death, however small, is needed for a rebirth.

So you want to be reborn, but you don't want to go through the pain — that is what is happening. You would like to have the whole sky; but you don't want to leave the comfort of the home. That is why you think about that room of yours in Frankfurt — it is just symbolic. You are continuously worried about what will happen to it. Nothing is going to happen to any room. Nothing is happening to you, so what can happen to the room!

But it is not a question of the room. It is a question of security, of comfort and convenience. You have become accustomed to living in a shell, and whenever a fear arises that the shell may break, you shrink away, withdraw. And then you say that you don't want anything, you don't want to change. But you do!

So do the marathon as well, and really do it. Howsoever much it hurts, let it, and accept it, and soon you will see that a very beautiful feeling is arising out of that.

To the sannyasin who felt resistance to the pain of growing, Bhagwan said:

Pain is a part of growth and is very necessary. Nobody can grow without pain, so if you want to grow, you have to accept it. If you don't grow, pain may not be there, but suffering will be. And that is the difference between suffering and pain.

Pain is beautiful because it has a potential to grow, and it is something on the way. Suffering is ugly, impotent, barren — nothing comes out of it. One goes on suffering and suffering and suffering, but nothing comes out of it; it is absolutely barren. Always choose pain, but never choose suffering. And that is the difference — you understand me? In the dictionary there may be no difference between pain and suffering, but in life there is a tremendous difference. Pain is beautiful — accept it, be courageous. Nothing is going to happen out of suffering so never accept it.

Seek some way to grow, because suffering accepted becomes hell; pain accepted becomes heaven, mm?
(she smiles tentatively)

It has been good; now you can smile!

BE TOTALLY IN IT

Another group member asked if he should try to remain the watcher, a witness, in groups.

No, don't be a witness, not at all. If you try to be a witness you are divided; you are not one and unitary, and all growth needs you to be unitary. So these groups will lose all meaning if you remain continually a witness. You are not in them, and it is as if you are acting a role and watching the role as well.

Be in the role, totally in it; let it take possession of you. Only then will you become foolish; otherwise you will remain wise — and wisdom never helps. There is a wisdom that comes out of foolishness; only that helps, and that has a totally different quality.

So put aside all that you know about psychoanalysis and mind — forget that you know anything about it. Just follow the group and the instructions as a small child, trusting. Then much will happen.

That knowledge is always there later on and you can bring it back. It can be useful to understand what has happened, to interpret. Knowledge can be good as a retrospective thing, but if you carry it in the moment then it is a barrier. This way the knowledge is used and you are not used by it. Try it!

The trainee groupleader, who had come to darshan with the last group and to whom Bhagwan had talked about the need to have a structure for that which is itself unstructured, said that this group had been a shattering experience.

What has been so shattering?

CHAITANYA

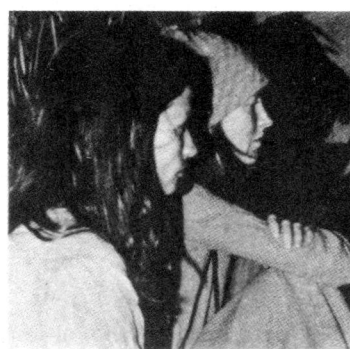

I went through an experience where I just lost myself . . . (he was hesitant, searching for the right word) . . . almost like a mindless daze . . . I wasn't able to contribute at all. . . . Eventually I got back some energy.

I had fallen earlier and that shook me up so maybe it was that. . . . I felt totally incapable of doing anything. But today I have a lot of my confidence back. It wasn't exactly fear, but the thought of doing anything was almost — unexplainable. But I think it was a part of this process. . . .

Mm mm. But you have understood completely wrongly.

The shattering experience happened not because you are incapable, but because you think yourself capable. It was not because suddenly unconfidence arose in you, but because you felt too confident in yourself. And to feel oneself too confident is a disease. That disease has been shattered. It is part of the ego to feel too self-confident and capable.

One has to accept the incapability, the helplessness; one has to accept whatever the situation is. And today you have again started in the old pattern: you are gaining self-confidence again. And again the shattering experience will come some day.

Now drop it! Don't try to be self-confident again!

EVERYBODY IS HELPLESS

What is wrong in being unconfident? What is wrong in being hesitant, in being in a state of helplessness, incapable? In fact that is how reality is. Everybody is helpless, and has to be, because everybody is such a tiny part, how can you think yourself capable? So infinite a number of possibilities surround you; so much unknown comes each day and has to be encountered. How you have lived up to now is a sheer miracle. There is no reason for it.

The feeling of being shattered came because your confidence was lost. The confidence is false; just on the surface like a crust of thin ice. The crust is very deceptive and any day you will fall into it, so it is better to know it. Just underneath is ocean, an infinite depth, an abyss. A thin layer of ice cannot protect you. It is better to be aware of it and to be aware of the danger.

It was not fear, it has nothing to do with fear. We have been taught, very wrongly, to be self-confident and to always be capable—or at least pretend to be. Man is helpless! The strong are as helpless as the weakest; the difference is not much. When a Napoleon dies, or an Alexander dies, he is just like any ordinary man—as helpless as a beggar, and there is no difference. The difference was only a pretension.

Drop that confidence. Even if for a few days that trembling remains, let it, but don't try to regain the old thin layer of ice. If you can remain with your incapability, your helplessness, I don't say you will never be weak again. The weakness arises with the idea that you are not weak. Then you have a comparison, an image, and when you fall short of it the trouble arises.

Once you accept whatsoever is, suddenly comparisons disappear: you are simply alone and yourself. Nobody is like you, nobody has ever been, or will be, like you; you are simply unique, incomparable.

This experience has been beautiful. Don't take it wrongly or you will again restructure yourself.

All these groups are to unstructure you, to destroy you—you as you are—and just to allow the spontaneity in you, as you were before you were born, as you will be when you die.

It was tremendously valuable but you threw it completely, and it won't be of much use. You may even become more structured than before, because now you know that the old structure doesn't work so well, you can make a stronger one around you.

Live without a structure, unpatterned, moment to moment, as a flow. These groups don't need a leader who is himself conditioned, structured. They need a leader who is just a flow, and who can help others also to flow; one who can create a milieu around himself in which others feel that they also can flow, that they can become helpless, like children, and that everything is accepted. But if you don't accept yourself, how are you going to help others to accept themselves? The first thing the leader needs is to accept himself unconditionally, whatever it is.

All great experiences are shattering. And only that which is creative is also going to be destructive. Only out of chaos a star is born. So be happy about it, be blissful, mm?

A sannyasin, very upset and weeping, told Bhagwan that her clinging and her possessiveness with her lover had been the cause of their separating. Her boyfriend, who was also present, added that he simply needed some time and space to himself, and so he had escaped.

Bhagwan explained to them at length the dynamics of their relationship over the preceding month. The girl had been ill, depressed, and her boyfriend had become more of an attendant than a lover. Now that she was back to her usual happy self she wanted love from him, but his love seemed to have been replaced by sympathy over those months of caring for her.

She had become very clinging, as she felt he was the right person for her, that he had proved his affection for her, but she was not leaving him a breathing space so he had left her....

Bhagwan went on to say:

So the thing is not to separate, but to understand each other. You love each other, I can feel it, but the love is in difficulty.

Ghosha, you have to remember a few things. One is that every man needs a space of his own. If you want to love a man and love him forever, and if you want him to love you, never fill his space completely. At least a part, one fourth, has to be given to him. The poor man needs that much!

And that's the difference between the feminine mind and the male mind. The feminine mind can be full with love, the woman's whole being can move into love, but a man has other loves also. The love for the woman is only one of his loves. He may also love poetry, music, painting, hunting, and a thousand and one foolishnesses. For a woman, one love is enough.

Once she finds a lover she surrounds him from everywhere. She wants to fill every part and every crevice of his being. But then the lover becomes afraid because he would like some independence; he would like to be alone somewhere, to be himself. So one fourth you have to leave if you want three fourths. This is a bargain, Ghosha!

Otherwise one day you will lose the whole. For a woman, love is her whole being. And this is a natural thing and has to be understood—a maturity is needed. If the woman had the capacity, she would make the lover a small child again and put him in her womb so she could surround him and have no fear of him escaping. But that cannot be done, so she creates a psychological womb around him—that is what home is.

And even if he is reading, she becomes afraid that he is more interested in reading than in her. Or if he is playing on his flute, she is afraid he is more interested in it. Everything seems to be competitive. She wants his total attention. But this is impossible for a man, and if you force him too much he will escape—or surrender, but then he will be dead.

If a man surrenders totally to a woman he is dead; a husband and no more a lover—he is a slave. Then the woman is not satisfied, because who is satisfied with a slave? She wants someone to whom she can surrender, not someone to surrender to her—he will be useless. So this is the dichotomy, the dilemma: that a woman wants the husband to be hers completely, but when he becomes hers, she is not interested.

It is good that Bhikshu is not surrendering, that he wants to remain independent and wants his own space — just a little space; he is not asking much.

And if you want to be with him, there is no need to cling. He will be with you. Clinging pushes people further away. You give it another try! And I will be with you this time. So whenever there is trouble you come to me; don't try to settle it yourselves.

Give it a try again, get married! Face each other a little.

(The two turn to look at each other for a few seconds, smilingly.)

Good! Hold hands and go to your places!

TUESDAY DECEMBER 23rd

BHAGWAN What about you? How are things going?

ALOK *I've been really rebellious and resistent to you. Whenever you say something in the lecture that I don't like, I cough.*

(a peal of laughter. Reminders are regularly given at the daily discourse to not cough or move unnecessarily as it disturbs Bhagwan's flow.)

ALOK *It is not as deliberate as all that, but I've discovered there's a very close connection.*

Very good! This is a good discovery!

ALOK *And....*

And?

ALOK *I like you.*

Very good. When you like me, what do you do?

(Alok looks uncomprehending, then thinks a little.)

You don't have anything to do?

ALOK *Well, I'd like to lick you!*

That's good. Nothing to worry about. . . .

Alok went on to say that he had had a conversation in the afternoon with the Christian in him. He wanted to feel in contact with Jesus, but his perfectionistic attitudes and fear of 'the wrath of God' were stopping him from entering wholeheartedly into life and into sex, and therefore he was miserable.

Mm mm. It is good to feel rebellious sometimes; it is part of growth.

It is natural and human sometimes to feel disagreement, to sometimes feel you would like to say no. But that is good; that is the way the real yes is born. If you say yes too easily, without saying any no, your yes will be impotent. So when a rebellious person becomes obedient, there is real obedience. When an obedient person becomes obedient it is nothing much. So that is very good. Don't be worried about it and don't suppress it. It's okay, it's okay. It will go.

If you can agree with me one percent, then you cannot escape. Ninety-nine percent you may disagree with me, but that's not the point. If I can get a small space within you, just one percent, that's enough. Then I will enter deeper, and you cannot do anything else. Then that one percent will become two percent, and two percent, three percent — and by and by you will see you are gone.

Christianity creates condemnation — and condemnation has to be dropped. One has to drop it, and to drop it without any effort. If you drop it with effort, then something of it will go on clinging, a hangover will remain. To drop a thing perfectly, just to understand it is enough.

You need to understand that you are body: body-rooted, body-oriented, living in the body. You may not be the body but you are living in it, and the body has its needs which have to be fulfilled. A religion that does not accept the body is only a half religion, and can only give you a half mutation. Half of you will remain undeveloped and that half will function as a rock around your neck.

One has to grow as a total unity. And if one has to grow as a total unity then everything has to be accepted, nothing can be denied. Of course, everything has to be used for a higher harmony. Sex is not to be left just as sex — that is vulgar. Sex has to be transformed for a higher harmony, and then it becomes love, and love becomes prayer. It goes on and on; more and more refined forms of energy. And ultimately sex itself becomes the energy we call God.

Sex is the lowest denominator of the same energy we call God. It is the first step to the same temple. And if you deny the first step, you can never reach to the second — then you can never enter into the temple. Sex has to be accepted, used, and left behind; not renounced — left behind. And remember, the distinction is great: not renounced, not dropped — left behind. You go on growing, and by and by you go so far away that the first step is left behind and you are in the innermost shrine. But that first step helped you to reach there, and you are grateful.

ALOK *But I neither totally truly accept the first step nor am free of it. I'm hung up on it.*

I understand. I understand — because still, deep down, the condemnation continues. You just have to understand.

For example, someone tells you for thirty years continuously that if you take the road on the left you will reach the station. And for thirty years you have believed that. Now you travel the road and you don't reach the station. You meet someone who says that this road doesn't go to the station at all; you have to go back to the crossroad

SEX BECOMES THE ENERGY WE CALL GOD

and take the road that goes to the right.

What will you say? Will you say that for thirty years you have believed this was the right road to the station, and now you can't leave it; that you are hung up? You yourself can see that the station is not there. You will simply say, 'Yes, you are right. Someone has wrongly informed me.'

And this much understanding is needed. Someone wrongly conditioned you about sex and about other things. Now you have become more aware. The people who conditioned you may themselves have not been aware; they may have been immature, may have been conditioned by others. They may have been in the same misery as you; they simply transferred the misery to you. Now please — don't you transfer it to anybody.

There is a temptation in the mind to unburden, to teach, to convince others, to argue.

If you need to, for three days close your room and sit silently facing the wall and look deep within down into your conditioning. Just see it — that it has not lead you anywhere, that you are simply split, divided. So one

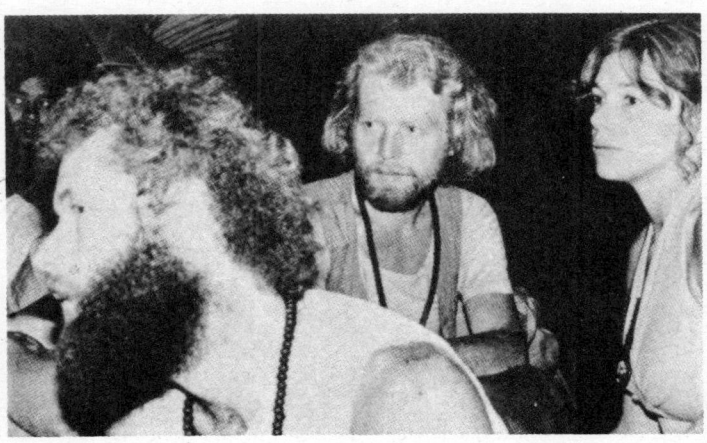

decides. One sees that the path has been wrong; one simply drops it. And once you have dropped it, start moving in the opposite direction. Because, in fact, action is needed to uncondition you, to recondition you.

So start moving in sex, in love, in relationships. Move, and just see where the condemnation is. It is all foolishness; there is nothing wrong. And, by and by, the more you see that there is nothing wrong, the old conditioning, the old habit will disappear. You will be freed. Just try, mm? It is going to go.

ALOK *But I've tried for so long.*

Because you try wrongly. You are still clinging to the old concepts. Because of those concepts you go on saying no to me. You disagree because you have certain ideas.

ALOK *I'm afraid that if I surrender to you, you will turn out to be just like the Jesus I knew.*

You have to try. There is no other way. You have to try me.

GIVE ME A TRY

ALOK   *I'm here.*

Mm, so move deeper into me. And disagreeing won't help because that means you go on clinging to your old ideas.

See the point that your ideas have brought you here where you are — in a miserable state, in a conflict, a divided mind. Now you are clinging to these same ideas and then you disagree with me because of them. And you ask me how to go deeper! You go on clinging to the bank when you want to go deeper and further away, to the other shore. Just see the point!

If you want to be with me then you will have to surrender — and it is a risk. I may turn out wrong. No guarantee can be given — because who will give it? I will — and if I am wrong my guarantee is useless! I can give you a thousand and one guarantees; it will make no difference. You will have to try me. Give me a try!

ALOK   (accepting) *I am....*

A sannyasin from Ethiopia said that he found he was still repeating a pattern that he had adopted as a child. Whenever his parents scolded him or said anything about him that he could take as being negative, he would just shut off, run away and console himself, saying that he could do without people, he could manage alone. He found he reacted to his friends just the same way.

It is just an old habit which has become rigid. Try to do the opposite of it. Whenever you feel like closing — open yourself. If you want to go, don't go; if you want not to talk, then talk. If you want to stop the argument, don't stop but jump into it with as much vigour as possible.

Whenever a situation arises which creates fear, there are two alternatives — either you fight or you take flight. A small child ordinarily cannot fight — particularly in countries like Ethiopia. In America, a child will fight so much that the parents will take the flight! But in old countries, in tradition-bound countries, a child cannot fight. The only way is to close, to wrap oneself inside oneself as protection. So you have learned the trick of flight.

Now the only possibility is that whenever you feel you are trying to escape, stick there, be stubborn, and give a good fight. Just for one month try the opposite and then we will see. Once you can do the opposite I will tell you how to drop both. Both have to be dropped, because only then a man becomes fearless — and because both are wrong. Because one wrong has gone too deep in you, it has to be balanced by the other.

So for one month you be a real warrior — about anything. And you will feel very good, really good, mm? Because whenever one escapes, one feels very bad, inferior. This is a cowardly trick — to close oneself. Become brave, mm? Then we will drop both, because to be brave is also, deep down, to be cowardly. When bravery and cowardice both disappear then one becomes fearless. You try it!

A sannyasin said that she had been experiencing a lot of fear, and felt some connection between this and the fact that she did not like herself very much — something she had just recently discovered. She said she kept judging herself through the eyes of others and was unhappy with herself.

LIFE IS TO ENJOY

What can you do? You are yourself whether you like it or not. You will not become someone else, you will remain yourself, so it is simply foolish, absurd. Whether you like yourself or not is not the point; no one is asking you if you do. So you will remain yourself; there is no way to get out of it. One has to accept it.

And there is nothing wrong in being oneself. The problem is there because you go on comparing. What is the point of comparing? Every individual is so unique that comparison is simply meaningless. Comparison is possible only if everybody is like everybody else. You don't compare a rose with a lotus; it is pointless — a rose is a rose, a lotus a lotus. Every human being is a different flowering, and you cannot be compared with anyone else. So drop the comparison and while you are here, enjoy. Why waste time!

And let the fear be, and by and by it will disappear. If you try to do something it will take longer to go. Fear is natural in a way, because man is going to die, and unless you know something within you that is immortal, unless the deathless is encountered, fear will follow you like a shadow. So simply accept it; it is part of humanity.

And rather than wasting time in these futile problems, start living! Relate with people and start enjoying small things, because this is how one comes to like oneself. If you dislike yourself you don't move into enjoyment, and because you cannot enjoy yourself you dislike yourself more. Then it becomes a vicious circle.

So get out of it! There is nothing to it. In a single moment, with a single decision, a man can be transformed — immediately. It is not a gradual process. This very moment, if you want to. . . . And that is the point, because if I want you to, that will not help. If you want to come out, this very moment you can, because the misery is created by you and is absolutely false.

Misery comes because you don't like yourself.

Somebody must have given you this opinion — your mother or father, your family — that you are worthless, and you have accepted their opinion.

Who are they to decide? Nobody except you can decide for you who you are. All judgements about you are just stupid, superficial. Nobody can look into you. They all look on the surface, and then they make a judgement — and you accept that judgement!

Then you start liking or disliking yourself. Both are nonsense. Life is to enjoy. And people go on preparing for some day when they will enjoy it, and they waste it. You try.

A sannyasin said that through meditating he had lately come to experience how his mind just went on and on; how impossible it was to still it.

Bhagwan said that there was no need to try to still the mind, to stop the thoughts. He said that just as the traffic goes by and one remains on the sidewalk, unaffected, just a watcher, so one should simply witness the thoughts as they went by. We are not our thoughts, and recognising that we are the witness is enough.

The very acceptance of the thoughts makes one more relaxed. The relaxation helps to create a distance, to separate oneself. To evaluate a thought as good or bad means that you are attached to your thoughts — so one should not put labels on them.

. . .put yourself aside, sit under a tree, and just watch the traffic. Soon, one day, the traffic disappears and the road is empty. Suddenly there is an interval and in that interval is meditation. But that interval cannot be created or cultivated. You cannot still the mind — you can simply wait in deep watchfulness and mind stills itself.

PUT YOURSELF ASIDE

Another sannyasin, this time a woman, asked if the suggestions Bhagwan had given to this man also applied to her. Bhagwan said that for her, witnessing would not help.

He has said before that the method of witnessing only suits a certain type of person. For others, total involvement is more helpful.

Many people who were followers of Gurdjieff and tried to adopt his method of witnessing simply went mad, because it is a tension, a strain for some people. Women tend to find it easier to adopt the method of total involvement; it is more akin to their nature. For men, usually witnessing is more useful.

Bhagwan told Anurag to be totally involved in the traffic of whatever she did, adding, 'Your enlightenment is to come in the marketplace!'

A third sannyasin, also a woman, asked if she should try the method of witnessing, but added that she didn't think she quite understood what witnessing was.

In reply Bhagwan said:

You just start one thing: every day for one hour sit in front of a wall, and look at the wall with half-closed eyes; just so you can see the tip of the nose. Sit very close so there is nothing else you can see.

Be relaxed, and if some thoughts come, just go on seeing that they are passing between you and the wall. You need not be concerned with whatever they are — fantasies, dreams, anything, nonsense. But you go on feeling that they are just between you and the wall. By and by, after two weeks, you will become aware of what witnessing is.

WEDNESDAY DECEMBER 24th

The Arica group, consisting of about thirty members, came to darshan tonight. Bhagwan first addressed one of the leaders, asking how he experienced the group.

Anup said that it felt very different doing the Arica work here in the ashram compared to groups he'd been in in the States. He said he'd felt there had been a lot more love, and that the trainers had felt okay about any mistakes they had made without feeling 'reduced'; and had been able to let things flow.

The term 'reduced', ego-reduction, was coined to describe the process that usually happens in Arica groups when the trainers and trainees collect to discuss the progress of the group and to give feedback, and tell each other how they feel they are functioning. Any negative comment or criticism can be called potentially ego-reducing Anup said that they had not felt the need to do it this time.

He continued, saying that he had found that he was on a power-trip. He added that he felt the training would need to be longer than this one had been; that these three days had been just a taste.

BHAGWAN Techniques work only when there is deep love. Left alone, techniques never work, because in fact it is love that works, not the technique.

Techniques are just excuses, and once love is there then there is no difference between the leader and the led, the teacher and the taught. They both become one and work together; it is an experience that is shared. It is not that the leader is higher than the led—maybe he knows a little more, but he is also learning.

Love never comes to a state where you can say that

LOVE NEVER BECOMES WISE, THAT'S ITS WISDOM

now you know it. Love never becomes wise—and that is its wisdom. It is always learning and learning and learning to the very end. It continues to be a learner.

And when the leader himself is learning then there is no power-trip. The power-trip, the ego-trip, arises when the leader starts thinking that he has arrived, that he is to guide—not help, but guide, lead others. Then the whole thing becomes wrong. Once techniques are in the hands of the ego they become destructive. The same techniques in the hands of love become creative. It depends. With love, even poison can be used and it will be medicine; with ego, even elixir will become poisonous. So it is a very delicate job to be a leader.

The leader is taking a greater responsibility than the led. He is not only responsible for the group but for himself also. And his responsibility is greater because there is every possibility to make it a power-trip.

So many gurus all over the world are living in a power-trip. And they enjoy it, but one day or other they will come to realise that the whole life has been a wastage. Whether it is through money that you attain the power, or through knowledge, or renunciation, or through meditation, it doesn't matter. Power is poverty, and some day or other the illusion disappears; one is disillusioned—one finds oneself simply empty.

So remember this from the very beginning: if you really want to help, drop the ego completely. In the very dropping you become a tremendously valuable leader. The leader is no longer there, but now you can be of help. And whenever you help, there will be no resistance against you; the other will find opening. Whenever you see that someone is resisting you, just don't say to him that he is resisting, rather, find out where in you you are creating the resistance he feels. Your subtle ego must be creating a shadow between you and him.

Whenever you see that the person you are trying to

help is not receptive, then look within yourself. Do something to yourself, change yourself, be more humble. If here, within, you become more humble, there, resistance is gone. It is very easy for a leader to become aggressive, and if you are, you can destroy but you cannot create. It is a great training for a leader — greater than it is for the led. It has been good and much more will happen.

And that too is right — three days is not enough time. The next group can be of seven days.

In fact all changes start near the fourth day, because mind has a certain resistance. On the first day it is very, very resistant. By the second day it learns that it is simply foolish to be resistant: you are simply wasting your energy and time; no one else is harmed but you. So on the second day one relaxes a little.

On the third day, because one is beginning to relax, one starts understanding that more is possible, and why settle for less? On the fourth day one relaxes. This is ordinarily. A few rare people who are receptive, can be open on the first day; a few people, very egoistic, will not even be on the seventh day. But as a general rule the fourth day is the most potential day, and after that day things start on a different plane.

Anup said he felt that this group had been a lot more receptive than other groups he had experienced in the States.

Mm mm, it is going to be totally different. It is going to be totally different because they are sannyasins, they are not just curious people. They have a commitment, they have dared. They are consciously trying to change themselves; it is not only a question of learning.

You can learn in two ways. In one, you remain the same, and when you learn something it becomes additional richness to you; it fulfills and feeds the ego. You remain the same. It is just that your possessions increase—you possess more knowledge.

Then there is another type of learning, where through learning you dissolve. Rather than becoming more you become less. And if you have really learnt, then you are not there, only learning is there. The real seeker is not after accumulated knowledge.

That's why I insist for sannyas, because after someone has taken sannyas he is showing a great gesture of affirmation, of surrender, of yea-saying, of receptivity. By the very gesture of sannyas he has become different. The same person will take things in a totally different perspective now. He will be less resistant, more cooperative, and he will feel more responsibility. So it is going to be different.

And then it becomes a family. If these twenty or thirty people (indicating the group before him) come in a group, just separately, then they are seeking their own ends and the group is just like a crowd waiting at the airport for a plane to arrive. There are thirty people sitting together but there is no inter-connecting link. They are all separate and it is just a jumbled-up crowd.

But when everybody is a sannyasin they are not a crowd, they are a group. That is the difference between a crowd and a group. A group is where each individual is related to the other in some way or other—a river flows there and you are all in the same boat. You are not seeking your goal, and the other is not seeking his—you are all seeking a common goal. It is not competitive, it is cooperative.

There is a vast difference—a family feeling of

belonging to one goal; that you have a certain identity. It becomes a family, a community. A community or a family functions differently. The energy is multiplied and each person's change will affect all. If one changes in a crowd, then only one changes. A crowd remains aloof, because each is an island in himself, not related to anybody else.

In a family—and sannyas is a family—one changes, one goes higher, and he is related to others, so others are pulled up. It is an unknown force. By and by you will start feeling that when one member changes, everybody goes higher; everybody has become more confident, less resistant. One person's realisation of any insight is shared. It is a very unconscious process, but by and by, working with people you will become aware.

I have been talking to many types of gatherings. I have talked to crowds where each person is listening to me but there is no inter-relationship between the people. So it is as if I am talking to one person. There may be ten thousand people sitting there but I am talking to one person, because each person is one; there is no inter-link. That gave me the idea that this wouldn't do.

Then I started creating a family. Now, when I talk to you, it is not that I am talking to one person; I am talking to a family. And I can see—it is so visible—that one person starts feeling high and suddenly the whole group feels the vibrations. One person starts smiling and suddenly the smile spreads; its ripples reach everybody. I can see that if there is someone sitting there who is not a sannyasin he becomes like an obstacle; the flow stops there. He is not part of the whole.

So this is going to be totally different. And these are the implications of sannyas, but one only becomes aware by and by. Good Anup.

Bhagwan addressed the darshan group:

I'D LIKE TO TAKE SANNYAS

So, because there are so many people, if somebody has something to say, something that has happened, one by one you can come out.

A seeker comes forward. He is the person who asked Bhagwan at a previous darshan whether a master was necessary to help one to become enlightened, and to whom Bhagwan had replied that he should not waste time but find a master to whom he could surrender....

EDWARD *I'd like to take sannyas.*
(sounds of cheering and laughs of pleasure from the group)

I was waiting for you! (more laughter)
Close your eyes...and if something happens in the energy, allow it; any movement comes to the body, allow it. And relax deeper and deeper inside yourself.

After a few moments Bhagwan presented him with a mala and his new name:

Good! And this is your new name: Swami Prem Ninad.
It means music of love. Prem means love, ninad means music — but not ordinary music. It means natural music. For example, a waterfall — then it is ninad. So it is not a man playing on a guitar. Then it is not ninad; it is ordinary music, not of nature. Wind passing through the trees — then there is music, then it is ninad.

Ninad means music of nature; not created by man, untouched by man — wild, virgin, mm?

A German sannyasin said two of his friends who had been in the group were not present as they had both become ill during the group; one on the first day, the other on the second day.

Sometimes it happens that when some changes start in the mind, the body reacts. There is something unfamiliar and the body wants to reject it. So many times illnesses happen.

But it is good and positive. After their illness they will feel of a totally different mind. Always remember in the group that if somebody becomes ill — during a group meditation or technique — remember always to give him the feeling that it is good and nothing to get depressed about. In fact it shows something has started to work, and the body wants to change with the new mind, so a few things have to be thrown out. Maybe there are a few poisons in the body, and when it starts to throw them out, you become ill.

Tell them that within two or three days they will be perfectly okay — and better than before, mm?

Vani, how are you?

VANI

Good — now! Outside I'm lost. I felt lost specially today because for the first time I brought some people I work with, some crew members. (she is a supervisory air hostess)

They were here, in the talk this morning?

VANI

Yes — and they left.

Mm mm, it must have been beyond them.

VANI
I work with these people very closely and I just can't share anything with them. I feel okay when I'm alone, but when I'm with people I want to share, to communicate. It's impossible...
This time I tried — I even stopped meditating, because it's even more impossible if I meditate. And I've tried to talk... it doesn't help.

In fact, you have to understand that when you start growing, there will come a distance between you and the people you have been working with. And the distance will create many problems, because they are in the majority, and they will think you are going a little crazy or eccentric or something. And whatsoever they think has a certain weight because they are in the majority. They will all think the same — and you become alone.

If you try to convince them, talk to them, argue with them, that is not going to help much, because whatsoever I am saying and doing has nothing to do with arguments. If one can feel, one can feel; you cannot convince anybody about it. It is not a philosophy. It is a totally new way of being and living.

So unless they are ready to change they will not be able to understand. So don't try the impossible. You are trying to change them, to change their minds so that they can live like you. But if they live like you, only then their minds can change. There is no other way.

SOMETHING GREATER IS POSSIBLE

So the only sensible thing to do is not to be worried about them. And while you are with them, act — just play a role. There is no need to be true, because if you are true, then the distance will be very very big between you and them. Just go on acting as you used to do, so there is not much of a problem.

And don't be bothered about what they say, because now you know that something greater is possible. But it is beyond their comprehension. So feel compassion for them, and don't be worried about it.

In Sufism, they say to pray and meditate when nobody watches you, not even your wife or your husband. In the night, midnight, when everybody has gone to sleep, sit silently on your bed and meditate — so that nobody becomes aware of your inner life. Once they become aware, first they will condemn. That is natural, because anything that is not of the common masses is suspected.

So don't be worried, and don't bring them here because that will create trouble. Nobody can be brought to me. People can come, but nobody can be brought. And never do that, because if you do they will be more resistant. In fact, they will be almost deaf to me, to what I am saying, and they will go convinced that Vani is mad. That will be the only conviction they get. (a chuckle)

And while you are working, play a role. That too is good. The capacity to play a role is good. Just remain a witness and go on doing things. And soon I will tell you. . .when I feel the time is right, I will tell you to leave everything, but just wait.

First conquer the situation and then leave. Never leave any situation defeated, never, because then the experience has been incomplete. Conquer the situation! When you start saying to me that there is no problem now, now everything is going fine, then I will tell you to leave — not before! And don't try to deceive me, because that is not possible, mm? Good Vani!

How was the group?

BOB

> *The group was perfect. I was very resistant at first, because I was having lots of phone calls from the United States, because my loved ones are very sick.*
>
> *I was very distracted... then I would come back to the group and everything was so peaceful that I didn't have the chance to throw anything. Then gradually I began to appreciate the group more and more, because instead of throwing off all this energy, I found I could centre more, and the news was not something that could turn me away from that. I felt very good about it.*

Mm mm. Sometimes it happens that in a situation where there is every possibility of getting sad, depressed, angry or negative, there is every possibility to lose the coolness and collectedness. If, in that situation, you are working on a certain technique, in the beginning it may seem that it is impossible because the situation is so raw.

But this is my observation: that in such situations, techniques go very deep if you just persist, because the contrast always makes things more clear. It is just as if on a blackboard you draw with a white chalk — it looks perfect. You can draw the same figure on a white wall with white chalk — and it will disappear.

It is the observation of centuries that on the darkest nights of life people attain to the highest peaks of bliss.

WHERE THERE IS RESISTANCE THERE IS TREASURE

When there is every possibility of getting depressed, deeply depressed, if you are doing something, the disturbance will not be a distraction; it will itself become the background, and your effort will shine against its contrast.

You are a photographer so you can understand it — that the background needs to be the opposite. If the background and the figure are the same, then the figure loses much — the intensity, the sharpness; everything is lost..

It has been good. In the beginning there is always resistance, and it is a good sign that your mind is feeling unconsciously that you are moving in deep waters: the fear is there and you start resisting. Resistance is a very symbolic thing. It shows that something is going to happen, otherwise the mind never resists. If the mind knows the territory is familiar and you have travelled it before, then there is no fear and the mind doesn't resist. Once the mind becomes aware that you are moving into unfamiliar territory, something uncharted, something that you don't know — then it resists.

Always remember, where there is resistance there is treasure. Once you see the resistance, gather courage, because you are moving somewhere and something is going to happen. Forget everything and follow in the direction from where the resistance is coming, and you will never come out of it empty-handed. But the ordinary tendency of the mind is that whenever you feel any resistance to anything, you simply escape. You miss many riches that life was going to shower on you.

A comfortable life is the poorest possible. And by comfortable I mean a mind that goes on avoiding resistances and always finds a convenient way to live. Then you will vegetate, you will not live. Are you going back soon?

BOB   *Well, since your birthday...*
I've been moving with all these people here; I've been with as many people as I could be here, at the ashram, and also the next circle of people — those who maybe don't come here every day, but live very close — and I spent time with them.

Every morning I would get up and the most incredible things would happen; with no plan I would just be led from one person to another.

I've found so many things here. It is very very rich material that is happening here. I believe more strongly than ever...that an incredible film can be made from this. (Bob is a film producer)

Much is possible out of it. Beautiful people have come, and more beautiful people will be coming soon! Good!
So what about you? (much laughter from the group; we all know what that means!)

Become a sannyasin!
    (Bob nods his head slowly, in agreement)

Close your eyes....
(The mala is placed over Bob's head)

A DIALOGUE OF LOVE

This will be your new name: Swami Prem Samvada. Samvada means dialogue and prem means love — a dialogue of love. And I give it to you for certain purposes.

All that is beautiful you will attain through deep relationships, mm? — with people, with nature. If you can find a dialogue, then you will attain much.

A dialogue is not a discussion. A discussion is a fight; a verbal, intellectual fight. A dialogue is a deep sympathy, a deep rapport with the other person, so that sooner or later you start flowing with the energy of the other. Then the other is no more the other, and you are not fighting; you are cooperating, helping the other to be himself. You remain yourself and the other remains himself, and there

is a deep meeting — not an argument.

Samvada — it is one of the most beautiful words.

And dialogue is a very very deep love, sympathy, rapport. With somebody you suddenly feel love and you start flowing. It is illogical, but it is very meaningful.

Change to complete orange! Good.

A sannyasin said that he felt himself to be lazy.

Bhagwan said that these sort of concepts we have about ourselves are the result of our conditioning, they are not our true nature. He explained that when we are born, we are without identity, and we seek for one — through parents, family, friends. Someone, the father, may say that you are lazy. You may not like the label, but at least it is something. It gives you an identity, a feeling of being someone. Superficially you may not like it, but deep down you feel better because you know who you are.

As a child you adopt these judgements — both positive and negative — and start believing in them and acting accordingly. It is a hypnosis. And when you grow up you carry these ideas.

Everybody is just an emptiness. If you accept labels then you are caught; and every day you reinforce them. This can be a pattern. It is just a false notion, and if you understand that, you can drop it this moment. Man is total emptiness and freedom. You are free to be whoever you like, however you like.

So don't try not to be lazy, Bhagwan continued, because then you are still repeating the word and the idea of laziness. He said that if Rishi found that anything he did gave him the idea he was lazy, he should do just the opposite. For example, if when he woke up at five-thirty in the morning he felt lazy, he should start getting up at four-thirty.

Bhagwan said that when he was younger he was also lazy and found it difficult to get up in the morning. So for the next few years — not just a month or two! — he used to get up at three o'clock! He said he was surprised to see himself doing it because he thought he was lazy. When it became obvious that he wasn't, he dropped getting up so early.

He said there is nothing wrong in sleeping late, but one should make the choice to do so; it should be a decision and not something one finds oneself doing out of laziness.

MAN IS TOTAL FREEDOM

Bhagwan said that in his childhood, he always wanted to grow his hair long, but his family did not like it and discouraged him. So one day he went out and had all his hair cut off — shaved!

His family were surprised, and said they had not meant he should shave his head, but he said this was the only way for him to overcome his desire for long hair. Now he was completely rid of it!

He said these are just notions of the mind and can be easily dropped; and that one could never be free unless one dropped such ideas.

FRIDAY DECEMBER 26th

A sannyasin, looking close to tears as he talked, told Bhagwan that he was feeling very sad and was easily hurt, and had felt like this for several weeks but he was unable to say what he felt was the reason for this.

Bhagwan asked his wife, who was also present, if she could comment, as her husband was not very clear about what was happening. Bhagwan said that perhaps, unconsciously, he was avoiding facing up to the problem for fear that he would not be able to cope with it. He added that women are more perceptive than men about things pertaining to relationships, so perhaps she could be helpful.

Turiya said that she was feeling a need to be alone lately — a feeling which was new to her — and that she thought this might be upsetting her husband, adding that she felt distant from him and wanted to have her own space. She said she used to cling to him a lot before.

Her husband said he felt rejected, 'wiped out', but did not seem to see a connection between these feelings and his wife's desire to be alone.

BHAGWAN   Now I understand exactly what the problem is. (to the husband) Because Turiya has been always afraid of being alone, she was clinging to you and you enjoyed it, the ego enjoyed it. The male ego enjoys it very much when a woman goes on clinging.

ALONENESS IS A GROWTH NEED

A woman is like a creeper, and the tree enjoys it tremendously—that the woman is dependent, mm? She was afraid of her aloneness, that's why she was clinging to you. Now, the more meditative she will become, the more she will like to be alone — because that is the only way she can get rid of her fear. So she wants to be alone, to be left alone, and you feel as if you are not needed, rejected. But you are not rejected at all, and it is not that you are not needed.

In fact she is trying to stand on her own feet for the first time, and if you allow her and help her to stand on her own, only then will love be possible. Up to now it has not been love. She was clinging to you because of her fear, and you were enjoying that because of your ego — neither you nor she were in deep love. Now for the first time love is possible.

If you help her to be alone, to get rid of the fear, she will always be grateful to you. And when she can be alone, and out of her aloneness she calls you, then there will be love, because then there is no question of fear. Only then can she share herself with you.

And it is going to be good for you also, because it is just the ego that is feeling hurt. Nothing else feels hurt, it is always the ego. The ego is like a wound — very touchy. You just touch it and it feels hurt. So she has been fulfilling your ego; now she wants to be alone and that hurts.

Try to understand. Let her be alone, leave her alone and give her more and more space. Whenever you feel that she needs to be alone, just move away — and she will love you tremendously for it because that is a gesture of love. When somebody needs to be alone you should leave them alone. If you love her, you understand the need—it is a growth need. And she will be grateful for it, more grateful than ever. Remember always that if someone loves you out of fear, that love is bogus, because love cannot arise out of fear. It is an empty gesture. Love can arise only out of deep understanding, not out of fear.

So this is going to help you both. And it was to come. Whenever a couple comes to me, the whole of their old pattern has to change, because they have lived in a certain relationship and now they start growing. That old relationship cannot contain you; you are becoming bigger and bigger. Your dresses were made for children and now they are too small and you feel confined. So don't cling to the old patterns; drop them. Help her to be alone.

(addressing Turiya) And Turiya, you remember not to hurt him unnecessarily. When you want to be alone, simply say you want to be alone. This too has to be understood, because many times we want to be alone but the way we express it is very ugly. We tell the other to go away or tell them that we don't need or love them any more. We may say these things, when in fact all we wanted to say was that we wanted to be alone.

So when you want to be alone, simply ask him and be very loving so that he can understand. If he is in a misunderstanding he will create trouble for you, and then growth becomes impossible.

You are both growing, and much love will happen. You are getting ready for it. Just a little waiting and patience is needed for it, mm? Don't be worried. Within weeks you will see a totally new quality of love coming between you, flowing between you, and much understanding, Everything will be good.

Bhagwan touched their heads and then enquired after their little daughter, Tanya, who was with them. He told Turiya to help Tanya to meditate, adding:

MY HEART IS BEGINNING TO OPEN

If from this age she can do some meditations, she will not have to come across many of the difficulties that you have. And if from the very beginning she becomes meditative, she will have a totally different life. Her choice will be different, her love will be different; her whole being will have a different dimension of growth.

This is the right time to start meditating. And at this age the mind is almost clean, pure, innocent; if seeds are sown in it they go very deep. The fruits may not come soon, but they will come one day.

When you learn something later on, your own knowledge always functions as a barrier; it goes on rejecting many things, mm?

Bhagwan broke off to hand a gift, a game, to Tanya. She reached forward shyly to take it, wriggled back to her mother's side, then in a sing-songy child's way said a quick 'thank you!'—her only English word!

PREM DHARMA

I've been feeling a struggle a lot in the last week. Feeling my heart beginning to open and flowing, and then coming in and clutching. So I'm feeling both happy and sad at the same time.

Enjoy both, mm? and don't choose. Once you choose you are ready for trouble. Sadness is as much a part of life as happiness. It is not to be denied, it has to be

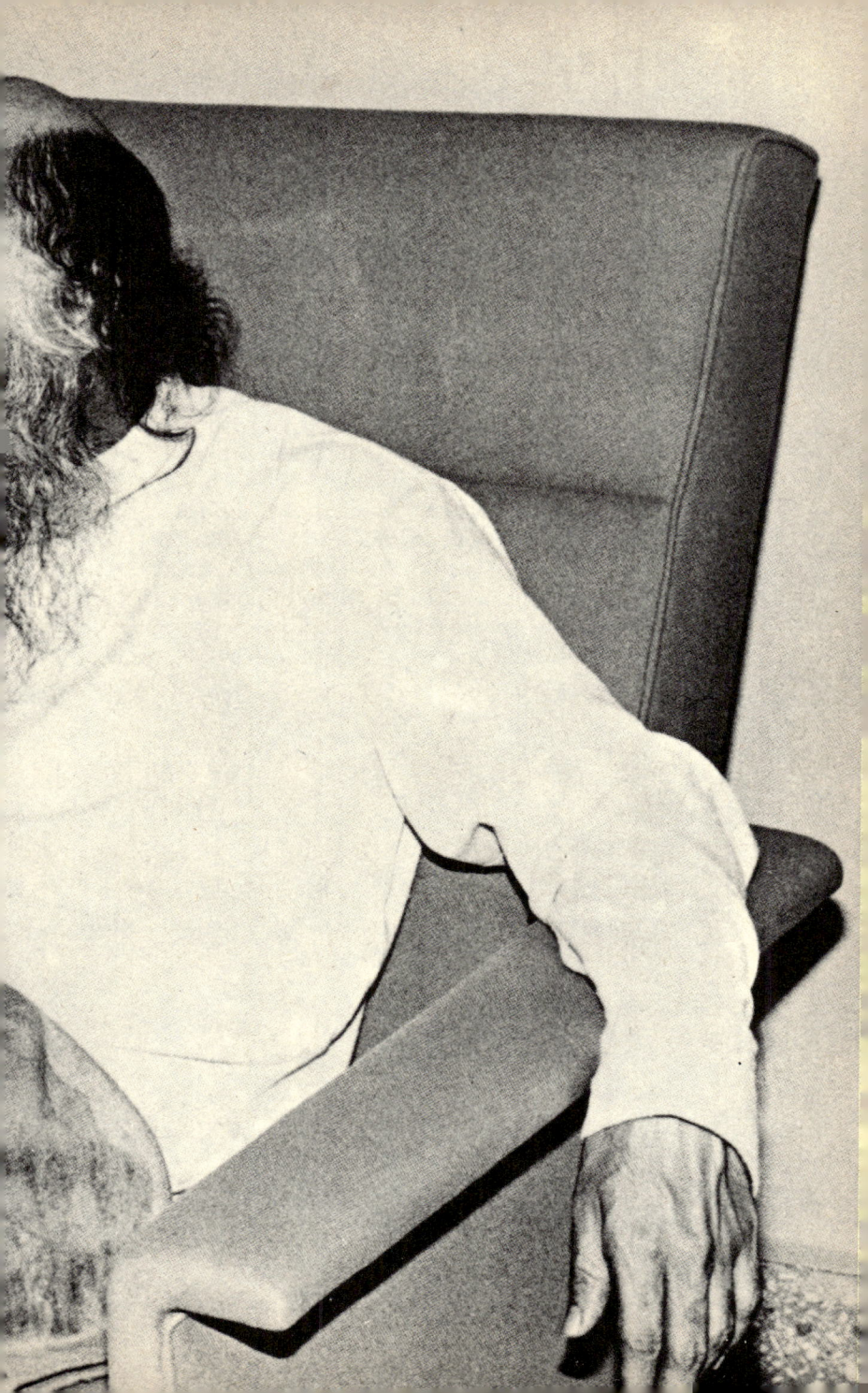

absorbed. It is a beautiful thing if you can fit into the total harmony.

A man who cannot be unhappy, who cannot be sad, lacks something. His happiness will just be on the surface, superficial; sadness gives you a depth. So don't reject it — because the mind has been trained to reject sadness. It has been trained just to be happy, which is foolish!

If you want to laugh you will have to be capable of crying. If tears cannot come, your laughter will be just a painted laugh. If tears can come to you, only then the laughter will be deep and from your innermost core. One grows both ways simultaneously, like a tree. The tree grows high and the roots go low, deep into the earth. Your roots will go deep in sadness and your branches will go high in happiness — and you are both. Accept both and enjoy both. If a man can accept the opposites then there is nothing else to learn.

If you ask me the one lesson that needs to be learnt, I will say be happy with the opposite — that will do. This is all there is to all philosophy, all religion. Try it! Good.

Mm, what about you?

Satya Radha sits gazing at Bhagwan silently for a few seconds.

(a little laugh) Mm! Say something!

SATYA RADHA *I don't know . . . I'm laughing and I feel very sad . . . especially when I listen to you. In the beginning it was so beautiful.*

YOUR WORDS ARE LIKE HONEY, A JOY

> *Every word was like honey and a great joy, and now I feel everything hurts me very much. The same words perhaps, but they go into me like a knife. I suffer very much.*

Mm mm ... suffer — because you have to pass with me through all the phases of life. You have to be sad with me, suffer with me, celebrate with me. You have to pass through all the climates with me.

I am not a particular season, I am the whole year. The summer will come and the winter, and there will be spring and there will be autumn — and you have to go with me all the year round.

There are persons who are like seasons; they have one taste. If they are summer, they are summer; if they are winter then they are winter. I am not fixed that way. And to me, people who have only one season are dead — they don't know what life is. Life is a tremendous change, a tremendous flow. Waves upon waves, and the ocean goes on and on and the waves go on shattering on the rocks and continue their song.

In different seasons, in different moods, you will have to live with me. When you have lived through all the seasons and all the moods, then you will understand what richness is.

So allow that too. If my words are like flowers, let them be like knives penetrating you. If my words were like soothing balm, now let them be like fire and flames. Because finally you have to pass through all the opposites to come back home, to come to a point where opposites meet, mingle and disappear.

A point will come one day when you will listen to me and there will be neither sadness nor happiness. My words won't be like flowers and won't be like flames. You will simply listen in utter silence, not even a sound, nothing will happen. You will be as if you are not — and only then you have heard the message. Before that — many climates . . . but every climate is good, so enjoy that too, mm? If you live with me in the day, then who is going to live with me in the night? Accept all the ways I am, and each new phase will break something within you, a block, a frozenness — and will help you to flow. I will hammer you in many ways. And surrender means that you are ready.

If I am going to help, you are ready. If you say that you are surrendered and will follow me if I am going to heaven and not if I am going to hell, then you are not surrendered. If you are ready to go with me anywhere, only then you are ready to go with me.

And this is my understanding: that unless you can touch the very bottom of hell you will never know what heaven is. That is why hell exists — to purify you, to destroy you and all that is unnecessary so that heaven can flower in you. It is paradoxical, it appears paradoxical, but the flower of heaven blooms in hell.

Ponder over it! (a chuckle) Good!

SUNDAY DECEMBER 28th

GEET GOVIND (a painter from Berlin) *I think some new things are starting in me, but I have not started....*

BHAGWAN Mm mm . . . start!
It is always difficult to start anything new, because the mind always tries to postpone. With the old, mind fits perfectly. With the new, there is a certain uneasiness. But don't postpone.

If you feel that something new is coming, that you would like to do something new, do it — because only by doing it will it settle in your being. In fact only by doing do we know who we are, and doing reveals your being. By dancing you come to know that you are a dancer — there is no other way to know. If you never dance you will never come to know that you are a dancer; you will miss that dimension.

Doing is always lesser than the being. As far as being is concerned you are infinite, you are all. But as far as doing is concerned, there will be a limitation. You will have to choose to do something and choose not to do something else.

You are a born painter; that is your natural flow. So if something is coming up new and fresh, you may have some hesitation, because you are a well-known painter — your name, your identity, your past, the fixed routine — and that can become an obstacle.

Sometimes, to become famous is very dangerous, because then you cannot play with the new. You become afraid. To become famous means that now you have too much invested in the past. Always remain an amateur, never become an expert. Always go on playing with the new and let your life remain a fun, and not a serious thing. Serious people are dead before their death.

So start immediately and don't waste time, whatever it is — because you cannot know unless you do.

It is just like a woman carrying a child in the womb. Unless the child is born she will never be able to know who the child is — whether a boy or a girl, beautiful or ugly.

There is no way to know. You can feel, a woman can feel, that something is in the womb, alive and kicking, but who is there nobody knows. Not even the mother can know.

Even an artist never knows what is going to be born. When it is born, only then you see. Then you recognise retrospectively that yes, you recognise the kick of it, a very vague feeling about it — but it was all in a deep mist.

So you start working, mm? I was waiting for it! As you start meditating, soon something will come up; it is surfacing.

GEET GOVIND

I am not sure if in Germany I can change my artist name. I will do it, I want to do it, but the galleries will say that I can't.

You have to!

DARING ALWAYS PAYS TREMENDOUSLY

GEET GOVIND *I have to?*

Mm, because that will give you a clean break with the past. You have to! You can say to them that that old man is dead! You can release to the newspapers that he is dead (a chuckle) and you start afresh, a new painter. You let those old paintings remain with the old man — nothing to do with you. If it is possible, change; if it is not then forget about it.

Start afresh, totally afresh. Dare! And daring always pays tremendously. It is going to happen, mm? Good!

PREM PRASTHAN *I feel that I've lost my balance and I'm teetering....*

Come here. Tell me what is happening.

PRASTHAN *Well, um, as far as I know I'm not that scared by it, but it's ... it's ... I feel like I'm falling over and then I catch my balance. Then I get back and everything that's in me, that's part of me, seems to be soaring up and down. As a result I'm finding it quite hard to feel comfortable.*

HAMMER ON THE ROCK

> *I suppose I'm fighting but I'm not aware of how; and I suppose I'm hanging on, but at the same time I don't know how I'm hanging on.*

Mm, I understand. Whenever you start changing, you pass through a chaos, because the old unsettles and the new has yet to be born. The old dies and the new is not yet born. There is an interval, and in that interval one feels very unbalanced, loses all identity, all sense of who one is; forgets completely where one stands. The earth beneath one's feet disappears as if one is in an abyss, falling . . . falling . . . and there is no bottom to it. And one would like to cling to anything.

And that is natural — that idea to cling to anything. But if you cling, you only prolong the interval. If you don't cling, the interval will disappear soon; it can disappear this very moment. It is not a question of time. It is a question of your trust.

If you trust me, don't cling. Accept the imbalance, the insecurity. Accept the discomfort and the inconvenience. Accept it and immediately it will disappear. It is there because you go on thinking that you were better off before — at least things were settled.

It is just as when a child is going to be born. For nine months the child has lived in the mother's womb, absolutely comfortable. Never again in his life will he be so comfortable. The whole of science cannot yet create such comfort as a mother's womb can give to a child: no responsibility, no worry, no struggle. Everything is supplied; even before the need arises, the supply is there. Not that you demand and then the supply is there. That law of economics does not apply there. Even before you demand, the supply is there. Everything is comfortable, it is paradise. And the child is completely asleep for twenty-four hours, deep in oblivion, in darkness, silent.

And then birth comes. The child cannot see what is going to happen. All that he can see is that everything is getting disturbed; he is being thrown out of his home — comfortable, heavenly.

In fact the biblical story of Adam's expulsion from the Garden of Eden is nothing but a parable of the birth of man. The womb is the garden and the expulsion is just the birth of the child, the trauma. And the child is uncomfortable, tremendously uncomfortable, terribly uncomfortable; the whole thing is like a shock. Psychologists say that it is a trauma. Before death, never again will such a trauma happen. Only death can be a comparable shock, and even it is not much of a shock because life tires one, exhausts. In a way, one starts wishing to die before one actually starts dying. So even death is not going to be so terrible as birth is.

This is again a birth. Religion is nothing but a way to be reborn — in consciousness. So if you fight, if you try to cling, the interval will be prolonged. Simply relax. There is no going back now.

The situation is as if the head of the child has come out of the womb and the whole body is still inside; there is no going back. You can only come out. And if you cling you simply prolong the pain and the suffering — and it is unnecessary. Cooperate.

Only death is comfortable. Life has its discomforts and one grows through them — pain, suffering. Everything has its own meaning.

So as I can see, I bless you. Nothing is wrong; everything is perfectly as it should be. Just be a little more courageous, mm? It will disappear. Don't waste time, and cooperate with the process. Accept it and move with it.

Finally, that which looked like insecurity in the

beginning, you will find is the only security. And that which looked like discomfort in the beginning, you will soon find is the only happiness there is. But you will have to move into it, mm? Don't be afraid!

Mm Devesh! Something about Diana? (Devesh's recently-arrived and much-awaited girl friend from England)

DIANA *I'm very pleased to be here. I'm basically a cynic, and I never expected to be so moved. I just came to see my friend!* (a little laugh of shyness)

Mm! Much is going to happen — you don't know! You are caught! Just help her, Devesh. First you make her comfortable, then I will make her uncomfortable! (much laughter) Don't scare her from the very beginning, that I will do! mm? (a chuckle)

(addresses Diana's friend) What about you?

VIRGINIA *Well, I'm also very honoured to be here. I've been to India many times, but this time I've come to try to get back onto a*

THE SEEKING BECOMES THE PATH

> *right pathway, and to have a spiritual tour of India as opposed to another type of knowledge.*

Mm, very good... you have been doing something about it on your own?

VIRGINIA
> *Um, yes, I've always been interested in this side of life. And I've had guidance from, have been lucky enough to have guidance, from indian people. But this time I've come back here because I've lost my path in England, and I hope that I'll find it here again.*

You will, you will find it. Mm, good. Just the very search is very very beautiful — whether one finds or not, that is secondary. One is seeking, and that is the significant thing because finally it is your very seeking that becomes the path.

There exists no path apart from your seeking. The very intensity of your search becomes your path. In fact the very idea of a path is fallacious. It gives you the idea that the path already exists there somewhere for you to follow, and you just have to walk on it. That is not true....

VIRGINIA *Oh, that's not true?*

That's not true at all.

VIRGINIA — *There isn't one set path?*

No, no, really there is no ready-made path. As you walk you create your path, and each individual passes along his own path. There is no public path, no super-highways.

VIRGINIA — *But when you go wrong, do you come back to a central highway or not?*

There are no central highways. When you go wrong that simply means that you become unconscious. When you become aware, you are right. Awareness is right, and unawareness is wrong. Whenever in your life you become a little sleepy, clouded, and the clarity is lost; whenever you don't know what you are doing or why, and why you are existing in the first place — then you have gone wrong, that's all.

If you regain your clarity and your vision and you can again see through and through, you have regained the path. In fact, it is not a question of anything outside you.

INDIA IS YOUR INNER BEING

It is something inside you, an inner focusing of energy. The very search is enough.

There is a saying of Jesus, 'Ask and it shall be given, knock and the doors will be opened unto you, seek and you will find.' In fact the doors are not closed. They are already open, only you have not knocked. The answer is already there, only you have not asked. And that which you are seeking is already present in you, only you have not looked.

So an intense search, a sincere search, becomes the path. And unless you come to know this you will again and again lose your path, mm? because that path that you think you have found is not the real path. A real path cannot be lost. That which can be found and lost was not found in the first place.

And for the real path you need not go anywhere. You only need to be inside, to go inwards. That is the real India — your inner being.

India is not a geography, and if you go to see India you are wasting your time. India is an inner space; it is just a symbolic word for inner space. When you start travelling withinwards then you are moving towards India. So whomsoever reaches to himself becomes an Indian. Just by being born in India one does not become an Indian.

Good! Help, Devesh!

Anything Pratiti?

Pratiti said that lately when meditating at home she feels a choking sensation in her throat. She said that all the energy goes to that point and breathing becomes difficult. She wondered what she should do if this sensation happened again.

HAMMER ON THE ROCK

You feel like dying?

PRATITI *Absolutely. If I don't say to myself to stop and to move. . . .*

Nothing to worry about. You are just on the verge where one comes to face death.

One has to face it one day or other, and anything that goes deeply will bring you to death. If you love somebody very deeply, someday or other, love will bring you to face death. That is the fear of love. So people go on playing with love but never delve deeply into it. If you pray, one day or other, death will be there. So people go on imitating; they don't pray. If you meditate the same will happen. Wherever you move deep you will have to pass the point of death, because only beyond death is life; that barrier has to be crossed.

So next time it happens to you just die! Don't try to stop it, and don't try to bring yourself out of it. Don't start fighting with it. Relax and just repeat inside that you are willing to die. Welcome it and be receptive. Not even a slight effort, mm? And once you allow it to happen, suddenly you will see that death has gone and the choking has disappeared; the energy is flowing and you have come to contact a new source of energy.

And this handkerchief, (he passes her one of his handkerchiefs) you have to put around your neck where you feel. . . .

This is to remind you that I am there, don't be afraid, mm? And it will go, don't be worried. It has to be faced;

death has to be faced to know life. Looks paradoxical, but that's how life is.

Darkness has to be faced to know the morning, and the darker the night, the closer the morning. So pass through it, mm? Good.

LEELA   *I feel very afraid.*

That's very good. Come here.

Feel afraid, there is nothing wrong in it. Close your eyes, and feel afraid, and let whatsoever happens, happen . . . allow it. . . .

Leela sits upright in front of Bhagwan, eyes closed. Her body begins to shake, tremble, and spasmodically jerks forward. Bhagwan watches her for a few seconds, shining the torch on her, then. . . .

Mm, good. Nothing to worry, mm? It is natural. Something new is growing, something new is happening — so you feel afraid. With the unfamiliar there is always fear; with the strange, with the unknown, there is fear.

Only with the known is there no fear, but the known just means the repetitive, the routine. Something unknown is entering. Allow it and don't feel embarrassed by it. You are suppressing, trying to hold it in so that nobody knows what is happening to you. You are trying not only to hide it from others, but from yourself as well. That won't help.

Drop all hide-and-seek, all games. Be true and sincere. Whatsoever is happening, allow, mm? And from tomorrow your meditation will go very deep. It is just that you are holding, and that's why you are afraid. Whenever you hold something, you are afraid in coming to me, because I will not be deceived. You have been a thief. . .that's why there is fear. (chuckle)

Don't try to hide anything. We are here to become absolutely true, authentic, nude and naked — that is the only way to become pure and innocent again, mm?

What meditations have you been doing?

LEELA   *I haven't done many because I've been sick.*

Now you are perfectly okay? That illness may also have been a trick of the mind! Sometimes mind creates illnesses so that you can hide. You can say, 'I am ill, what can I do?' So you can escape from meditation. (a chuckle) Don't be worried. You start from tomorrow working hard!

MONDAY DECEMBER 29th

The Primal Therapy group, halfway through the fifteen days of their therapy, were at darshan.

The course actually consists of a total of twenty-five days which includes the ten days of the camp. For the last two days of the camp, members of the group maintain silence and remain in isolation (except of course during the meditations). This continues for the remainder of the group.

The entire period is intended to be a meditation, with each thought and activity being observed and brought into the sessions. Individual and group meditations are given as is felt appropriate. Through the process one is helped to remember, or relive, one's past. This reliving is linked with body feelings and sensations. One is taught to unify the body and the mind to form an integrated experience of oneself.

Bhagwan has described it as not so much a therapy as a situation where people can let go into their fears and madnesses, their obsessions and secret hankerings, in a safe and protected environment and where help can be given to see beyond them.

Bhagwan turned first to address a sannyasin who is training to assist in the therapy.

She said she was liking it, but felt she was not yet totally involved in it, that she was still holding herself back.

BHAGWAN No, you have been growing, and I am happy. You continue. When you work with people, you can work as a duty or you can work with them as a love. There is a lot of difference between these two. Duty is lukewarm, love is passionate. Duty can help, but love can transform. Duty can touch only the surface of the other person because it comes from your head. Love can transform because it comes from your heart.

Whenever you are working with people, remember that each person is unique. You will never find such a person again; it happens only once. Each person is historic because he will never be repeated again. So each moment of contact will also be historical because it is unrepeatable; it is tremendously valuable. So whenever you are helping, help out of love. Flow, and forget helping. Start caring — that is the difference.

If you help, you will be at the most a nurse. If you care, you become a mother. Help is a quantitative thing. Care is qualitative, and it shows an intensity; it is a flame. So be deeply in passion.

Each individual is representative of the divine. Love him, worship him, respect him, and whatsoever you do, do in deep humbleness. Then you will be helped more than you are helping. Then you will grow more than the person can grow through your help.

And there is no other way in the world to learn something than to become a teacher. But take it as a very very sacred and holy affair. Be really sincere and authentic about it. I'm not saying be serious. I'm saying be sincere, because once you become serious you cannot help. Be sincere but non-serious, playful. Take it as a fun — but don't forget the sacredness of it. When fun and sacredness meet, there arises a quality in you that can help. This is the alchemy of help: fun and sacredness meeting in you.

And that feeling is right — that you are still not total in it. One never is. The more you are in it, the more you will feel that something is lacking. Life is a continuous flow, and there is no end to it. Something more is always possible.

There is no end to it and it is good; otherwise, if an end came you would be dead. But the feeling is good, so bring more effort, more energy into it. You will become more and more total in it, but never total. Do you follow me? You become more total, but never total. Nobody ever is. Good!

Bhagwan turned to the other assistant helper who said he felt he would like to act as a vehicle; to allow things to happen through him. But for this, he felt more moments of being quiet and inactive were needed. He wondered whether the structure of the therapy as it was would allow this.

Mm mm, make it part of the work! It is helpful. Activity helps and passivity too. After each intensive experience, a few moments of passivity are tremendously useful and meaningful.

In fact, that is the whole meaning of the active work: to bring you to a point where you are exhausted, tired. Tired of activity, tired of aggression, tired of outgoingness; so tired

that you would like to relax within yourself. You would like to simply sit and do nothing, or lie down as if you would like to disappear for a few moments, to withdraw.

So these moments of withdrawal are very very meaningful. So make it part of your work. First be very active, because only then those moments are available. The activity should be so intense and so passionate that you are really burned out, otherwise if you simply sit without intense activity, nothing will happen; you are not ready.

After the activity, sit in silence together. You can hold hands and be in a circle, not doing anything. Just a few moments will revitalize you. You will be able to feel that the energy is not coming from you, but from something deeper than you, higher than you, greater than you. You are at the receiving end. It is not coming from you; it is being given to you.

Two sannyasins had had very powerful emotions come up connected with their parents. The first, a boy of twenty-seven or so, said he realised how much he missed his mother, and that he felt a deep split. He was visibly moved and tearful while he spoke to Bhagwan.

It has been very good. . . .

The mother is the first love, and through the mother you start loving the world. Through the mother you start being capable of love, and whenever you come to love somebody, your mother's love will be present there.

You have touched something very basic. Cry, and be happy about it. Don't suppress it. It will bring many things up. If a man cannot love his mother very deeply

WOMAN BECOMES A MOTHER, MAN BECOMES A CHILD

then he cannot love any woman, because all women are representatives of the mother, reflections of her.

In India we have a saying that if you really love a woman, eventually she becomes your mother. Only then love is fulfilled. Each husband becomes a child, each woman a mother. That is the culmination — and that is where man and woman departed.

A child is born and goes away from the mother; they separate. Then the child returns and becomes a child again, has a second childhood, and finds the woman again turning into a mother. Each woman has to complete her circle by becoming a mother, and each man has to complete his circle by becoming a child. When the circle is complete, love is fulfilled.

Watch, even a small girl is motherly. She starts playing with dolls, plays house and things like that. She is already a mother, a miniature. In the West something is missing, and that's why the whole family life is on the rocks, has almost gone. The family has disappeared because the base of it is that the man should love a woman so totally that he becomes her child, and the woman becomes his mother.

But this is possible only if you love one woman, intensely, deeply, intimately. If you go on changing your woman every day it is not going to happen; then all relationships will remain casual. That is where the western man and woman are missing. The conflict and the confusion and chaos is so much that they both think they are being cheated by each other. Nobody is cheating anybody — it is just that the circle is not ready until it is completed.

If you cannot become a child again, you will not be able to love your own child. If a woman cannot become so deeply in love with her husband that she becomes a mother to him, she will not be able to love her own children — and then the vicious circle continues.

You have touched something very deep. Dig it deep

and let flow, mm? Good!

The next sannyasin, a woman, said that she was feeling very very sad but she did not know why.

Bhagwan shone his torch on her face and sat with his eyes closed for a few minutes. She continued to weep. . . .

You cannot feel what it is, what the sadness is about? Can't you pinpoint where it started, and why?

She said that it might have something to do with her father leaving home when she was six years old. It had been a shock to her as she had had no idea he was going. . . .
Bhagwan said that the only way to get rid of past wounds was to become conscious of them. . . .

If you become conscious of them, they dissolve. Otherwise they are always hiding there, and they go on influencing your life — though you don't know it.

For example if you loved your father, a deep wound is left there. It is natural and has to be so, because a child, and particularly a girl, misses the father very deeply. When the parents separate, it is not so difficult for them; in fact it may be more convenient. There are moments of conflict, of violence, so that two people may think it is no use to be together when they are hurting each other — and unnecessarily. So they may feel relieved. But nobody thinks about the child.

The child is both the mother and the father. Half of the child comes from the mother and half from the father. The child is a synthesis of the polarities of male and female. When the mother and father separate, and the child is not yet grown up, a rift happens in the child. It is not only a divorce of father and mother. It is a divorce within the child between male and female, and that becomes a wound.

If the child is grown up — and by grown up I mean if a girl is so grown up that she has fallen in love with some man — then there is no problem. In this man she has found a new synthesis of man and woman. So if the father and mother separate, there is not going to be such a deep wound. But a small child is helpless, and the wound is so deep. She goes on hiding and hiding and hiding it, until by and by she forgets all about it. One has to forget. To live you have to forget many wounds, but they are there inside. They go on continuously functioning from behind the stage, prompting your head.

You love a man, but your father left you when you were very small. Now you cannot believe in any man, cannot trust him, because the first man you trusted deceived you. So on the surface you think you love the man, but at the back a deep distrust is there. It goes on prompting you, telling you to be alert and not to be deceived again.

These are unconscious things that go on inside. You don't know that they are there, but they influence you. You cannot trust totally, you cannot surrender totally. You cannot move totally — you are always half moving and half ready to move back, always fearful, divided.

These deep wounds have to be lived through, that is why you are so sad. Don't try to repress it. Be sad, as sad

as possible. Be consciously sad. Go behind the stage in
fantasy, and then you know, and something can be done.
When you know something, you can tackle it because it
is no longer a problem really. The past is past and cannot
be undone — but your wound can be undone.

Your father and mother cannot meet, but the male
and the female within you can meet and the rift can be
bridged. And once that happens, you will be able to forgive
your father. You may even become capable of feeling a
deep compassion for him. Because that poor man must
have suffered, otherwise what man would leave the woman
he loves?

Gurdjieff had written on his house — and it was to be
read by all his disciples — that before you enter here, you
must be capable of forgiving your father and mother. It
looks foolish. How can it be meaningful? But it is, because
to come to a master, you come to a man who is both
father and mother. If you have not yet forgiven your father
and mother, how can you forgive me? Impossible!

And the master is even more important because he is
both father and mother. He is a union, a synthesis of male
and female, yin and yang. When one becomes capable
of being a disciple, only then can one come to terms with
one's own father and mother. Only then can one come
back to a loving relationship.

But your knot can be undone, your complexities can
disappear. They will disappear on their own. Don't try to
escape from them, mm?

Something to say?

DEVANAND *I left the group . . . and I'm going home in a few days.*

DON'T LISTEN TO THE MIND

Mm mm . . . go home. Mm? Go home—and because you left, there is nothing to say.

DEVANAND *I felt I got something out of the group.*

No, you escaped from the situation. You are a coward and cowards always go on trying to find rationalisations.

You were just going to touch some layer within you and
you escaped. Your cleverness is not going to help you; in
fact it is your enemy. Just the very moment that you were
coming closer to some wound, to some strata which would
have been very meaningful and significant, you escaped.

Next time when you come, be ready — you will have to
do the group again. You have to do it once completely,
because it is going to help you so much. You cannot see,
that's the trouble. You are almost blind, you cannot see.
What have you gained by dropping out of it? Just by going
home, what are you going to do? Even if it was a little
painful, you were not going to be killed by these people.
Whenever somebody wants to grow, there is some
discomfort. One has to get hurt, but others are going
through it, so you were not alone.

That is why I am insisting so much on the group —
because people have become so cowardly that they cannot
grow alone. In the past, people were really brave. They
worked alone, and nothing like a group existed. By and by,
as people became cowardly and lost all courage, groups
had to be started.

When did you drop out of the group?

DEVANAND   *Yesterday . . . so I've missed*
one day, no, two.

It was unworthy of you. This was going to give you
many valuable experiences. If you can gather courage
I think you should complete it. Or is it difficult to
gather courage? You are really very very scared.

All this time the sannyasin had sat palefaced and hunched-up,
without much display of emotion. To any ordinary observer he did

DON'T LISTEN TO THE MIND

not seem too perturbed by Bhagwan's words or the idea of resuming the group.

DEVANAND
I'm not that scared. I just feel . . . my mind told me not to do the group. I just woke up one morning, and my mind said not to go back to the group.

So don't listen to the mind! You have been listening to this mind for your whole life and where has it led, what has it given to you?

This is rot — what you call the mind. It is nothing to do with you, just a crowd; accumulated rubbish that you call your mind. What is the need to listen to it?

You just tell the mind that for seven days, (the duration of the remainder of the group) you are not going to listen to it. And then don't listen to it, just go to the group every day. Try, mm? It will be a good experience and you will feel more comfortable about yourself.

You will get out of your bondage, the bondage of the mind, and you will feel free. The mind is your slave, not your master. Who is this mind to tell you not to do the group? If you want to do it, do it, and the mind has to help. If you don't want to do it, don't, and the mind has to help you.

If you don't want to do the group, tell me. But don't bring in the mind.

DEVANAND
I can't tell the difference between me and my mind.

You can! Why did you start this group? You wanted to do it! Then the mind became afraid because it became aware, by and by, that things were going to be dangerous — so it told you not to do it.

There is a sannyasin here whose mind tells him every morning not to do the dynamic meditation. But he goes and he does it, and it is a beautiful experience because now he has become aware that he can put aside the mind. You can put aside the mind that feels fear, and then you regain your power and your mastery. Just try!

DEVANAND

I feel that all my life I've been trying, making an effort, pushing myself hard in everything I did. But I can't tell the difference between what is my mind and what is me.

Who is saying this — you or your mind? Right now close your eyes, and be honest.

Devanand sat for a few moments with eyes closed, then said he couldn't tell the difference.

(laughing) It is your mind! The effort was being done by you, because every effort for growth comes from the being, and all laziness comes from the mind.

So look at it again tomorrow morning and decide. If it is your mind, then put it aside and go to the group and finish it. And if you feel it is you who does not want to do the group, forget about the group. It is up to you to bring some clarity to it, mm? And be sincere.

If it is you, you will feel very happy about not doing it, and if it is the mind, you will be unhappy. You look unhappy, that is why I am insisting on it — that it is the mind. You should have been very very happy if it was your being that wanted to drop out, because when you follow your being, happiness comes to you.

FOLLOW YOUR BEING

But you have to clarify this. On it, much depends — your future growth. If you start listening to the mind your growth will stop, mm? Try, try hard to see what is what. Good.

TUESDAY DECEMBER 30th

A sannyasin who had been celibate for several months on Bhagwan's suggestion, said she had been feeling very sexual lately and did not know what she should do about it.

BHAGWAN   Just do one thing whenever it happens again. Sit straight—on a chair or on the floor—with the spine straight, but loose and not tense.

Inhale slowly and deeply. Don't be in a hurry; very slowly go on inhaling. The belly comes up first; you go on inhaling. The chest comes up next, and then finally you can feel that the air is filled up to the neck. Then for a moment or two just keep the breath in, for as long as you can without straining, then exhale. Exhale also very slowly but in the reverse order. When the belly is being emptied, pull it in so that all the air goes out.

This has to be done just seven times. Then sit silently and start repeating, 'aum, aum, aum.' While repeating aum, keep your concentration on the third eye spot— between the two eyebrows. Forget about the breathing, and go on repeating in a very drowsy way, aum, aum, aum— like a mother sings a lullaby so the child goes to sleep. The mouth should be closed, so much so that the tongue is touching the roof; and your whole concentration is on the third eye.

JUST TO BE IS A BENEDICTION

Do this just for two or three minutes and you will feel that the whole head is relaxing. When it starts relaxing you will immediately feel inside a tightness dropping, a tension disappearing. Then bring your concentration down to the throat; go on repeating aum, but with your concentration on the throat. Then you will see that your shoulders, your throat and your face are relaxing and that the tension is falling away like a burden dropping; you are becoming weightless.

Then drop deeper, bringing your concentration to the navel and continuing the aum. You are going deeper and deeper and deeper. . . . Then finally you come to the sex centre. This will take at the most ten minutes, fifteen minutes, so go slowly, there is no hurry.

When you have reached the sex centre the whole body will be relaxed, and you will feel a glow as if some aura, some light, is surrounding you. You are full of energy, but the energy is like a reservoir; full of energy but with no ripples. Then you can sit in that state as much as you like; the meditation is over—now you are simply enjoying. Stop the aum and simply sit. If you feel like lying you can lie down, but if you move that position the state will sooner disappear, so sit a little and enjoy it.

This brings what scientists call the alphawave in the mind. It has a certain rhythm—ten cycles per second—which is also the rhythm of the magnetic field of the earth. When you are also in the same rhythm, you become part of the magnetic field of the earth. This is what relaxation is.

Sometimes it can happen without any effort. It happens while making love, doing meditation; sometimes while dancing or singing and sometimes for no reason at all. But whenever your rhythm coincides with the magnetic field of the earth, you feel very very happy and glowing, just beautiful. Just to be, is a benediction.

So whether one achieves it through sex or meditation

or dancing, through listening to music or watching beautiful scenery or looking at the stars, is irrelevant. The whole point is that when your body becomes too tense — for any reason at all — just do it and it will give you total relaxation.

When our rhythm and the rhythm of the earth are different, the tension arises. A child is not sexual because his rhythm is still the same as that of the earth. But when he grows he will go far away from being natural, will become part of the society and will start becoming tense and worried. Anguish and then sex will arise. The more tense a society, the more sexual it becomes.

That is why the West has become so sexual. Because there are so many tensions, they have to be released, and there seems no other way to release them. But there are a thousand and one ways. So you just try this, mm?

The next sannyasin to speak with Bhagwan spoke to him in both Hindi and English. Only that which he said in English is recorded:

RAJ

> ...I want to jump and yet I haven't jumped. I want to do what you want me to do, and yet there's a part of me that resists, and I'm in so much confusion....
>
> Sometimes I just go into my room and want to hammer something. Then I say, 'No, I am yours completely....
>
> ...and you said once not to make a problem out of things, so I think there is no problem and I will go to the ashram. So I go for two days, and then next day it's a big problem....

FEEL COMPASSION NOT CONDEMNATION

> *I have questions and answers by the hundreds.... I can only come on Sundays now, and the other day you said not to miss any meditation because you may miss something. So I thought I'm again in the trouble ... and it goes on, Bhagwan. ...*

(laughingly) I know, it is natural. Nobody can surrender totally, nobody. If you can surrender totally then right this moment you will become enlightened. Nothing remains to be done then.

So you cannot be total in the beginning; it is not so easy. Even if a part can surrender that is more than enough. One should be happy about it.

When I say, 'Don't create a problem,' I mean this: that a part of you is surrendered, another part is not — that's why there is conflict. The conflict is natural, because now you are divided, and the part which is surrendered knows the beauty of it, and would like the other part to surrender too. But the other part is completely unaware of it and is afraid, so conflict arises.

Don't pay much attention to the other part. A little part is surrendered — be happy about it, be grateful. Even that doesn't happen to millions of people. They waste their whole life, and never come to know what love is, what surrender and trust are.

Through your gratefulness other parts will follow by and by. Emphasis should be on the part that has surrendered — that should be your centre. The other parts that are not surrendered should be left to the periphery. You should be indifferent.

And the second thing is: whenever you meditate many things will happen, and the idea is bound to come that something has happened to you. Nothing is wrong in the idea, that too is natural. One starts feeling that one is purer, holier; nothing is wrong in that. The problem arises if you make it an ego-trip. There is no need to make it an ego-trip; let it be a simple statement of fact. It is so, but don't get too attached to it — you need not prove it to anybody. Don't evaluate or judge it.

The problem arises when you start feeling 'holier than thou'. Holiness is good, but when it becomes comparative then it is bad. Do you follow me?

When you take a bath you feel a certain feeling of coolness, of freshness — and there is nothing wrong in it. But when you see a beggar, dirty, and a condemnation arises; when you cannot see that man's humanity, you simply see the dirt, and no compassion arises in you but rather condemnation; when you feel that you are purer than this man — then it is wrong, then it has become an ego-trip.

And it is good also to help this person to try to have a bath; to create a situation where if he can be made interested he also can take a bath. So, good, feel compassion for people but not condemnation. In both ways you feel holy, but in one way you are creating trouble for yourself. Sooner or later that pureness will disappear and only ego will remain there. In another way, when you feel compassion, your holiness will grow, your purity will grow every day. Ego is the only dirty thing there is.

So I say don't create any problems out of these. Enjoy everything that comes naturally.

The next sannyasin sat wide-eyed and hunched-up in front of Bhagwan. . . .

DHEERENDRA *The other night I got very frightened. I was in my room lying*

AFTER THE DARK NIGHT IS THE DAWN

> *on my bed, and for some reason I started thinking that I am not my body alone. The room stood out very strongly, everything in the room stood out strongly, but it wasn't warm, it was cold.*

(smilingly) It was a hotel room?

DHEERENDRA   *Yes.*

(laughing) It has to be cold! Mm, then? . . .

DHEERENDRA   (still looking tense and intense) *I felt like running away from you . . . feeling closed . . . I know I'm closed.*

It was an effortless meditation. It suddenly happened and that's why you got frightened.

Now try it on purpose and consciously tonight. Be in the same room; lie down and start thinking that you are not the body, that you are separate from the body. The moment that you start thinking that you are not the body, everything will become very present and strong, because the warmth is within the identification with the body.

Suddenly you are in a strange land: only things are there, and your own body has become like a corpse—that's why you got frightened. Try again tonight. Go in deeper and deeper, and don't become afraid. If you become very afraid, take the locket (the locket, which is part of the mala all sannyasins wear, has a picture of Bhagwan in it) in the hand and remember me. Continue the feeling that you are not the body, and by and by take the next step—that you are also not the mind. Thoughts are there, but you are not them. You are the observer of both the body and the mind, you are a witness. Go on feeling it as deeply as possible.

In the beginning it will look like death—it is. But soon you will see that a new sense of life is arising. The fear will disappear and instead you will feel a weightlessness. You will feel a new sort of freedom as if suddenly wings have grown to you and you can fly, and the whole world is yours. But before you attain to that, fear will be there and it will become very very terrible. One has to pass through it.

Now for seven nights do it, and become as frightened as you can—but don't run away from it, don't escape. Go deeper. You will feel like sinking, dying, suffocating. Take the locket in the hand and accept it, that it is okay.

To come to oneself, one has to pass through many fears. After the dark night there is the dawn, the morning.

It has been good, you should be happy. When will you do it, at exactly what time?—so I can watch you.

DHEERENDRA *Ten o'clock.*

Ten o'clock. Then be particular—exactly ten o'clock. And if you feel me there, don't get frightened. (a chuckle) Mm? and don't get scared!

WEDNESDAY DECEMBER 31st

BHAGWAN   (to an initiate)   Your energy is really moving beautifully. This is going to be your new name: Swami Dharmananda.

Dharma means the Ultimate Law that sustains life; what in Chinese they call Tao. Ananda means bliss. Dharmananda means bliss that comes if you live according to the Law. If you fall in tune with the Ultimate Law, suddenly there is bliss. In fact all misery is because you are not in tune with the Law, you go astray from it. The further away you go, the more miserable you become. Hell means the furthest point from the Law, or God, or nature—and the nearest point is heaven. To become one with the Law is to go beyond both heaven and hell. That's what in India we call 'moksha'—total freedom.

If you fall into the Law as a fish falls into the ocean and becomes part of it, then you are blissful. Dharmananda—

remember the meaning because that is going to become your sadhana, your path. Become as natural as possible, as spontaneous as possible, and live moment to moment, mm? Very good!

A seeker, not yet a sannyasin, said, in answer to Bhagwan's query of whether she had tried meditation, that she had, and had liked it. Bhagwan talked about meditation and its transforming effects:

. . . we are living so minimally that it can be said to be almost nothing. Life can become a pinnacle of bliss, it can come to peaks of happiness.

In the talmud it is said that when you face God again, He will not ask you what mistakes you have committed, He will ask you how many opportunities to be blissful you have missed. That is the only sin—to miss an opportunity to become blissful. Because unless you become so blissful that a natural gratitude arises in you, you will not believe in God.

When you feel very very blissful, celebrating each moment of life, by and by you start feeling thankful—not towards anything in particular, just thankful towards the whole. That is what prayer is. You cannot believe in God unless you have come to a point where you can be prayerful. People ordinarily think that through prayer they come to God; ordinarily they think that if they pray they will understand God. But just by doing prayer nobody can understand.

Prayer must happen, and that is possible only when your life has become so beautiful and so happy, that with

each breath there is thankfulness. Said or unsaid, that is not the point. You may never mention the word God, you may never kneel down to pray—that is not the point. But with each breath you feel a deep gratefulness, you are grateful that you are—and the prayer has started. This prayer is not something to do, it is a way of being. Then you come to know the whole, and without knowing it, we live in vain.

There is much possibility as I can see, mm? You can grow. You have a very simple, innocent, loving heart. It can take a jump immediately and then become a flame and flower . . . . And be a sannyasin!

The girl said her one objection to becoming a sannyasin was the wearing of saffron-coloured robes. Bhagwan spoke about the significance of the colour, but first said that as her husband was a sannyasin, it would be very helpful for them both if she too were to take sannyas.

This has been my observation, that if the husband or the wife becomes a sannyasin and the other does not, it creates a very small rift. In the beginning one may not be aware of it, but one has started moving in a different way, and I don't like that, mm? because later on that can create trouble. So I always emphasise that if a couple can go together into sannyas it is more beautiful.

My sannyas is not a renunciation or an escape from life. On the contrary, it is to live life as intensely, as passionately as possible. So if a couple can become sannyasins things grow very fast, and they become closer than they have ever been before. You can never become close to a person unless you start moving in the same direction. You may love a person and you can move into

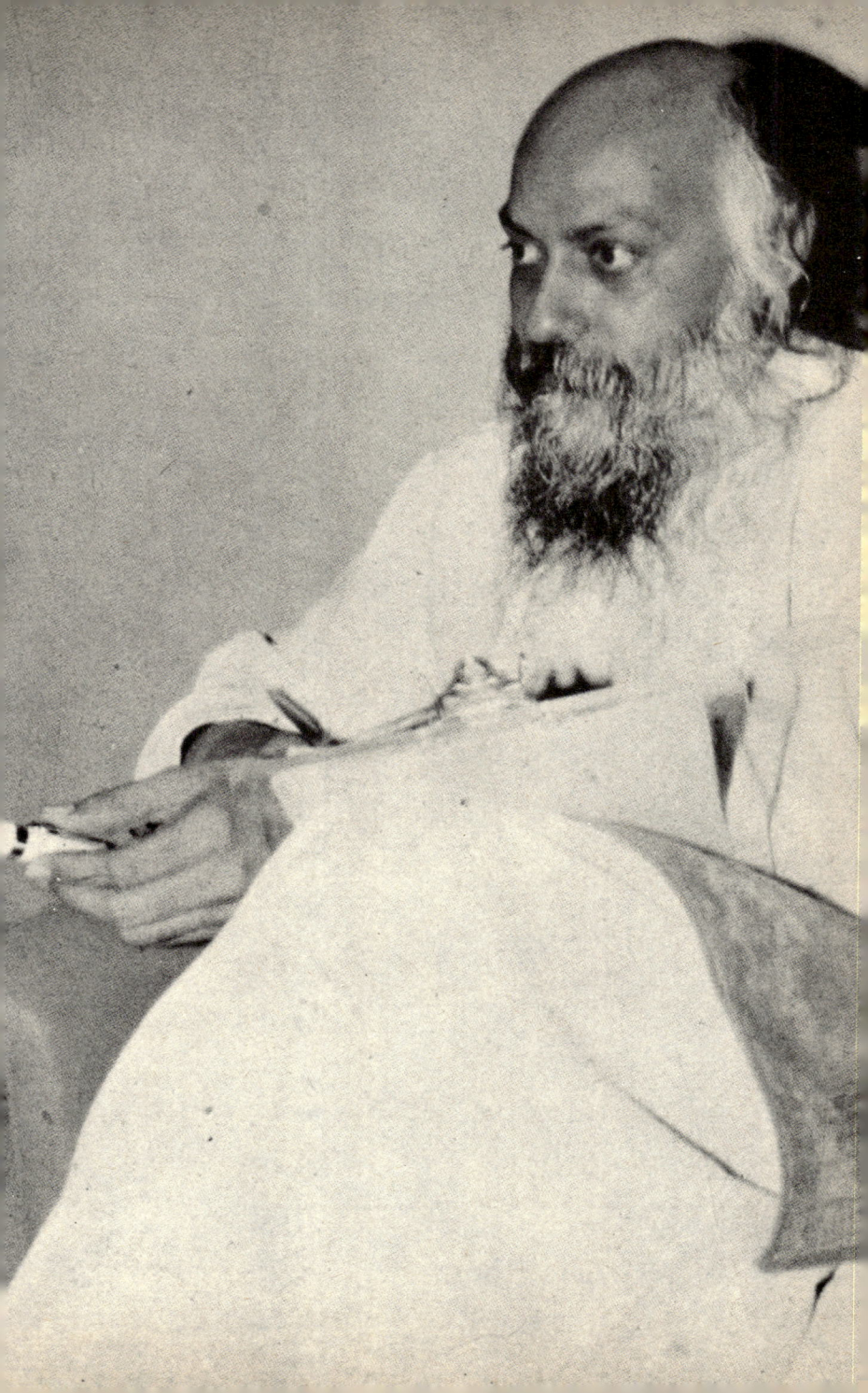

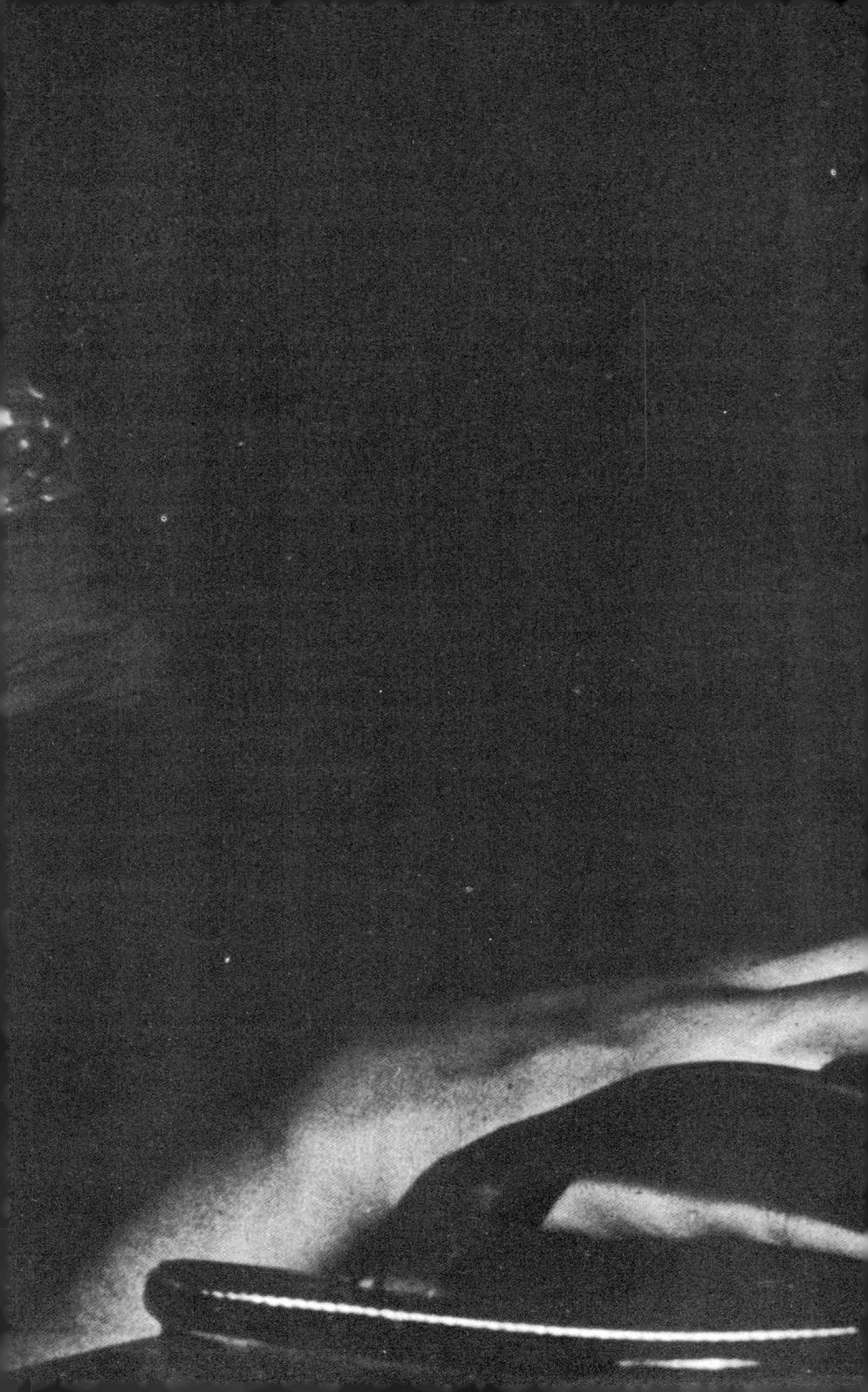

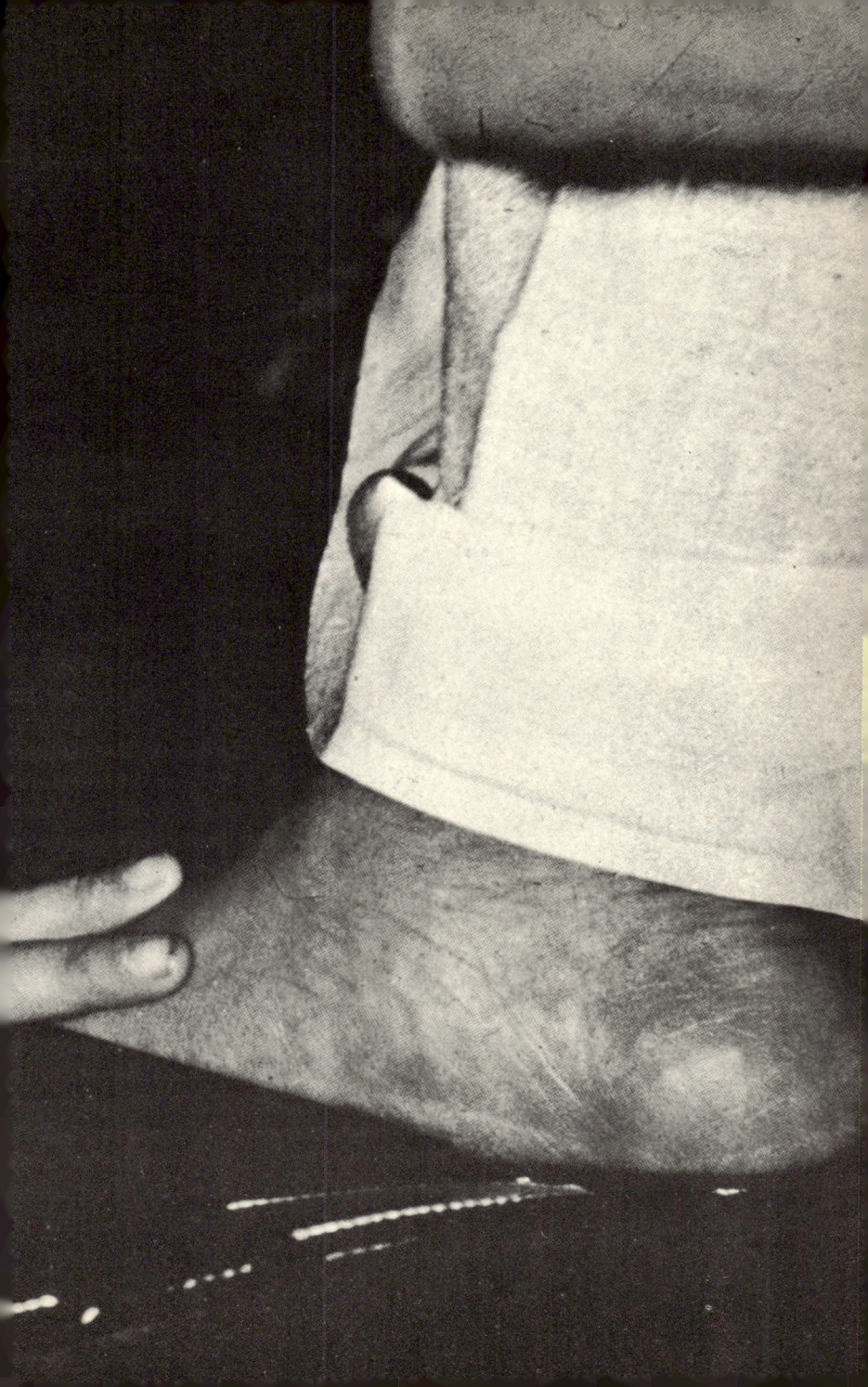

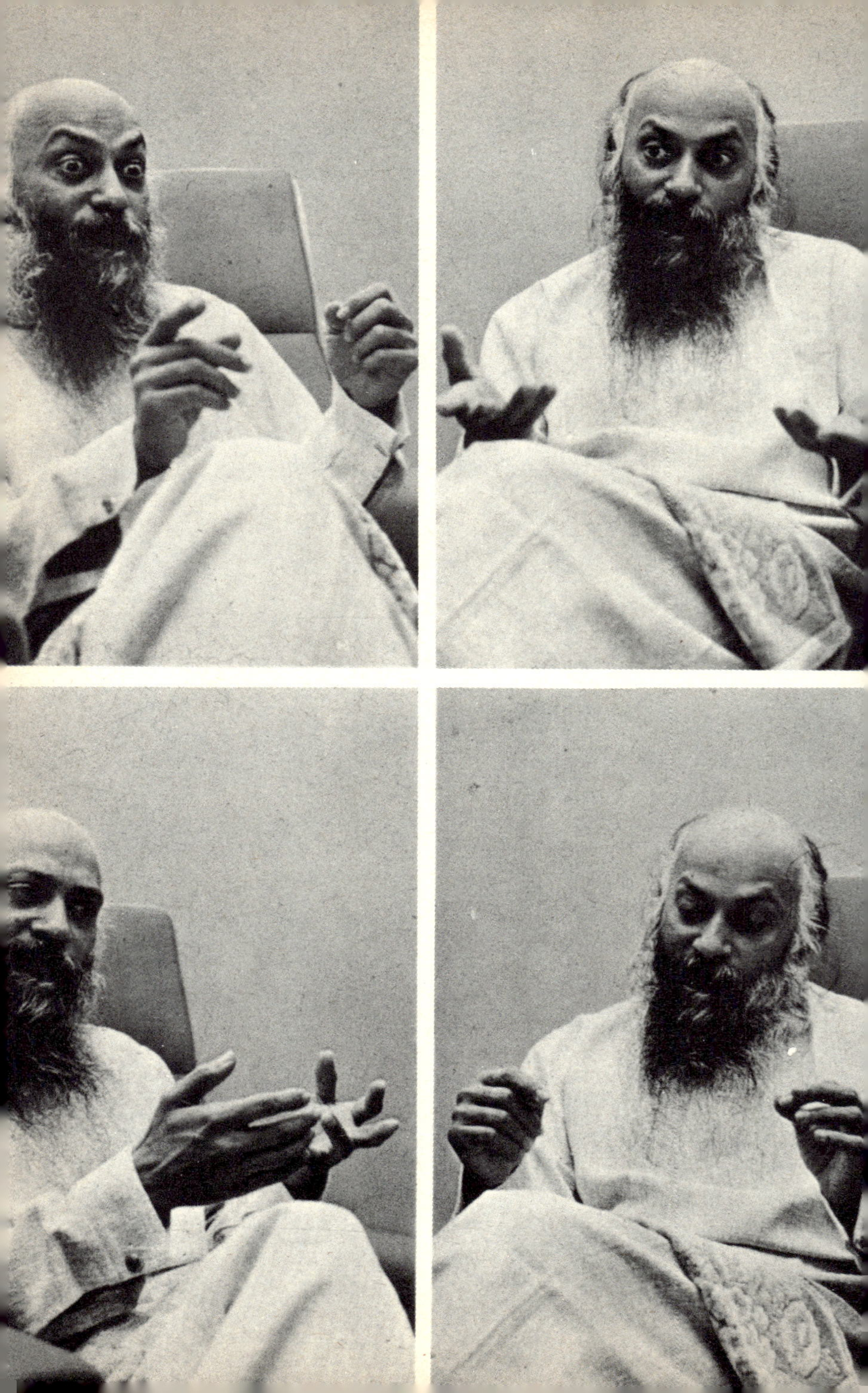

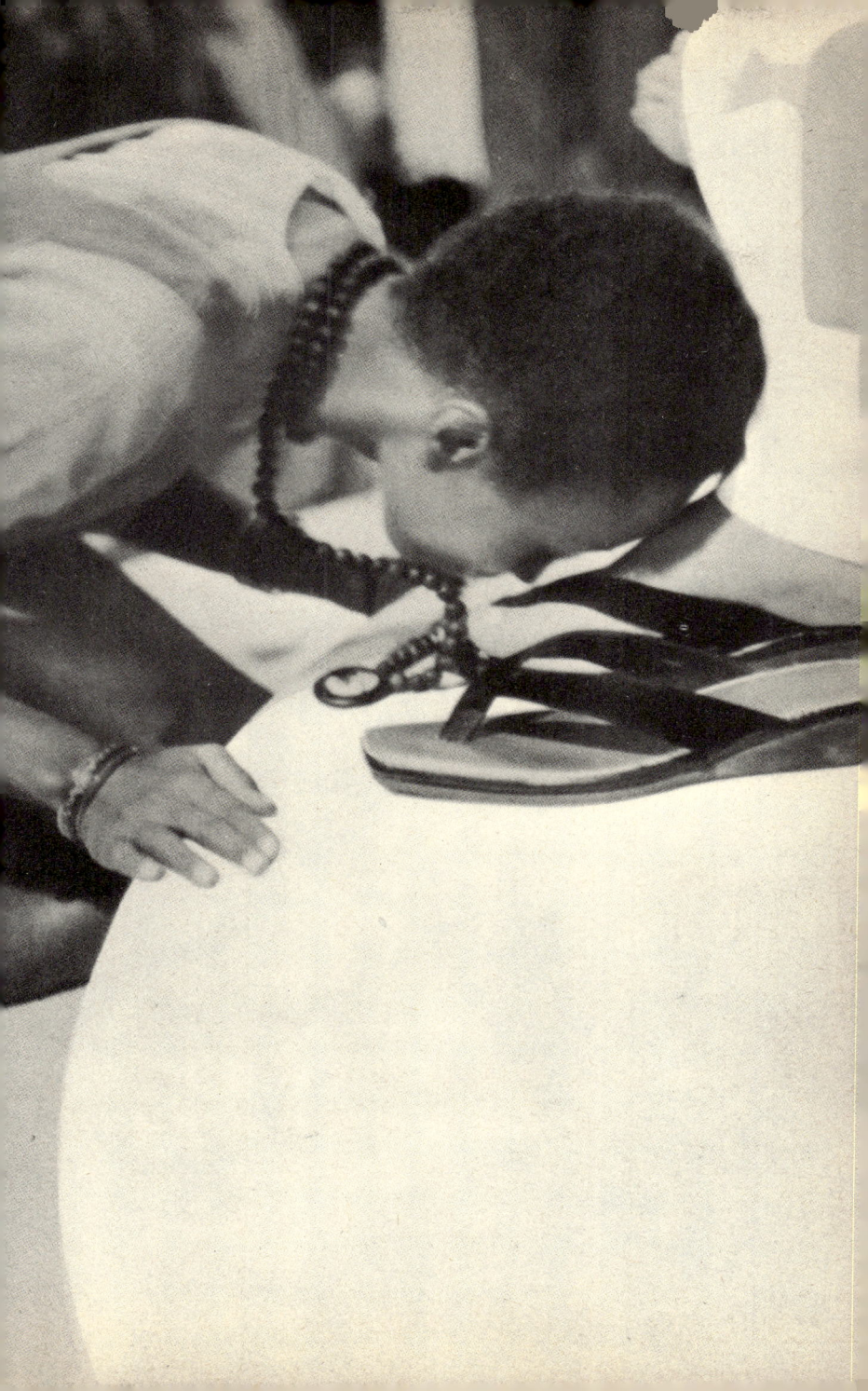

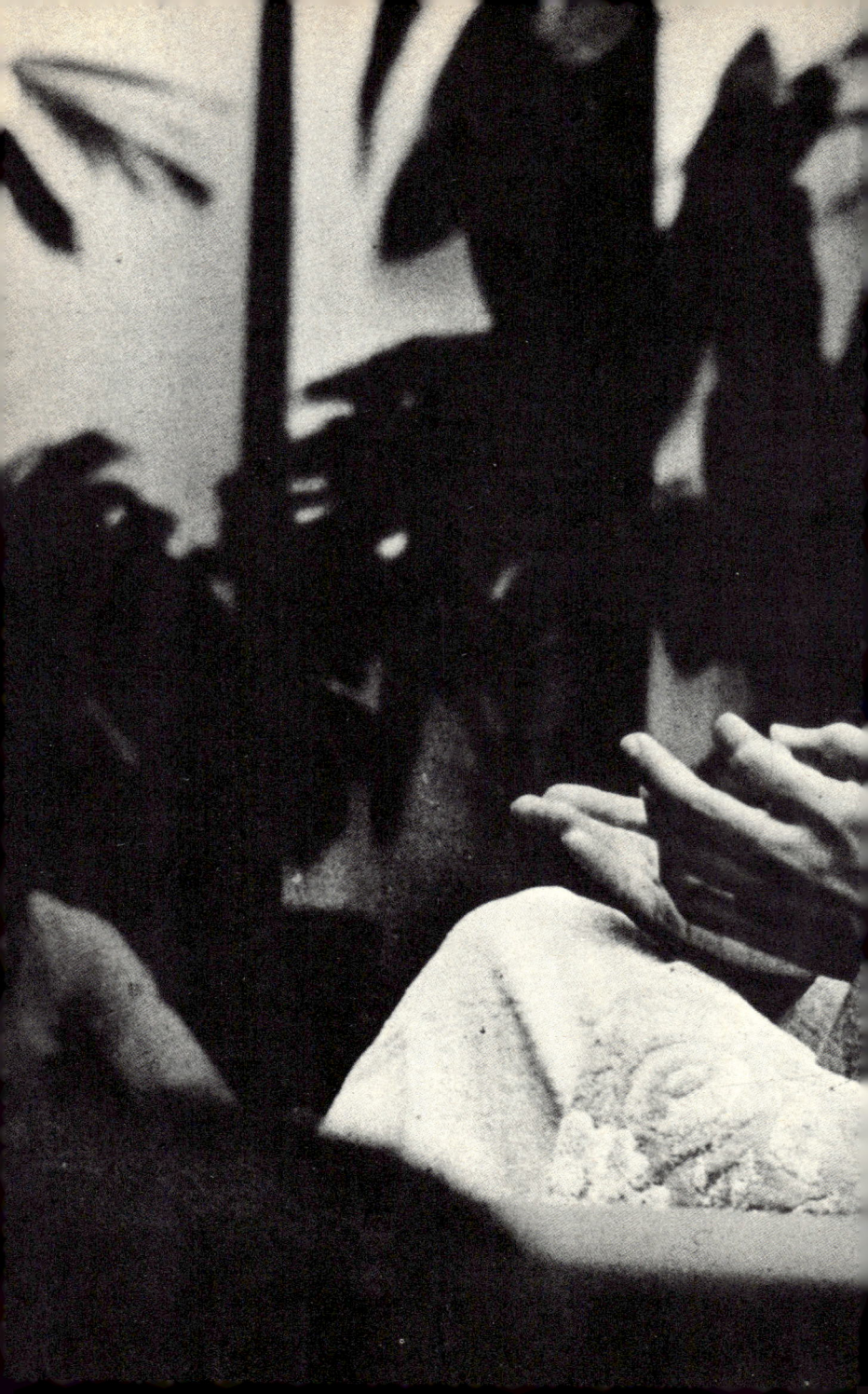

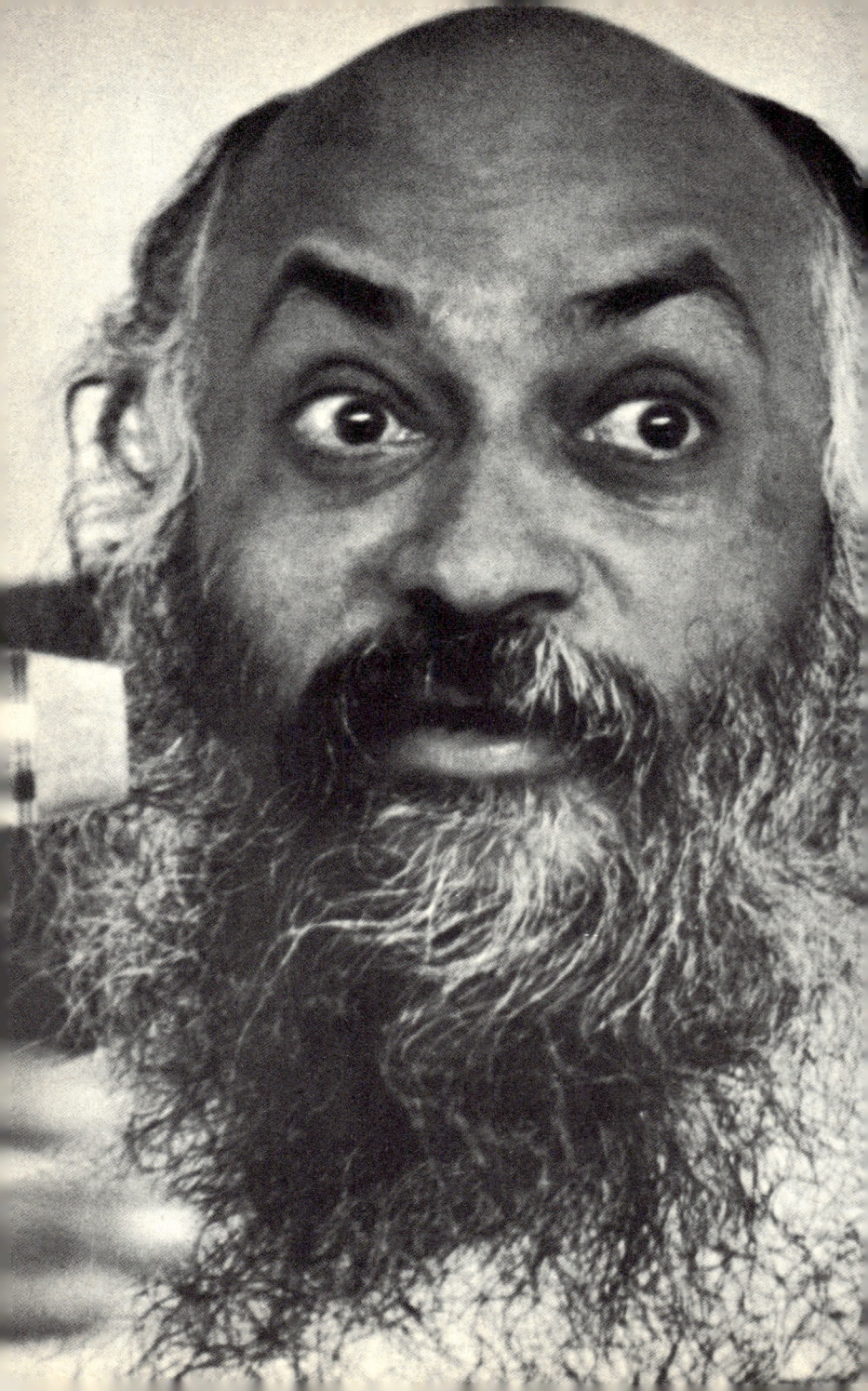

I TRY TO CHANGE YOUR WAY OF LIFE

separate dimensions, but then your meeting will be just sometimes, and on the periphery—then you go your own way.

When a couple starts becoming so deeply in tune with each other that they are growing in the same direction, then love grows and becomes more and more divine, less and less lustful. Then love has a purity, a fragrance, and then it is eternal. You can die, but the love never dies.

But wait until you can accept it in toto. The saffron robe is part of it and does tremendous work. It changes your whole person; it is not just a change of dress. A dress is not just a dress, it is a very style of life. Your clothes are you: they show your choice, your mind, and they are not just accidental.

A man who lives at ease, relaxed, will always have loose clothes. A man who lives in tension, who is always struggling and fighting, will have tight clothes. If you want to fight, loose clothes won't be helpful, they will become a hindrance. And if you want to relax, tight clothes won't allow you. Watch a person who has loose clothes walking. He has a different walk, a grace in it. A person who has tight clothes walks as if he is trying to overtake himself.

In the old palaces, for the king there were certain stairs, and for the servants others. For the servant the steps were very little, for the king there were very big steps, because he would be wearing such loose clothes that he had to move very slowly.

Each and every thing that you do—your clothes, your furniture, your room, your hair—is you. You are written on everything. So when I change the name and the clothes I am trying to change your whole way of life. In a very subtle way I am trying to create a break between your past and your present, so that the past drops and you can start afresh.

If you love your husband, soon you will start loving orange clothes, mm!

ANXIETY IS A SOCIAL BY-PRODUCT

Members of the Enlightenment Intensive group were present. Having spoken to those at darshan who were not part of the group, Bhagwan turned to address the participants. . . .

Were you in the group? Come here! Anything to say, any experience? . . .

SHANTIDHARMA *I was having difficulty the first day as my left eye became very bloodshot, but after that it was good. I became more and more unidentified with my mind. I've also released some anger . . . I screamed a few times and released some of that anxiety in the pit of my stomach.*

Sometimes it happens that if you release anger, your eyes can be affected. Exactly at the same time as you become very angry, they become bloodshot. Only one eye became bloodshot; that means that only one part of the mind, the right side, carries anger. If the right-side mind carries anger then the left eye will become bloodshot—but that is a good sign. It shows that the anger has been released.

If you can release anger, anxiety is automatically released. In fact anxiety is nothing but a social by-product because you are not allowed to be angry. When you want to be angry, you cannot; when you want to be loving, you can't be; when you want to dance or cry or laugh, you cannot—and that creates the anxiety.

Anxiety is absolutely human. No animal is ever in anxiety. When you are feeling afraid and you would like to escape from a situation, you cannot because it won't be 'manly', so you fight. Animals never do that. First they have a mock fight to judge who is the stronger, mm? because if it can be solved that way why unnecessarily fight? They are more intelligent than human beings.

Then one dog realises that the other is stronger, so he simply pulls down his tail and escapes. Nobody is going to say that he is a coward. In fact he is intelligent, simply intelligent.

But when fear arises in you, you cannot accept it; you go on denying it—hence anxiety. Whenever you fight anything natural, anxiety arises. So try to accept the natural more and more, try to be more natural. In fact, try to be more like an animal. Religions have corrupted humanity because they have been teaching men to become like angels, and when you try to become like angels you fall even below animals. Become more and more natural like animals, and suddenly you will find that in your spontaneity you have become an angel.

Because of your religious training, (this sannyasin was a former catholic priest) you have created much anxiety for yourself. Once you understand, it will be released.

There is a saying of Chuang Tzu: 'Easy is right.' It is profoundly true. Uneasy is wrong, easy is right. So become more and more like a child, like an animal. Animals have a tremendous beauty that human beings have lost. Nothing has been gained, just anxiety and madness and a thousand and one neuroses.

Drop all unnatural ideals. If you can accept yourself as you are, anxiety disappears. That's my whole teaching— to accept oneself as one is. Don't go on top-dogging yourself. If there is a fight between the top dog and the lower nature—what religions have called lower—then never listen to the top dog because that is the ego. Always listen to nature and always move with it.

This experience has been good but much more has to be done.

Shantidharma said he was going to do an Encounter group next. Bhagwan said he should not be shy in the group. . . .

One has to expose oneself in total nudity. When you have nothing to hide, anxiety disappears. That's the beauty of truth. If you lie, there is anxiety; but if you are true, there is none. Whenever you say a truth you don't need to remember it, but whenever you tell a lie you have to remember it. And one lie leads to a thousand and one other lies.

SHANTIDHARMA *One of my difficulties is that I'm working in a situation where there isn't that total openness and acceptance. So when I'm functioning in that atmosphere it is hard for me to be totally open. Like, it's easy here, but when I function professionally it's very difficult.*

It will not be. Once you know that it is easy, it is not a question of here and there. Once you live it and you have the taste of it, then it is always easy wherever you are — because it pays tremendously.

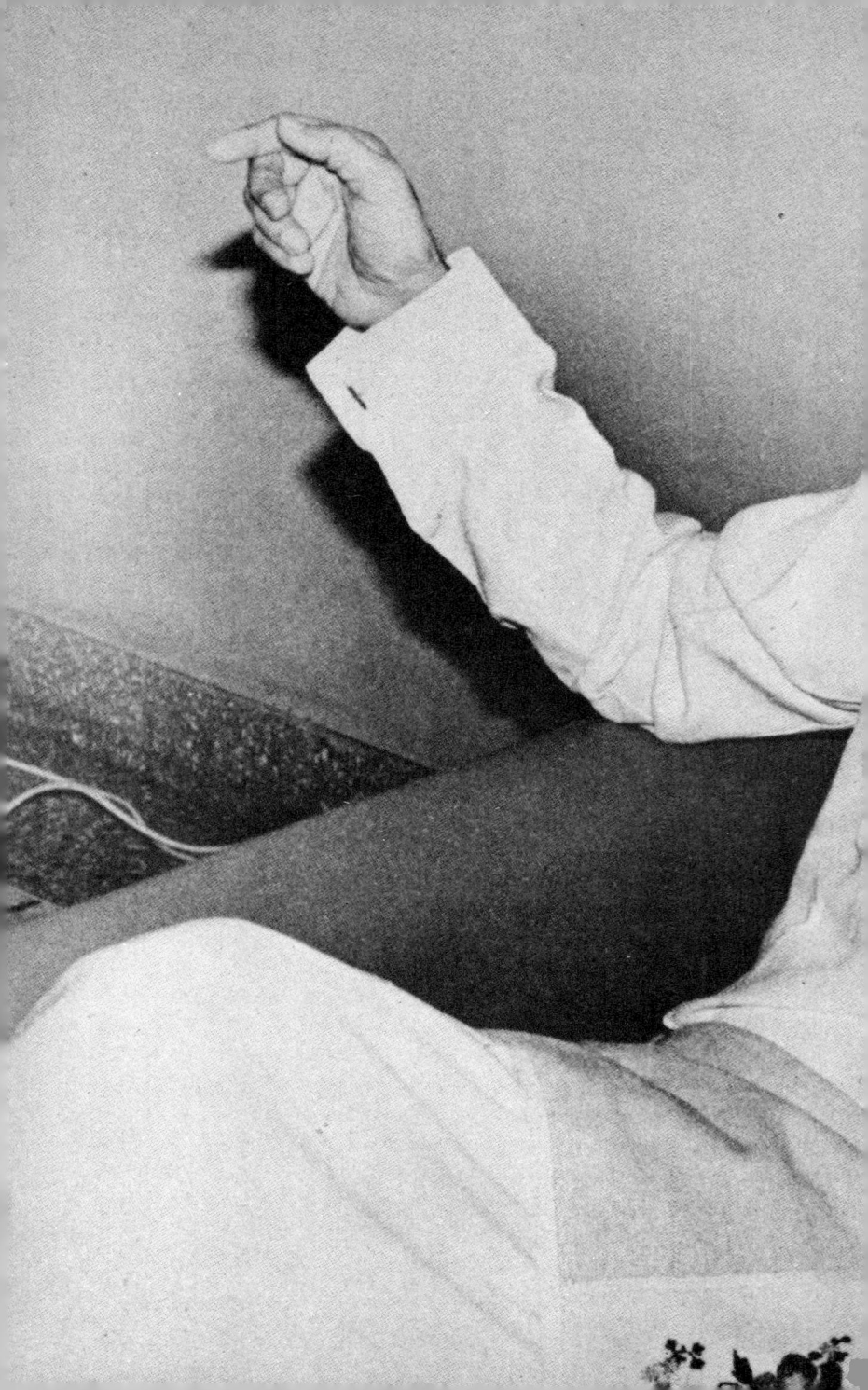

Right now you don't know what it is, so you are afraid. Once you know that to be natural is so beautiful and so blissful, then you are ready to lose anything at any cost. If you lose your prestige, your power or your money, you are ready, because it isn't worth it.

It is as if you have been carrying pebbles and then I show you a treasure, diamonds. Will you say to me that it will be very difficult for you to drop the pebbles? You will immediately drop them! You were in an illusion that they were diamonds, and because you had never known real diamonds there was nothing with which to compare them. Once you know the real diamonds, who bothers about pebbles?

There is a very old story in India about a prime minister who became interested in meditation. He left his post and went to the forest. The king became very interested in what happened to this man who had left such a great post, so he came to see him.

The prime minister was sitting with his legs spread, under a tree. When the king came he didn't stand up, but remained sitting. The king said that he thought he would have become religious, but he had become uncivilised and had lost even his manners.

The prime minister laughed and said, 'Who bothers? I was paying you respect not for you, but because I was on an ego-trip. Now I have dropped out of that ego-trip. Whatsoever you call me — mannerly, unmannerly, civil, uncivil — to me it is irrelevant. I have simply dropped out of the game.' It is said that the king was very impressed.

This man must have found something which was more valuable, because that is the only way you can drop things. Whenever you find a higher value, the lower drops. Whenever you find a more blissful way of living, the miserable way of living drops. If it doesn't drop, it simply shows that you have not found it yet, that's all.

So forget about your profession, your world there.

Be here with me so totally that you can taste something of the natural, the spontaneous. Then when you go back nothing can destroy it. You may throw everything else, but that you cannot throw.

Once you know what freedom is then no prison can allure you, however decorated. So just be natural here. Good!

Bhagwan enlarged on what he had said to Shantidharma when he spoke to the next questioner, who said he did not like being the way he was.

KLAUS *... My energy tends to be always negative and the positive side is never strong enough to come up. The ego is so strong here.* (pointing to his head)

Mm mm . . . it is not strong enough.

KLAUS (in disbelief) *What?*

It is not strong enough, and you have not suffered enough. You need a little more misery. This is the point to understand: if something creates misery one never carries it. You are still enjoying it. You are saying these things — that it is negative and ugly, and your energy is lost — but deep down you are still enjoying it. Otherwise, who is forcing you? There is nobody!

If you feel so miserable, get out of it! And don't say that it has become a deep-rooted habit. There is no question of habit. If the house is on fire, you simply run out. You don't say that you have lived in this house for thirty years and it has become such a deep-rooted habit that you can't go out. If you say that, it simply shows that you are not aware that the house has caught fire. You may have heard the rumour, but you cannot see. And you are not true enough to yourself so you accept the word of someone else.

My suggestion is that you don't try to get out of it, please, until you see the fire. Nothing is wrong in it, enjoy it! When you are doing negative things, enjoy it. When you are really in hell, then any day you will jump out of it. So if you ask me my advice, I will say go deeper into your hell — and go happily. Enjoy it and do it consciously. That is all that my teaching is — to do it consciously. Don't think that you are something wrong — that is creating a division in you. What is wrong in it? Enjoy it.

KLAUS *Hurting other people?*

I AM FOR ABSOLUTELY EVERYTHING

But you are enjoying hurting others, so hurt. If they want to hurt you they will; that is for them to decide. You simply enjoy it. And you are enjoying it. Whether I say so or not is not the point, because unless you enjoy a certain thing you cannot continue it. There is no question of habit or anything.

It is a simple trick of the mind: that you go on enjoying but you also want to show that you are very wise and that you know that these are very negative things and rubbish, but what can you do? — you cannot get out of it. That is not true. I can see you enjoy it. I am never against anything. I am for absolutely everything, so just enjoy it.

KLAUS (tentatively) *I don't dare, that's my trouble.*

That's what I was saying — that your ego is not strong enough! You are not courageous enough. You are not really thinking that you hurt others and you don't want to. You are a coward. You are not worried about others; you are worried that they will hurt you, that they will react. So you are hiding under a philosophy, a good philosophy of not wanting to hurt people.

In fact all you want is to hurt but not to be hurt — that's the whole game. So see it as it is. I may look hard, but I want things to be understood exactly as they are; then one can move very easily.

You are not the only negative person in the world, and if you don't hurt people, somebody else will. And nobody can hurt a man who is not ready to be hurt.

There are people who want to hurt, and there are people who want to be hurt, so don't worry about it. Simply accept yourself.

I know one day you are going to get out of it, but that is not going to be by your effort. When you have created such a hell around you that you cannot live in it a moment longer, then you will jump out of it, leaving no trace on you. That's the only way, so accept it.

God must be trying to do some negative things through you. He has chosen you; what can you do?
(the group laughs)

And the effort to try to change yourself is egoistic, so drop all this nonsense and enjoy your being as you are. One day suddenly you will understand the whole nonsense of it. I am not saying that it is nonsense. I am saying that you will understand one day. My understanding cannot be yours. I cannot give it to you, and you cannot borrow it from me.

So I would like you to understand yourself. The only way is to experience the intensity of it. My understanding is this: that if from the very childhood every child is allowed to be really angry, anger will disappear from the world. The child will come to know the poison of it for himself. He will feel almost burnt, and he will suffer through it. Nobody wants to suffer, so he will drop the nonsense.

Because a child is taught again and again not to be angry, he becomes angry but it is only luke-warm; it is never enough to bring him out of it.

So let things be as intense as possible, and then they evaporate of their own accord. Try it! Don't move against yourself. It is perfectly good — be negative.

(The questioner begins to relax, to smile.)

I WANT TO SURRENDER SO MUCH

You are feeling happy already!

Who else was in the group? Come here!

ANUBHUTI (looking tearful and soft) *I've been in a relationship for almost two months, and right now I'm just upset because I have a fear so strong that I can't surrender. What happened today was that we were playing, wrestling, and I hit him* (her boyfriend) *in a very tender spot. I did it with my body, not my mind, and immediately I became so afraid that he was going to get me, to be angry and I ... blacked out ... made me start crying, and I was just lying on the floor....*
I'm in so much fear that I just can't surrender, (sobbing) *and I want to so much.*

He has not reacted in any way?

ANUBHUTI *He didn't know why I was crying and acting that way.*

Tell him everything!

ANUBHUTI *I told him....*

And tell him this also, that you are feeling difficulty in surrendering but you would like to, mm?

Talking to him will help. Don't hide it inside yourself. When you love a person you have to tell him everything. In love, no secret is allowed. Even this much privacy is not good. You should not carry your wounds alone. If he loves you he will understand.

Surrender is never easy, because the whole ego has to drop before it. Without surrender nothing is achieved—no love, no prayer, no meditation. So surrender is the key. And that's why the whole world is so miserable—because people cannot surrender. They have missed the key. They remain beggars when they could have become emperors.

Don't try too hard, that may have been the trouble. When you try too hard, surrender becomes more and more impossible, because—and this has to be understood—surrender cannot be willed. Will is against surrender. It is as if you are trying too hard to go to sleep. The harder you try, the more disturbed will be your sleep, because the very effort makes you more awake. So the way to go into sleep is not to try at all. Surrender comes the same way.

So just talk to him, mm? Then just lie together, cuddled, and don't try, don't will. It will happen . . . leave it to me.

Another member of the Intensive group said that the first day of the course he felt very negative and on the second day he actually left it—just for five minutes—until he realised that that would not help. Things became progressively better, he said, and now he felt very open.

He continued:

THE OUTSIDE 'I' DISAPPEARED

> *The outside 'I' disappeared
> . . . then I felt just that, well . . .
> I is me . . . it's not explainable.
> But it was very beautiful.*

It has been beautiful.

It always has to be that way: first the negative and then the positive. If you escape in the negative you miss the whole point—and you almost missed it. But if you can prolong that period of pain, then a turning is bound to come, because every valley has a peak, every peak a valley. Every night has a morning, and the darker the night, the more beautiful will be the morning. So one has to pass through the dark night, the negative part, where hate and anger and all aspects of negativity arise.

This is what is meant by austerity. This is what is meant by being courageous enough to hope against hope, to go on and on and on—till suddenly the turning point comes. One never knows when it will come. One never knows the bottom of one's negativity, but when you have touched the bottom, suddenly you are moving upwards again.

It has been really good. You were fortunate that you did not drop out, because when the positive comes it is tremendously beautiful and blissful. Now try to carry it on back home.

Once a month take twenty-four hours for an Intensive. Go on asking yourself the question, and you will pass through the same cycle from negativity to positivity. It will be faster now, and by and by within seconds you will be able to pass from the negative to the positive—because you have become efficient in diving immediately to the bottom, and you know the bottom so you are not afraid in any way.

So try to continue it. This is going to help you tremendously on your path. Once a month at least, give twenty-four hours to it, and this time will become your most cherished.

Siddharth asked if he should move to the second question, 'What is another?' He said he felt it to be the same as 'Who am I?' — the first question asked in the Intensive.

It will be the same. If you have touched the positive through one question, all questions will be the same. Again and again you will touch the same point. The question is one; it has a thousand and one forms.

The question is one and the answer is one; there are not two questions and two answers. So you will reach the same point through either. The questioning is just trying to dig into your being.

It is just as if you dig in one place and after thirty feet there is water. Then you dig another place and again, after thirty feet you reach water.

You are the water and your mind is the earth around you. Sometimes the earth may have rocks in it, sometimes the earth may be soft and you will reach sooner, but you will reach all the same. So keep just one question, there is no need to change.

The next sannyasin, Smrati, said that although she had done most of the therapies available in the ashram, she continued to have small areas on her breasts, hips and thighs, that she felt were blocked.

The therapy referred to in the following conversation is known as Rolfing, or Structural Integration. A very heavy and deep massage, it works on the soft tissues of the body, releasing tension in the muscles and allowing the body to find its natural shape.

Especially in early childhood, mental stresses and strains are registered in the body as well as in the mind. These stresses and strains help to create the shape of the body. For example, if anger is held in, the shoulder muscles come under tension, and a deformity, though it may only be slight, is formed.

As the work progresses, usually in courses of ten sessions

GO ABOVE SEX NOT BELOW

each, there is much emotional catharsis, as material that has been suppressed for years is released. The technique in itself is extremely powerful, and with the addition of daily meditation and the effect of Bhagwan, its potential is increased dramatically.

Rolfing is available through a sannyasin who is also currently training other sannyasins in this field.

You have to pass through Rolfing . . . it is going to help you. It will be very painful, and that is why I was not telling you to do it up to now—you had to pass through the other therapies.

Rolfing is painful because it has to relax the body structure. When for many days you have carried a certain emotion, then it becomes part of the body. It is no longer a part of the mind only, so it cannot be dissolved just through the mind. It has to be dissolved in the body also. The body and the muscles take a certain structure; that structure has to be broken, unstructured.

Something about sex has happened in your childhood, and has gone so deep in the body that all the erotic zones— breasts, hips and thighs—have become frozen. The frozenness is just a protection, like an armour around the body, so it is as if you have become sexless. You are an almost perfect celibate.

This is what celibates all over the world have been doing. They freeze certain parts of their body—they have developed certain methods to do this—and once those parts are frozen, they are no longer worried by sex because the energy is not there. But this is not good, because they become deadened, dull. One should go above sex, not below, and this is going below. This sometimes happens, particularly to women, because they have a passive sex.

You may in your childhood have been offended, violated in some way, but you may or may not remember, because sometimes you forget what you don't want to remember.

You have become so afraid that the very parts which feel sexuality have become frozen. They can be dissolved only through Rolfing.

If you can have the Rolfing done here it will be better, because the Rolfer is a sannyasin and he will be more careful about things. Rolfing is just a technique to relax, but if the Rolfer is meditative he can work deeper than an ordinary Rolfer can do.

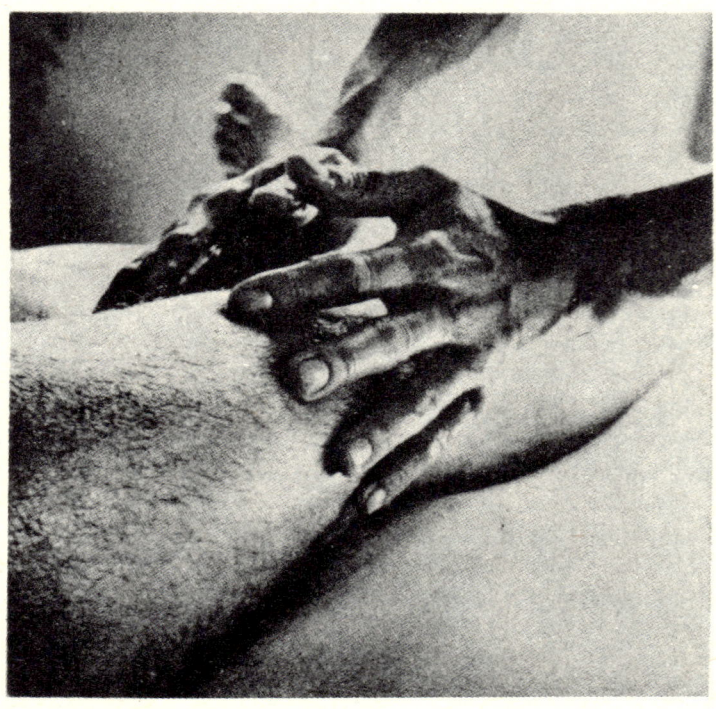

THURSDAY JANUARY 1st 1976

A sannyasin brought his guitar to darshan and sang and played to Bhagwan. He sang a song full of hare krishnas and LSD, kama sutras and cosmic consciousness. Bhagwan sat listening, sometimes with eyes closed, sometimes looking at the sannyasin, or occasionally looking at the faces of those in the group watching the guitar-player.

The song finished. Bhagwan commented that it was good, but could have been better. . . .

BHAGWAN   You bring too much of the mind in; it should be more of the heart. Even nonsense songs are beautiful. There is no need to bring in chemistry, physics and philosophy, no need. You bring in too much of the mind and then the whole music is missed.

Music is not of the mind. Mind is a jarring note in music, a distraction. You cannot become lost in it; it becomes more like thinking and less like singing. Sing anything wild, anything of love, even gibberish, but nothing of the mind.

You can go on repeating 'hare krishna, hare ram' — just two words — in different ways, different arrangements, so it is like waves and becomes a wild ocean splashing on the rocks and you are lost in it. There is no need to manage, manipulate. Let the music be in control of you. Simply be lost in it and you will attain to a deep orgasm, you will explode. You will become the universe. Cosmic consciousness you become of course, but you don't talk about it. Do you follow me? Become so in tune with the music that it carries you to the furthest shore of being.

Otherwise you are misusing the music; it is an abuse. You are bringing something of the mind and pouring it in. That is corrupting it. Music is an innocent thing. It knows nothing of philosophy, nothing of chemistry, nothing of marijuana. It knows nothing of LSD, of cosmic consciousness. These are mere words, just bullshit.

Move into it. Become one with it! Start dancing! Be lost in it, and whatsoever you are saying will start happening. You will explode into a totally different dimension of being where stars are moving, and where there is pure existence.

Music is a meditation and it is sacred. If you bring mind into it, it is a sacrilege. So don't do it; drop the intellect.

But it was good. Next time when you come go wild with the music. Just drop your head, that will do!

A sannyasin, an economist for the United Nations in Geneva, said she did not know whether she should be in Poona with Bhagwan, or with her work in Geneva.

She wondered whether she had her priorities wrong in feeling responsible about her work. She added that her work wasn't important, and that no one would even read it. . . .

No, feel responsible. There is no need though to make it a burden or a tension. One should always feel responsible, whatsoever one is doing. Whether the work is going to be used or not is not the point, because just in feeling responsible for something you mature.

RESPONSIBILITY IS SINCERITY OF THE HEART

GAYATRI

> *I feel I've always been responsible, that I've just been a façade of responsibilities.*

You must have taken responsibility in a very wrong way. It is not a burden.

When you feel responsible, it has nothing to do with others — it is not a duty. It is not that you are trying to prove something, or that your whole life depends on it; nothing like that. Responsibility is just a sincerity of the heart — so that whatsoever you are doing you do with your whole heart. When one does something, one should do it totally — then it becomes a meditation.

If you do something irresponsibly then you are wasting an opportunity to be meditative. You work six hours in the office and you may work indifferently. I am not worried about whether the work suffers or not. It may be useless work — because almost ninety percent of government work is useless, and as far as the U.N. is concerned, it is one hundred percent useless — that is not the point.

When you live six hours of the day in a dull state of mind, it is not easy to get out of this dullness. By and by it becomes part of you, your very style of life. If this film of dullness spreads all over your life, you are poisoning yourself. Being responsible means doing the work consciously, lovingly. Do it totally so that those six hours become a sharp, intense awareness in you, and then you carry that awareness into the other parts of your life. By and by your life becomes a life of response, of aliveness.

That word 'responsibility' is very beautiful — it means alive. A dead man is not responsible. If he is lying in the middle of your path and you ask him why, he will not answer. He is not responsible; he is not answerable to anybody now. If you are responsible, you become alive.

So you see, my emphasis is not on the work; it is on you.

Gurdjieff used to tell his disciples to do foolish, absurd work — and to be responsible. For example, he would tell a disciple to dig a hole. The whole day the disciple dug; it was hard work and he was perspiring. By the evening, Gurdjieff would come and tell him to fill it up again. So the earth had to be put back into the ground.

The following day, again Gurdjieff would say to dig another hole. The disciple wondered what was going to happen, but again, by the evening Gurdjieff would be there telling him to refill the hole.

And he used to say to be responsible! What Gurdjieff is trying to say is that if you look for the use, then the whole of life is useless. It is just digging holes and filling them up again. Eat every day, and then throw it out of the body; fill the hole in the stomach, then throw it out. Every night go to sleep, get up again every morning. And this goes on and on until one day, one dies.

The whole thing is just like that. But Gurdjieff says that that is not the point. He says do the work as responsibly as possible, as if much depends on it — do it with full alertness. He would allow a person to stop such absurd work only when he saw that he had become responsible. It would take months sometimes; for three months the person would be just digging and refilling a hole. People would escape from Gurdjieff sometimes because it was maddening — you knew from the very beginning that it was useless.

But if you stuck to it, by and by a tremendous beauty arose. The hole became irrelevant; the emphasis now was on consciousness. Doing it lovingly, by and by you forgot about the end. You simply enjoyed this moment.

Responsibility means to be alive in this moment whatsoever you do, mm?

So after two weeks, you go and be responsible — in my

sense of the word—and enjoy it. When nobody else is going to enjoy it, at least you can!

What about you? Something is heavy in your head?

(The sannyasin in front of him sobbed despairingly)

Mm, tell me, tell me . . . bring it out.

VEETMAYA   *I don't know anything.*

(with a kindly chuckle) You know at least what is in your head, mm?

VEETMAYA   *It's all crazy in my head, all crazy!*

Mm mm. It cannot be more crazy than all these people. (indicating the group) Mm? Look at them! Can you be more crazy than them? (the group laughs) No, you cannot be! (laughs)

VEETMAYA   *I feel that everything I have to say is . . . stupid.*

Don't be worried about stupidity. Just tell me.

VEETMAYA
> *I really don't know where I am or what I am. I've always been feeling it's a big movie, (a wail) but I don't know where I am in it.*

You are in the audience! It is a big movie and you are in the audience!

> *Yes . . . but I don't know what I want . . . I don't know what to do. I don't know what is real and what is unreal . . . I don't know.*

Nobody knows in fact. One has to understand this: that one has to live without knowing it. By living, by and by you will come to know it. There is no other way. One never knows what is real and what is unreal. Live life — and by and by, that which gives you happiness is real, and that which gives you pain and suffering and nothing else is unreal.

I know nothing is clear, I can understand your difficulty — and it is everybody's difficulty. Everybody is in the same boat. I don't think you are stupid. It is good that you understand that you don't know. This is good. One has to grope in the dark. Truth is not something that can be given to you; you have to seek and search.

VEETMAYA
> *But I don't know where to search and how. . . .*

WHATSOEVER YOU ARE, BE REAL

Love, cry, laugh, weep, dance—these things you can do. By and by you will come to feel it.

VEETMAYA — *I don't feel really happy, and I don't feel really unhappy in anything I do.*

Then this is the thing to be tried! Feel really unhappy. Don't you ever feel really unhappy? I can give you a few people who can make you really unhappy, mm? (a laugh)

VEETMAYA — *I often felt very unhappy with my boyfriend in Germany.*

Were you unhappy with him? So love will give you something . . . at least it can give unhappiness. If you can be really unhappy, then you become capable of being really happy.

So whatsoever you are, be real. If you can cry, really cry. If you laugh, really laugh—and be authentic. Move to the very depth of it.

VEETMAYA — *I'm so afraid to . . .*

Then be afraid totally. Nothing is wrong in that either! Whatsoever you do, whatsoever you feel like being, be in it. Don't start thinking about it; live it. By and by you will have a feeling of who you are.

Even if at the end of your life you come to know who you are, it is early. So never expect that in the beginning someone can tell you that this is you. If it were so easy then everybody would have known. One has to struggle for it. One has to grope, one has to go astray many times. There are many hazards, many pitfalls on the way; a thousand and one wrong doors and one right one. It is a puzzle.

Life is a labyrinth, mm? But if one goes on, persists, one day the right door opens. That is the reward for your whole struggle. There is life in its tremendous glory and splendour!

But that cannot be given to you. You will have to seek and search for it. But don't be depressed in any way — this is how it has to be. Mm? Mm. . . good!

Everything that happens around a master has to be extraordinary. Extraordinary because, particularly for the westerner, to be in the presence of an enlightened being like Bhagwan Shree, is in itself extraordinary. It is, literally, 'out of this world', and a mind-blowing experience. . . .

Perhaps the only remotely comparable experience is what happens to a person in love. If love has never been experienced, then the whole phenomenon will sound somewhat unbelievable, perhaps a little crazy, fanciful. Yet even the most sceptical of observers has to admit the power of love to transform.

One of the most moving and most powerful experiences that can be felt near Bhagwan, happens when a disciple kneels before or touches the feet of Bhagwan. Again, particularly for westerners perhaps, the act is a very significant and meaningful one — to symbolically surrender the ego, to place oneself before another human being in an attitude of respect and vulnerability, in deep gratitude and love.

Energy flows particularly strongly from the hands and the feet. This is why Bhagwan places his hand on the lowered head of a sannyasin in benediction. The sannyasin's body is lower, which facilitates the flow of energy from the body of Bhagwan to him. By being in contact with the ground, excess energy can be safely discharged into the earth.

LIFE IS A LABYRINTH

Some months ago, while talking to a sannyasin, Bhagwan touched the sannyasin's foot with his own, applying pressure for several seconds. He made no comment as to what was happening, but some days later the sannyasin returned to say that an hour or so after this incident, his hands and feet and the lower part of his legs had broken out in a rash, in little sores. Bhagwan confirmed his feeling that it was connected with the transmission of his energy to the sannyasin.

Bhagwan then related the story of how Meher Baba went into a state of unconsciousness or semi-consciousness for a year, after being touched by Baba Jan, the only enlightened woman of this century. Later in his life, Meher Baba also became enlightened.

Although not as dramatic or tangible as these experiences, many people do experience that something very beautiful and overwhelming happens to them while kneeling before Bhagwan.

He radiates a warmth that seems to penetrate the very depth of one's being, creating a feeling of vulnerability and openness and receptivity. One feels an onrush of tremendous joy, an overwhelming sadness, an at-oneness with that from which one was never separate.

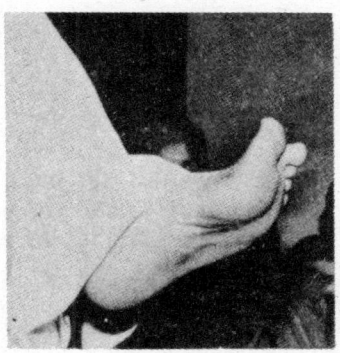

FRIDAY JANUARY 2nd

A sannyasin said he needed to return home as he was unwell. He was apprehensive about going, and felt he would miss Bhagwan's physical presence. He was also afraid that he would fall back into his old patterns again. . . .

BHAGWAN   No, no. I will not allow that, don't be worried. That is my responsibility, mm? You will not fall back.

Once you start growing you cannot fall back, but the fear does arise. In fact the more you grow, the more you become fearful of falling back. The fear is natural, but it comes only to those who are attaining something. Those who are not attaining anything are unafraid, because they are already beggars and they have nothing to lose.

YOU WILL NEVER BE THE SAME AGAIN

Once you start attaining something you have to protect that wealth, and so fear arises — but it is a good sign. Whenever a man becomes afraid that he is losing something, it means he is gaining something.

But go back — you will not lose it. This is one of the criteria: that if anything is achieved there is no way to lose it again. If you have come to know something, how can you unknow it? If you have experienced anything, is there any way to unexperience it? There isn't. And a spiritual experience is such a deep and intense phenomenon that once it starts happening, you will never be the same again. Even if you are thrown back into darkness, that light will still be there.

It is good sometimes to go back to the old situation, to the old people, the old friendships. To go back to the old world where you have lived before — before something started growing in you, before the seed started sprouting — is good. Go back to the past where there is every possibility that you may become the old.

Going is good because that will show you if you have really attained something. You may go back to the old world, but you cannot become the old, and in contrast you will see your growth more illuminated. You will see that you have attained something that cannot be lost. That which can be lost is not worth attaining. Only that which cannot be lost is worthwhile, because only that is your nature.

So observe what happens, and you will come back very very happy . . . and by going there this fear will disappear. I am in favour of people going again and again to the old situation, because it gives you a criterion to judge.

In the past, a tragedy happened to the East. People started becoming so afraid of the world that they simply started escaping. They moved to the Himalayas, to the monasteries; and then they started feeling a little silent,

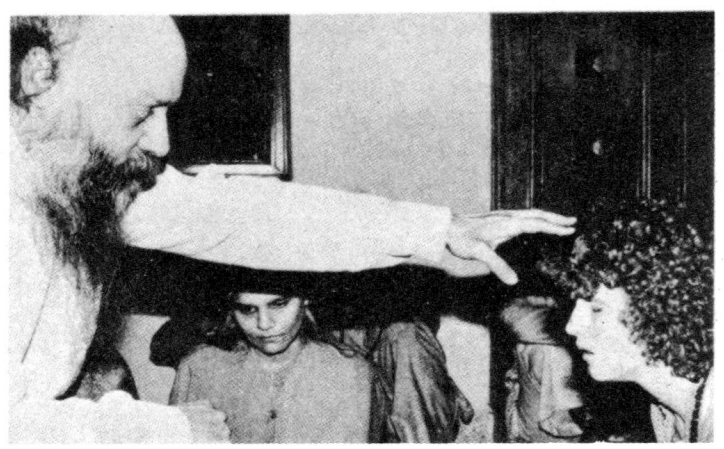

happy, unworried—living in such a peaceful atmosphere. Then they became afraid to come back to the world, to the old. This fear is bad because it shows that they had not really attained. Perhaps because of the Himalayas— the silence, the peace and the natural beauty; the tremendous quality of eternity of the Himalayas—they fell under the illusion that they had attained something. That is a reflected glory; they are simply reflecting the glory of the Himalayas.

To me, this is a basic training: that they should be sent again and again to the bazaar, to the marketplace, to test what they have attained. If it remains in the marketplace, then it is yours. If just by moving to the marketplace it was lost, then it was of the Himalayas, not of you.

For so many centuries people were so afraid that in the East, religion became completely separate from life. Life became of the market, religion of the monastery, and they became unbridgeable; both became lopsided. A marketplace which has no meditation in it will become absolutely ugly. It will be alive but it will be ugly.

A SANNYASIN IS A TIGHT-ROPE WALKER

A monastery which is not courageous enough to go to the market will be silent—but dead. So the monasteries became dead and the marketplace remained alive, too alive—alive with madness.

This is the situation that happened in the East and it can happen in the West too, because now the West is moving on the same lines; the same spiritual search has come. Before that tragedy happens, I would like to work in a totally different dimension, so that life, the ordinary life, is never divided and separated from the religious life.

Have you seen the way a tight-rope walker balances? That is true meditation. When he feels that he is falling to the left, immediately he leans towards the right to gain balance. By the time he has gained balance again he sees that now he has moved too much towards the right; he immediately moves towards the left to regain balance. And this is the way—moving between left and right he remains just between the two.

Watch a tight-rope walker—that is the whole life of a sannyasin. One should always be leaning to both sides and always gaining balance.

So go, mm? And I am coming with you!

Bhagwan spoke next to a sannyasin who is to begin massage in the ashram.

Continue working, mm? Massage is something that you can start learning but you never finish. It goes on and on, and the experience becomes continuously deeper and deeper, and higher and higher. Massage is one of the most subtle arts—and it is not only a question of expertise. It is more a question of love.

First learn the technique, Prageet will teach you that—and then the remaining I will teach you. (chuckling) Learn the technique—then forget it. Then just feel, and move by feeling. When you learn deeply, ninety percent of the work is done by love, ten percent by the technique. By just the very touch, a loving touch, something relaxes in the body.

If you love and feel compassion for the other person, and feel the ultimate value of him; if you don't treat him as if he is a mechanism to be put right, but an energy of tremendous value; if you are grateful that he trusts you and allows you to play with his energy—then by and by you will feel as if you are playing on an organ. The whole body becomes the keys of the organ and you can feel that a harmony is created inside the body. Not only will the person be helped, but you also.

Massage is needed in the world because love has disappeared. Once the very touch of lovers was enough. A mother touched the child, played with his body, and it was massage. The husband played with the body of his woman and it was massage; it was enough, more than enough. It was deep relaxation and part of love.

But that has disappeared from the world. By and by we have forgotten where to touch, how to touch, how deep to touch. In fact touch is one of the most forgotten languages. We have become almost awkward in touching, because the very word has been corrupted by so-called religious people. They have given it a sexual colour. The word has become sexual and people have become afraid. Everybody is on guard not to be touched unless he allows it.

Now in the West the other extreme has come. Touch and massage have become sexual. Now massage is just a cover, a blanket, for sexuality. In fact neither touch nor massage are sexual. They are functions of love. When love falls from its height it becomes sex, and then it

WHEN YOU TOUCH, YOU TOUCH GOD

becomes ugly.

So be prayerful. When you touch the body of a person be prayerful—as if God Himself is there, and you are just serving Him. Flow with total energy. And whenever you see the body flowing and the energy creating a new pattern of harmony, you will feel a delight that you have never felt before. You will fall into deep meditation.

While massaging, just massage. Don't think of other things because those are distractions. Be in your fingers and your hands as if your whole being, your whole soul is there. Don't let it be just a touch of the body. Your whole soul enters into the body of the other, penetrates it, relaxes the deepest complexes.

And make it a play. Don't do it as a job; make it a game and take it as fun. Laugh and let the other laugh too.

Soon you will be helping many people. . . .

SATURDAY JANUARY 3rd

Bhagwan was talking to a sannyasin as we entered the porch. Anup was saying that he had a friend who was paralysed, and wondered if anything could be done to help. Bhagwan suggested the friend should become a sannyasin and handed a mala and the paper with his new name on it to Anup, then continued . . . .

BHAGWAN   If you are lying in bed all day and you can't move, you will continuously want to, because movement is life. Nothing else is so important as movement. Rocks are dead because they cannot move. The trees are a little more alive because a little movement is possible, but they are rooted in the earth. Animals are not rooted in the earth so they are more alive, they can be free.

Man is even more alive, because not only is he not rooted in the earth, he is not rooted in matter. His consciousness is a freedom, a sky with no boundaries. So movement is very essential and basic to life.

When you are paralysed, the very paralysis, twenty-four hours a day, becomes an auto-suggestion. Again and again you remember that you cannot move. Again and again you repeat to yourself that you cannot move — and this repetition cooperates with the paralysis. So just the opposite has to be done.

Whenever he feels that he cannot move, he should close his eyes, and in fantasy go for a long walk, or a run.

TO BE REALLY ALIVE, BE A DANCER

While going for a walk, it may be raining—the raindrops are falling on you making you completely wet. The whole thing is that all the senses should participate—smell, touch, vision—everything. This becomes a miraculous cure.

If he loves dancing then it is perfect, because dancing is exactly the opposite pole to paralysis. People who don't know how to dance are already half-paralysed. Paralysis is no movement and dance is pure movement. To be really alive one needs to be a dancer. That is the beauty of watching a dancer. Suddenly you feel the ecstasy of the movement, so alive, so delicate, so tremendously moving—as if gravitation doesn't exist. If he is a real dancer you feel that he can fly.

One of the greatest dancers, Nijinsky, would take great jumps that were thought physically impossible. Scientists observed him and said that such a big jump was not possible with gravitation. They asked him how it happened. He said he didn't know except that a moment came when he was not; when he felt he could fly.

When he jumped—and the height of the jump was a miracle—the greater miracle was his coming back to earth. He would come so slowly as if . . . a dry leaf is falling from the tree and comes slowly . . .

Bhagwan had paused for a moment to find a suitable parallel to describe the dancer's movement. He looked at the trees around the darshan porch and in front of him, and then went on describing how a leaf falls, moving his hands gracefully in a gentle zig-zagging downward movement. Just as completed the sentence, a dry leaf rustled its way quietly down the branch of a tree on to the ground below.

. . . not like a stone. It is as if he defies the whole law of gravitation.

So tell him that if he can imagine dancing, that will be the cure.

Many times it has happened that a person has been paralysed for ten years, and the doctors have told him that he will not be able to move for the rest of his life. Suddenly one day the house catches fire and everybody is running out. The paralysed person forgets, and out of fear he also runs from the house.

People see him running and can't believe it. They say, 'But this is impossible, you can't run!' Then he becomes aware of what he is doing and falls down. How can he run? — one can never go against the experts! But he has run!

Every paralysed person can be hypnotized, and in hypnosis he starts walking. That means that the body is functioning perfectly, it is just that the belief somewhere is not cooperating.

So tell him, mm? And I will be working on him....

DHARMA CHETNA (trying to hold back tears) *My life seems to be governed by fear. I think lately it has got better a little bit, but it's still very much there. Can you help me?*

(a little chuckle) Mm, I will help, that's why I am here!

Everybody's life, more or less, is governed by fear, because there are only two ways to live life. Either it can be governed by love, or it can be governed by fear. Ordinarily, unless you have learned to love, it is governed by fear.

FEAR IS ABSENCE OF LOVE

Without love, fear is bound to be there. It is just an absence of love. It has nothing positive in it; it is just absence of love. But if you can love, fear disappears. In the moment of love there is not even death.

There is only one thing in life that conquers death and that is love. All fear is concerned with death — and only love can conquer death.

So one thing I would like to say to you is, don't pay too much attention to fear because it becomes an auto-hypnosis. If you go on repeating that you live by fear, your life is governed by fear, you are dominated by fear — and fear, fear, fear — then you are helping it. Take note of it: that your life is governed by fear — finished! It simply shows that love has not yet become so powerful that fear disappears.

Fear is just a symptom, it is not a disease. There is no cure for it; there is no need. So it is just a symptom, and it is very useful because it shows you that you should not waste your life any longer. It simply says to you to love more.

So I will not talk about fear. I will help you to love more — and fear disappears as a consequence. If you start working directly on fear you strengthen it, because your whole attention will be focused on it. It is as if somebody is trying to destroy darkness, and becomes focused, obsessed, with how to destroy darkness. You cannot destroy darkness because it is not there in the first place. Note the fact that darkness is there — and then start working on how to bring in light.

The same energy that you are using to fight fear can be used to love. Pay more attention to love. If you touch, touch as lovingly as possible; as if your hand becomes your whole being and you are flowing through your hand. You will feel energy passing through it, a certain warmth, a glow. If you make love, go wild and forget all civilization. Forget all that has been taught about love; just be wild and love like animals.

Once you realise that the presence of love becomes the absence of fear, you have got the point and there is no problem. These six weeks be as loving as possible, for no reason at all — just be loving, mm? And it will go. . . .

KAMAL   *I've had a tension in my head, like a pressure, a cramp... and I'm in a mess.*

Mm mm. What is the mess?

KAMAL   *I'm not very loving and . . . I don't feel very good about myself.*

Mm . . . that may be the tension — because love is a release. If you are loving you remain relaxed. If you are not loving you become tense. Tension means simply that there is some energy that needs to be shared. If you don't want to share it then it accumulates and becomes a headache. Always remember that the more you share, the more fresh energy will be flowing in you.

I was reading the life story of a poet. He says he used to live in a very old house, two hundred years old. It was in a very primitive condition — no modern facilities, no electricity, no running water. The house had a beautiful well with very fresh water, very pure.

When electricity came to the town they closed the well, hoping that if some day it was needed it could be

EACH RELATIONSHIP IS A MIRROR

re-opened. After fifteen years, just out of curiosity, the man opened the well, just to see how it was. It was one of the most ancient wells in that locality and it had never been dry. When all the other wells were dry, the whole town had come to drink from this one.

When he looked in, it was completely dry. He couldn't find an explanation so he asked the experts. They said that if you don't go on carrying water out of the well, sooner or later it dries up because the small springs that feed it with water become closed. Then by and by the water evaporates leaving the well dry. Each day the well needs to share—then it is always flowing, with new water always coming in.

The same is true for human energy also. Each man is a well of energy. Love means that you allow somebody to throw a bucket in you, to draw some energy from you. Don't be a miser about it, otherwise soon you will start feeling that you are drying up. Then you will become tense and a deadness will gather around you. You become more and more afraid of sharing, because you think that if you share you will become even drier. You are in a vicious circle.

The whole logic is wrong. Whenever you feel something tension-like is gathering, share. Catch hold of any stranger, because in fact all are strangers. Some strangers you have known for a few years, some for a few months, some a few days, some you have just come to know, but all are strangers. Even your husband with whom you have lived for years is a stranger. Two strangers living together by and by become familiar, that's all.

Run and share with anybody, but never be miserly. I have been watching; you are becoming a little miserly. And you can like yourself only when you love. In fact when somebody likes you, only then can you like yourself.

Each relationship is a mirror; it reveals your identity to you. Each relationship brings you something of your inner heart which was unknown to you before. Man is such an infinity that thousands of relationships are needed — the father, the mother, the brother, sister, husband, wife, friend. Thousands of types of relationships are needed to reveal you from every corner, from every aspect of your being, so that you know all your faces. Even then, all that you know about yourself will be less than you are. It can never be more than you, and it can never be equal to you because you are such an infinity that all the mirrors of the world cannot exhaust you. Something will always remain elusive.

Share more, and let sharing be the only law. To be a miser is to be a sinner. That is my definition of being a sinner. Mm? We are here for such a short time; why be a miser? Share, and whatsoever you give, give wholeheartedly and much will come automatically. Not that you ask for it or demand it; it just comes. The whole of existence re-echoes you.

So try it for one month. Just be a sharer, and then see.... Then you will love yourself, because that is the only way: if you love others you love yourself. If you don't love others, by and by you will come to hate yourself.

PRABHU PRAKASH

Something which happens to me is ... I feel like I'm getting higher, you know, lighter and more present, and better.

But each time it happens, it's too much for me. So each time it happens I find some way to get myself down again, and I don't know how to deal with that.

No, don't try to deal with it — accept it. As it is, accept it. When it goes high, you go high. When you start

SOMETIMES EFFORT IS A HINDRANCE

bringing yourself down, watch that too, with total acceptance. No need to make any interference.

Just accept coming to the height and going down to the valley. Accept both as if you are unconcerned whether it is high or low. Watch as if it is happening to somebody else, not to you. Then immediately it will disappear.

If you go on doing something it will not disappear, because effort cannot help here. There are places in your inner growth where effort is needed, and there are places where effort is a hindrance. This is a place where it won't be helpful.

For one month accept whatsoever happens, and you will see that your highs are growing higher and higher, and simultaneously your depth will become deeper and deeper — but now you will be able to enjoy both.

If you enjoy only the peak, who will enjoy the valley? If you only enjoy the day, who is going to enjoy the night? Don't become obsessed with the day. Remain flexible so that you can enjoy both the day and the night — and remain indifferent.

PRABHU PRAKASH *It is difficult to remain indifferent because I feel I am harming myself.*

No, no you are not. By not being indifferent you are harming yourself. Try for one month to just be indifferent. This is something that you have to experience before you can understand what I am saying. These are just moods that come and go; you remain unperturbed, a watcher. Everything is going well. This phase comes to everybody. . . .

PRABHU PRAKASH — *It seems like a fear to me. When I'm in a certain space I can't really handle because it's new, it's different and it's ... I become afraid, you know?*

Now there will be no question of handling it. You have to be indifferent. Let it be. Wherever it is leading it is okay. Accept either higher or lower, and just see what happens.

SUNDAY JANUARY 4th

Bhagwan first addressed a seeker from Holland. People from many many different countries are drawn to Bhagwan—from Africa and Amsterdam, from Liverpool and Luxemburg, Melbourne and Montreal, they come, they are pulled.

Bhagwan has said that all the time he is calling people to him who have been with him before in past lives, who are ready to work and move with him again; or seekers who have worked extensively on themselves in this life or one past. Certainly the far-reaching influence of Bhagwan is apparent. When they first meet Bhagwan, often sannyasins feel a certain sense of familiarity, a rightness somehow, and with other sannyasins too—a feeling of having met before.

BHAGWAN You have been doing some kind of meditation back home?

SHARON   *Yoga.*

Good, very good. So you are ready, now meditate. Yoga in itself is not enough. It is a good preparation, but preparation for something else.

It prepares your body/mind, but if you go on preparing and preparing and never doing the thing for which yoga was preparing you, then it can become an obsession. It has happened to many people in India—they are always preparing as if to go on a journey, but never go. The journey goes on being postponed and the preparation continues. Yoga is perfectly good, very essential and necessary, but it is not enough. It gives you the jumping board, but you have to jump further. Mm?

How long can you be here in India? Be here. If you are really interested in inner growth, be here for a few months. I can see that much is possible—you are ready to move. But you seem a little afraid, mm? What is the fear? Just close your eyes so I can feel the energy.

Sharon closes her eyes and shakes with silent sobbing as Bhagwan shines the torch on her face for several minutes.

Mm, good, the energy is really good—but there is something you have to do. Do you have some question to ask?

SHARON   I think so, but I don't know what it is.

Yes, the question is there, but you may not be aware of what it is. But you will become aware. . . . Have you started meditating here?

(Sharon nods in the affirmative)

Much will soon come up. And what about sannyas, or is there some hesitation still in the mind?

LOVE IS THE PATH

SHARON *I don't understand it, but I think I want to take it.*

(Chuckling) Mm mm, you will understand it by taking it. There are two types of people: the first try to understand sannyas, then they take it. Another type take it first and understand later — and this is the better! Mm? So should I give it to you, and then understand?

Sharon, red-eyed, nods her assent. Bhagwan places a mala around her neck. . .

Good! Change to orange. This will be your new name: Ma Prem Marga. Marga means path, and prem means love — path of love. Love is the path.
Become more and more loving — that's your real yoga. If you become more and more loving then yoga is not only of the body — it goes on transcending the body. Otherwise, sometimes yoga can become just a technique. Make it love!
Who is your teacher?

Marga said that she had mainly been studying on her own.

You have been studying on your own? That's very good, very good. Now start meditating, and soon your question will come up. The day it comes up, come immediately, mm?
Change to orange and become now the new name and the new person. Then you will understand by and by. There is no hurry. . . .

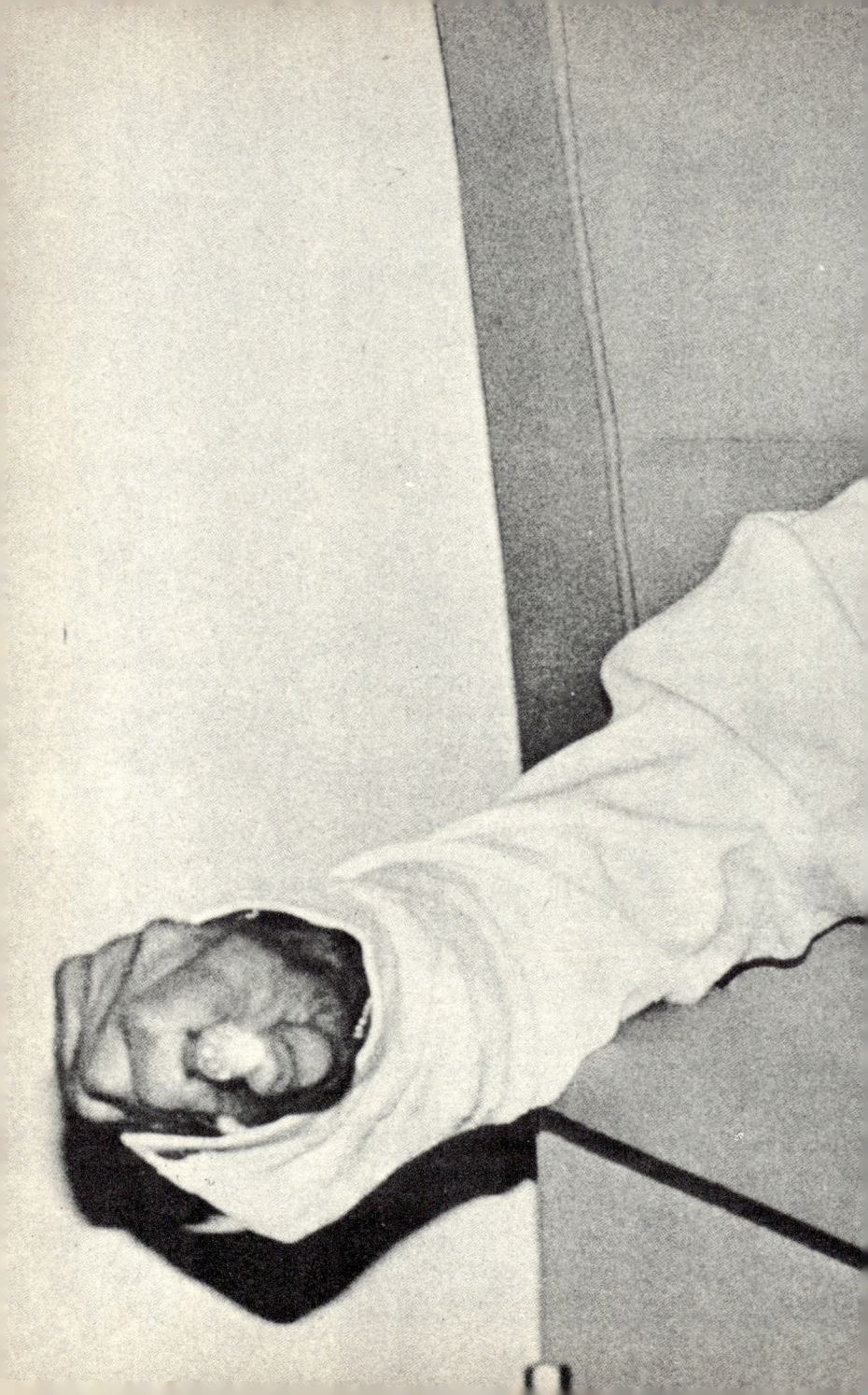

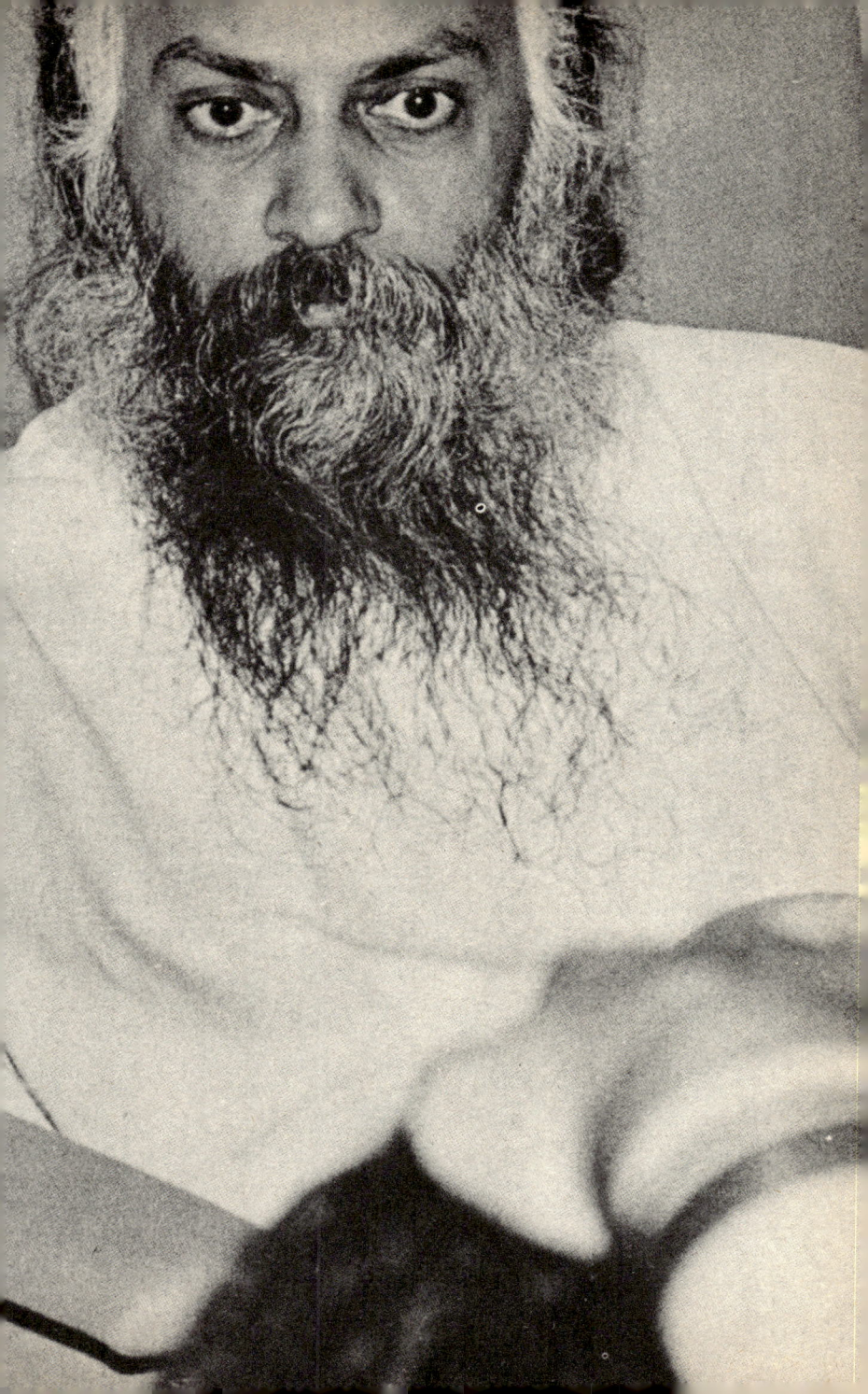

Bhagwan spoke next to a sannyasin who had come to darshan several weeks ago in turmoil about her love relationship. Bhagwan had talked to her about the impermanence of relationships and had told her that as her meditation she was to try to live in the moment, and not to seek security.

ASHA — *I've been watching . . . and I feel really phoney.*

Phoney?

ASHA — *Mm. I don't really want to change at all. I've been looking inside, and what I'm really up to is adjusting the environment, and manipulating most of the time, keeping myself really well defended.*
The only time that I don't feel well defended is if things go beyond my control; if people go off and do what they want anyway; that kind of thing.
I find myself reacting a lot to you; things that you say that I've accepted before—I can feel them inside myself. I've only been to two lectures, and at one you talked about some cabinet minister who said, 'Well, what is there to change?' And, um . . . I felt deeply hurt, you know, because I felt, 'That's me, that's what I say, that's what I'm saying.' I feel that's really what I'm up to.

DIAGNOSIS IS THE TREATMENT

Mm, it's good that you have become aware of it. You were not aware of it before and this is a good insight. Now things will start being different.

Once you understand that you are trying to manipulate, then the base disappears. Manipulation is so useless and futile a thing. If you succeed, nothing is gained; if you fail, there is much frustration. So whatever the result, whether you succeed or fail, the ultimate result is frustration.

You can go on manipulating only if you are not aware; it is an unconscious process. In some other thing's name—love, helping people, creating order—you can go on manipulating, and the process can continue, but it needs something to hide behind, a good name. Once you start feeling the truth of it then you will see that you are phoney. To understand that one is phoney is a great insight, and if you remain with it. . . I will not say to you to drop it, to become authentic, no—remain with the phoniness and you will find that it is disappearing, evaporating.

Once you understand that something is untrue, you cannot live with it; it has to go. So don't do anything about it, because whatsoever you do will be phoney, will again be a subtle manipulation. Just go on understanding that this is phoney and accept it. Be phoney consciously, and the next insight will be that when you try to be phoney, when you consciously make an effort to manipulate people, one day suddenly you will see that you are incapable of manipulating.

I am happy . . . this is a good insight, a very essential insight. You have got the point, you have diagnosed your own illness. In the inner world the diagnosis is the treatment, there is no other therapy needed for it.

Now try only one thing: not to forget it. I'm not saying to drop it—go on manipulating, but now watch and don't do anything to change it; remain with it. It will be difficult to remain with it—even for three days it will be difficult, arduous — but it has to be done. One has to pass through it. Good, Asha.

A sannyasin said that he found his mind making judgements all the time — about other people, and concerning insignificant and petty things.

Just one thing to do: whenever you feel any judgement coming in the mind, change the breathing pattern, and immediately you will see a change and that the judgement has disappeared.

Whenever you want to change a pattern of the mind that has become a long-standing habit, breathing is the best thing. All habits of the mind are associated with the pattern of breathing. Change the pattern of breathing and the mind changes immediately, instantly. Try it.

Whenever you see that a judgement is coming and you are getting into an old habit, immediately exhale — as if you are throwing the judgement out with the exhalation. Exhale deeply, pulling the stomach in, and as you throw out the air, feel, visualise, that the whole judgement is being thrown out.

Then take in fresh air deeply, two or three times, and just see what happens. You will feel a complete freshness; the old habit will not have been able to take possession.

So start by exhalation, not inhalation. When you want to take something in, start inhaling; if you want to throw something out, start by exhalation and just see how immediately the mind is affected.

And don't be worried about it, because the very worry gives it emphasis and feeds it. Simply do this and immediately you will see that the mind has moved somewhere else; a new breeze has come. You are not in

the old groove so you will not repeat the old habit. And this is true for all habits. For example, if you smoke, if the urge comes to smoke and you don't want to, immediately exhale deeply and throw the urge out. Have a fresh breath in and you will see immediately that the urge has gone. This can become a very very important tool for inner change. Just try it!

MONDAY JANUARY 5th

An English girl, not yet a sannyasin, had prior to darshan sent a letter to Bhagwan about her relationship with Devesh, a sannyasin with whom she had been having a relationship in England.

BHAGWAN   I read your letter. I can understand your inner indecisiveness. Whenever there is something very important the mind always hesitates, because anything more important than the mind is always a danger to it.
   The mind wants to manipulate and control everything, but there are a few things which it cannot control. The only way for the mind is not to move in these directions, so it stops.
   Love is one of those things which is bigger than the mind, higher than the mind, beyond the grasp of the mind, beyond comprehension. Love is something absurd for the mind — it should not happen in a logical world. If people were rational then love would not happen at all. Because people still persist in being irrational, love happens. Whenever a person is absolutely rationalised his heart is gone and he becomes a shrunken phenomenon inside. He is like a dead rock. He lives — yet lives not.
   So this is always a problem: love happens, and then the mind starts hesitating. It starts finding ways and means and rationalisations to avoid it — and it is a great rationaliser. It can even convince you that there is no love.

EXISTENCE IS ABSURD

The same will happen with anything that is not rational—and life itself is irrational. Existence is absurd; in fact there is no reason why we are. Existence is given for no reason at all: suddenly we are and then suddenly we disappear. The whole thing is more like magic.

So my suggestion is—I call it a suggestion because you are not yet a sannyasin, otherwise I can order you . . . (great cheers and laughter from the group)—that you don't listen to the mind. Love deeply.

As I see you both, you fit somehow. Very few people fit, but you do, so don't miss this opportunity.

Diana looks moved. She had been listening politely, but now her face flushed a little, softened; there was a sense of a slight let-go, a relaxing. . . .

Abandon the mind completely. You are loving, but very grudgingly, mm? One step forwards, one step backwards. You go a little towards Devesh but you are always ready to withdraw. Mm?

DIANA *That's true.*

That withdrawing is not allowing you to experience what love is, because love needs you totally—either all or nothing. But part-love is never satisfied with the part, it asks for the whole.

If you go on hanging like this it becomes your habit, an unconscious mechanism; then you are puzzled as to whether you love or not. If you love half-heartedly or just in part, it looks more like liking than love. Liking is of not much value; it has no passion in it, no life.

So drop this now and move. It is dangerous I know, because you are moving into the area of another, you are losing your control. You will no longer be on your own and that ego, that self-sufficiency of the ego will not be there. But as you leave your control, simultaneously the other is leaving his. In fact when you live with another person, it is not a surrender from the woman to the man or from the man to the woman. In fact both surrender to love, to something in between. Both are enriched, nobody loses out.

You have been fooling around long enough. Now drop all this! One can miss the opportunity. There is a time, a right time, and there is a right person—but you can miss it. You may continue searching but nobody knows whether you will again be able to find the right person, in the right moment.

And Devesh loves you. There is no need to make any bondage, no need to make any legal institution around you. I am not in favour of marriage—there is no need for it. There is a higher union which is more than marriage. . .

DIANA   *What about children?*

First move as deeply into love as possible. Till then avoid having children, because children should come out of a tremendous love, otherwise not. You can give birth to ordinary children, who are just by-products of a physiological and biological meeting of man and woman, but they are anonymous.

When two people move higher and higher in love, and a point comes where their personalities are no longer separate and boundaries dissolve, then they give birth to children. Then the children come from a higher plane. They have a personality of love—they are not only by-products of sex. They carry a deep harmony within them, and if you become aware, you can see whether the child is a by-product of a sexual meeting or a by-product of love. A different aura surrounds the child, a different vibration, because he has to carry that original quality of oneness.

When a child is born out of love you give something to the world. When a child is just from a sexual meeting, you simply over-populate the world; you don't give anything. Remember also, that when you give birth to a child out of deep love, out of surrender and meditation, something is simultaneously born into you. You become a mother.

Every woman who gives birth to a child is not necessarily a mother; it is not enough just to give birth. To become a mother your own heart should have bloomed. There are many women who have given birth to children, but there are very few mothers. To be a mother is a rare harmony and a unique experience. This is my observation: that if a woman can become really motherly — she may give birth to a child or not, that is not the point — if she can become motherly, that is her enlightenment and none other is needed. That is her buddhahood.

So love first and don't be worried about children, because then sooner or later you will start thinking about marriage. (laughter from the group) First love each other, and give each other total freedom. Don't be possessed and don't possess. Give the other full space to flower. Mm? Share as much as you can, and the sharing itself becomes a very very subtle possession which has no possessiveness about it; you are so certain of the other, you can trust. Meditate, love, and one day when you feel that you are overflowing now, that you cannot contain it any longer and you would like a soul to carry your burden, your fulfillment, then give birth to a child, not before. One should wait till one has become perfectly grown up. The world would be so beautiful if people would wait for the right moment.

And it seems that you are dominated too much by your family.

DIANA   *Very true.*

Mm? By and by one has to move away from the family.

Diana seems to respond to this, to look a little upset.

Not that you should not love them; this is how you can love them. It is the only way. It is just as when a child is born and he moves away from the mother, then one day he moves away from the breast. Then he is ready one day to move to the neighbourhood to play, and then to school. One day he comes home and he is totally different from when he left; he has become grown up. When he falls in love with another woman, that is the furthest he will go from the mother. In fact the day the child chooses his or her partner, that day he is really born, he actually comes out of the womb. Before that, the womb surrounds him in a thousand and one ways.

Everybody has to come out of the family otherwise they will not become themselves; they will always remain immature. One has to understand that to come back one has to first go away. When you

ONLY AN INDEPENDENT PERSON CAN LOVE

have become your own, an authentic being, then you can come back to the home. Then you can again love your father, your mother and your brothers. But now you are there to love them, and before you were not. How can you love when you are not?

This is the trouble — that the family dominates the child too much, and is always afraid that he will go too far away from them. So they force him, they try subtle ways to influence him, condition him. The child goes on resisting deep down, and because of that resistance he cannot love them, cannot really love them.

Only an independent person can love, and a family is fulfilled when a person has become grown up. So just listen to your heart. You are grown up, and whatsoever your heart says, risk.

Devesh is a vagabond, that's perfectly true, but a beautiful vagabond, mm?

(laughter. Devesh looks shyly down into his lap.)

The 'vagabond' comes from a background of English upper-crustness, politics and the British army, so he is a rather special person. Special, because he is completely unspoiled and has a beautiful childlike naivete about him; an unsophisticated air of enquiry and a sense of humour — not the typical dry sense of humour of the English, but one that is both penetrating and gentle.

He took sannyas sometime ago with applaudably little hesitation, and had managed to woo his woman into coming to see Bhagwan for herself.

Coming from a similar background, she also is somewhat reserved and cautious, but Bhagwan reassured her, last darshan, that she was caught!

Bhagwan continued...

Anything to say?

DIANA   *The only thing that worries me is that we spend so little time together—just three or four months of the year.*

What are you doing there exactly?

DIANA   *Well at the moment I'm minding an exhibition for the Arts Council, but that finishes in July. After that I don't have a job . . .*

So let Devesh be your job!

   Turns to address Devesh who is sitting next to Diana and in front of him.

So Devesh, after July be her job!

DEVESH   (Politely and quietly) *Fine!* (laughter)

   Take the responsibility, be her job! If Devesh is here (now to Diana) be here, if he is in England, be with him there.

But now start settling together. It is going to be
beautiful! I bless you, mm? Good!
And come soon for sannyas!

Pratima, what about you?

PRATIMA (trying to hold back tears) I seem to just be going around and around in self-destructive circles.

What is happening?

PRATIMA Just the same as was happening about three months ago with Siddhesh and with the whole...

What is happening with Siddhesh?

PRATIMA Well, we had become friends again and were getting quite close, and I was feeling not so aggressive. I felt he was opening and I was becoming more open, and we were spending a lot of time together.
Then I wanted more. I wasn't satisfied with what was happening, especially sexually, because he is not interested. He said he was more interested in seeing me as a friend, a sister, but he was not interested in that way. I just went berserk, and I did exactly what I did before.... (crying)

EVERYBODY HAS TO BE ALLOWED SOME INSANITY

So now what is the situation, mm? tell me. I will manage, don't be worried.

PRATIMA *The situation is that I feel completely stupid. It seems that something was happening that I wanted to happen, and then just for no reason at all I stomped on it . . . just went and stomped on it.* (violent outburst of crying)

Mm . . . when did it happen, this stomping?

PRATIMA *I don't know, I think it was yesterday. He left some things in my room and I gave them all to him. I just went completely insane and I threw things at him, and it was just for nothing!* (crying more)

(chuckling gently) And when did your sanity come back?

PRATIMA (laughing between her sobs) *I don't know that I've got any.*

(laughing) Otherwise how can you feel that you went insane? Now it is back, so ask his forgiveness, mm?

PRATIMA *I did, and he just said that he was sick of it all; that I'm just a complete stranger and I keep creating things, and he doesn't want anything to do with me. . .*

Just remember always that as you have your insane moments, he also has his. These are his insane words, don't be worried about them.

Everybody occasionally has to be allowed a little insanity. When you are insane you understand, but when the other is insane you don't understand.

He is saying these things because you have been hurting him, so he is sick of it all. Perfectly true—who is not sick of insanity? Mm? When you start becoming saner he will do the things you were doing; then his moment of negativity comes up. If you are in the day, he is in the night; if he is in the night, you are in the day.

Just look at the whole game of what goes on! Because he said he was not interested in sex, your ego was hurt. Very deep down, women are too identified with sex. They think that if somebody is interested in them, they must be interested in sex. If somebody says they are not interested in sex, the woman thinks he can't be interested in her!

Look at the paradox of it. If somebody simply says that they are interested in sex, then the woman is hurt. She says that then they are not interested in her; she feels hurt. If somebody is only interested in you, then too you feel hurt. Deep down there is a confusion. The confusion is that you would like somebody to be interested in you and hence interested in sex; via you, he should be interested in sex.

People come to me every day: the man is interested in sex, the woman is not. The woman thinks she is being used, and then she starts thinking that the man is interested only in sex so she starts withdrawing. If this goes on to a peak by and by the man gets fed up; he starts not being interested in sex. Then the woman jumps, because this is the last chance—if the man escapes, he escapes. Get hold of him! So she starts becoming interested in sex— but now the man says he is not interested.

You have been hurting his ego, now there is a chance

BECOME PARTNERS IN THE SEARCH

for him to hurt yours. You have been insane, throwing his things, and you must have said nasty things to him, so he is hurt. Now that you are coming back, he will take revenge. So give him a little rope to be insane and do things. By and by you will both become aware that you are wasting time.

So be open to each other and settle things. It is such a simple game, but you create so much out of it. That too is one of the parts of the human ego: that out of small things we create big problems. With small problems only a small ego can exist. So fighting and quarrelling, this and that, and creating big problems around you, you feel perfectly good. Great problems are happening—and nothing is happening; only Pratima and Siddhesh are fighting, nothing else.

So talk to him, take his things back; and you have said bad things, so take them back too. Allow him to be a little nasty so he feels good, and be finished! Become aware of what you are doing to yourself and why.

This is nothing but a negative tape in your mind. Once you get into the rut, it goes on repeating. So next time this negative tape starts functioning, close your room and sit there, and tell the negative tape that you will give it ten minutes, you will listen to it for ten minutes, then it is not to disturb you anymore; that you are fed up with it.

Rather than being fed up with Siddhesh, be fed up with this negative habit, and when you are in a negative mood, avoid meeting Siddhesh. Nobody is interested in anybody else's negativity. Take a pillow and talk to it, beat it, write nasty things on it, and be clear of them. When you have finished with your rubbish, then go laughing to Siddhesh; call him and tell him the whole story of what has been happening all day—and he will enjoy it, he will understand.

Everybody is here in search of his own happiness— become partners in the search. Why create fighting? There is no point . . . and you are not crazy! You understand, and people who can understand that they can feel crazy sometimes are not mad. You cannot convince a madman that he is crazy. If you can, that means he is already recovering!

One grows out of these sufferings—you are growing, that's all. And sometimes be crazy but don't make so much fuss about it, mm? So many crazy people are here; all the crazy people of the world are coming here, (laughter from the group) so nobody can say that he is the craziest. Impossible!

Just talk to him, and when everything is okay and flowing, come together, mm? Good.

Samvada, come here. How was the group?

SAMVADA

I started with a lot of resistance, but you'd told me last time that that was alright and to follow in the direction of it, and I was able to do that.

I found after I'd taken sannyas, within twelve hours people were coming and wanting to buy all my movie equipment; they wanted to take my entire past away!

Laughter from everybody. Samvada came to Poona only two months ago, ostensibly to make a film about Bhagwan and the ashram. He had filmed Bhagwan's birthday celebrations on December 11th and as he said at the previous darshan, was spending more and more time with sannyasins, till he took the jump himself, two weeks ago.

I'VE BEEN FEELING A LETTING-GO

SAMVADA

> So I've been feeling a sense of letting go of all of the things — my sense of self-image, of who I am, and my attachment to all these things. I don't understand it all yet, but I don't feel it means I won't be making films, or that I won't be being an artist or . . .

No, no.

SAMVADA

> I don't feel it's the end of that, but rather the beginning of it in a different way.

A beginning of a totally different way. And for the first time you will be able to do much creative work. Something better, something deeper will come, as if out of the blue.

In fact, all creative work can be done in two ways: either you do it through the mind, or through no-mind. You can do it through your thoughts, but all thoughts are borrowed. Howsoever you try to make it original and new, at the most it remains a modified form — nothing new is born.

If you start meditating, a moment comes when you don't think about it. Out of a non-thinking emptiness something bubbles up, something from you takes shape. It surprises you as much as it surprises others. All great artists, whatever the medium of work, are surprised when a new thing comes to them; they cannot believe that it is out of them. It is something from the beyond.

All great artists have been aware that they become possessed by some unknown force. It is nothing but your own depth—but you are unaware of it. The whole effect of meditation is to throw you back to your original depth so that something new arises. Then for the first time you will feel happy and blissful—because there is no other bliss than to be creative. Uncreative people cannot be blissful; at the most they can feel pleasure, gratification. Only creative people can have a pure and uncorrupted bliss.

So don't think about the past. It is good that it has gone, allow it. That is the whole meaning of sannyas—that the past be allowed and you can relax into something new.

Man is an infinity, but by and by we all become focused in a certain rut, a routine—then we function from that. It is as if you have many windows to your room, but you have opened only one, and you always look from it into the same direction. By and by you forget that there are other windows and other doors. The East is beautiful, the West too. The morning and the sunrise have a beauty, but the sunset has a beauty of its own—both are unique. You need to open all the windows and all other avenues of vision.

So dropping the past simply means creating a new window. The past will be available to you, you can still use it, but it will not be the only window. You will become more and more flexible, liquid, flowing. When one becomes multi-dimensional, whatsoever you do carries many layers of meaning in it. If you are fixed in one dimension, in one habit form, you go on repeating yourself.

I was just reading about a man who was purchasing a Picasso painting. He was a little afraid as to whether it was a fake or a true one. So he asked a critic who said it was absolutely authentic, and that he could vouch for it, because when Picasso was painting it the critic had been a guest in his house.

So the man who was going to purchase the painting went to Picasso and asked if it were true. Picasso said it

was true that the critic had been a guest, but that the painting was a fake.

The man couldn't believe it! He asked Picasso whether he had painted it or not. 'I painted it,' Picasso replied, 'but sometimes I paint fake Picassos. It is fake because I simply repeated myself, it is not authentic. It did not come from the beyond, it was just a technical repetition — so it is a fake!'

So you just float and leave the old structure, and many more avenues will become available. The old will be incorporated, because nothing that you have learnt can be lost — but there is no need to get fixed in it. In a subtle way whatsoever you have learnt remains a part of you, but it will not be your whole being. You will always be able to move away from it, beyond it, even opposite to it. Then you have an inner freedom. Good!

SAMVADA

*You asked me when I came
how long I would stay and said*

> *I should stay until it felt like my home...*

Right!

SAMVADA

> Well, a few days ago, just before the lecture I found a question I wanted you to answer, but I didn't get it in in time. It was in an old diary of mine and it said:
>
> *If a rose is a rose is a rose, is a rose a rose if it knows?*
>
> And I came that morning and you talked about the rosebush and not knowing, and I thought that I must have come home!

(laughing) You have come home! Good Samvada!

Bhagwan turned to address members of the Encounter Group who were present.

Encounter therapy is the basis for most of the other therapies in the field of humanistic psychology that are being currently used in the West and now here, in the ashram.

It represents a totally new approach in therapy, in that individuals are not regarded as 'sick', and therefore dependent. Rather, the accent is on taking responsibility for oneself. The onus is on the individual as to how far and how deeply he is prepared to commit himself.

In a group setting, people are helped to confront those areas in themselves—which are usually related to fear, or anger, or sex—where alone they might be too frightened to delve, or may be quite unaware that they even exist. In an atmosphere of caring and support, members are encouraged to work out their problems, their blocks, and 'hang-ups', experientially rather than intellectually, as compared with psychotherapy. Problems are expressed in terms of their present situation, in the herenow, rather than returning to the past and associated traumas—as is done in Primal Therapy.

The various aids used include body work—massage, and bio-energetics—gestalt and fantasy work, psychodrama, psycho-synthesis, and direct confrontation. Meditations are also used in the ashram groups.

The course lasts for seven days, twice a month, and is semi-residential.

Alok, how was the group?

Alok looks at Bhagwan for a few minutes without saying anything.

ALOK *In your lecture yesterday morning . . . well, I don't cough anymore. . . .*

This was greeted with laughter and applause. In his last darshan Alok had confessed that whenever Bhagwan said anything in the lecture that he didn't like or agree with, he would cough.

I know! I watched whether Alok is coughing or not!

ALOK   Well, yesterday in the
               lecture, towards the end of it,
               I looked up towards you, and
               in my heart . . . my heart ached
               and the words that came were
               that I receive Jesus in my heart.
               And then I felt, like, well, that
               I'd come home.

Very good, very good Alok.

ALOK   And um, I talked with God
               yesterday in the group. Teertha
               (the groupleader) was playing
               God, and I think I have to either
               trade my sex problems in for a
               new set of problems, or just lay
               them aside and play with them
               when I feel like it!

Mm good . . . just relax. Don't make them problems, just relax. They solve of their own accord.

If you are too worried about a problem, you go on poking your finger in the wound and it doesn't allow it to heal. There is no problem in fact. Man is a problem-creator. One can live without problems but the ego cannot, so it goes on creating something or other.

Leave them, just enjoy yourself, and they will disappear. The very enjoyment solves all problems. The very delight in life, in small things—eating, walking, talking, taking a bath, meeting with friends, falling in love, or just sitting looking at the sky—small things, but if you can enjoy them there is no energy available to bother about problems. You understand me? The whole energy moves into these delights and there is no problem left.

BE HERE AND DELIGHT

The problem arises because you are not using your energy in a creative way. Man needs a release and a continuity of sharing, so just delight. Be here and delight!

Jesus has knocked at your heart, that's why the coughing has stopped! It was the devil coughing in you! (laughs) Good Alok!

PRATITI *A fear of men is coming up. I'm afraid of men...*

Pratiti afraid of men? Men should be afraid!

Laughter from the group. Pratiti is the mother of a sannyasin who is also living here at the moment. She doesn't seem at all as one thinks of a mother. Italian, she is always full of energy and words — funny, touching words, that run and scramble about so quickly that it is difficult to catch hold of them.

In fact no woman is really afraid of man, only men are afraid of women.

PRATITI *So what is this I am feeling?*

Just an idea, nothing really. There is a certain point in man's fear, because he is the active partner and he can fail. He has to prove something, that he is potent. The woman is passive, she has nothing to prove. She is always a success.

For man, every woman is a crisis: he may come a success or a failure from her. He may not show the fear, he may show just the opposite, but every man deep down is afraid of women.

It depends much on the woman to give him a certainty, a security that everything is okay, and he is a beautiful man.

So you need not be worried about such notions, mm?

ANAND PREM

In the group I got in touch with some of my anger, and a part of my reality I hadn't contacted before. I began to see things differently . . . just walking down the road, the trees . . . and everything, seemed to look different.

Mm . . . whenever it happens that any accumulated negativity is released, it is as if a curtain disappears from the eyes and every sense becomes more sensitive.

You see the same colours but they have a different glow, a luminosity. Green is not just green; there are a thousand and one greens and you can see the difference. Each sound has a musical note to it; even the traffic noise becomes part of a harmony. The more your negativity is dropped, the more you become aware of a tremendously beautiful world around you. You have been living in it and you have missed it!

So make it a point now. There are many curtains, and they have to be dropped. Just like anger, there is jealousy, possessiveness, hatred. Drop them by and by, and just see how life becomes infinitely enriched.

WE CAN BE EMPERORS

We are poor because of ourselves; nobody is forcing any poverty on us. We can be emperors but we have decided to be beggars.

TUESDAY JANUARY 6th

A sannyasin said that he was feeling much better since last darshan, when Bhagwan had suggested he undertake much physical activity — running, walking, swimming, or whatever he enjoyed.

BHAGWAN   You have much energy and you had not been using it creatively. Whenever energy is not used creatively it becomes destructive, stagnant, and by and by a prison of solid rock is created around you.

There are two types of people — those with high energy and those with low energy. If the high energy people don't use their energy there will be problems: aggression, anger — anger for no reason at all, and against any and everybody — violence, hatred, jealousy.

Low energy people have a different type of problem — sadness, lethargy, a disinterestedness in life, and a dragging and dull attitude. So the problems of a low energy person need to be tackled in a different way. He needs more relaxation, and methods which don't use energy, but rather allow him to relax into the non-tense so that energy is not dissipated in any way. Buddhist methods, Vipassana, are for low energy people. For a high energy person such methods will be a problem. He would not know what to do — so much energy and nothing to do, so the energy becomes suppressed. Dynamic methods and catharsis are for high energy people.

ONE NEEDS TO BE A LITTLE PATIENT

The East is basically low energy: poverty, malnutrition, and centuries and centuries of passivity. The West is high energy. You can divide it into male and female, yin and yang. Male means a high energy person, and female means a low energy person—it has nothing to do with man and woman.

So you are a high energy person, remember that always. Whenever you feel any problem arising, that is simply an indication that you need more work, more creativity. It doesn't matter what you do, but do something physical—anything physical is beautiful. If you don't, then the mind uses the energy round and round in circles.

So swim or dance—do something with the body. Body movements are going to help you tremendously. It has been good, and you look perfectly well. But remember, don't forget!

A sannyasin said that many of the problems she had, or imagined she had, were dropping.

They do drop—one just needs to be a little patient. Everything drops of its own accord, because in the first place it has come of its own accord.

This should be a continual remembrance: that everything arises on its own and subsides on its own. You are just a witness sitting on the bank, and the river flows by. Sometimes it is in flood—when it is raining; sometimes it passes slowly—when it is summer. You are just a watcher, it is none of your concern.

This is what is the attitude of a meditator—to look at everything but not to jump into it. Whatsoever passes is good. Sometimes happiness comes, sometimes sadness, anger, jealousy—you need not make them your problems. You have the attitude as if you are waiting at the railway station in the waiting room. So many people coming and going—good and bad, saint and sinner—it is none of your concern; you simply sit in your chair unconcerned. You are waiting for your train, and these people are not coming for you—you don't even know who they are. You are not in a judging mood of who is good and who is bad, because you judge only when you think this is your home.

Let the whole world be just a waiting room. We are waiting for our train, and sooner or later we go. Whenever your train arrives you move. . . .

The mind is just a waiting room, so be aware of it. Soon you will come to a great insight that everything arises on its own, and if you interfere you delay the process. So let this be the motto: Acceptance—no interference. What can you do? The rain is coming and clouds have gathered in the sky; there is much thunder and lightning, but what can you do? You simply watch, and then sooner or later they disappear.

Your mind is also a sky. You are beyond it. You can watch your thoughts moving just as you watch clouds float by. You are the watcher—and when you see that, you will see that there are no problems left.

You follow me? Just try!

The Tao group were present at darshan this evening. It was the first group to pass through this particular process and the feeling was one of a very positive experience.

The groupleader described the format, or nonformat, as: 'The substance, purpose, and process of the Tao group is committed to nothingness, no pre-planned structure or method. The creation and evolution of the group emanate from each moment to be discovered. Whatever happens will happen.'

The Tao group meets for seven consecutive days, and is available twice a month.

I'M TOTALLY HAPPY

Amida, come here! Something to say?

Amida is a beautiful person. Having worked extensively on herself for many years through Arica training and EST, she has undergone incredible changes since coming to Poona. At her first darshan she was lively, with lots of energy, but looked as if life had taken its toll on her. There was a nervousness, a sharpness about her.

Tonight the lines of harassment and hasslement on her face had gone. She looked quietly glowing, serene, centred. . . .

AMIDA (gazing at Bhagwan for a few minutes) *I'm totally happy...*

You make me happy also!

VIPASSANA *I've been looking for areas in myself to work on, and I feel like there is nothing!* (laughing)

There is nothing. This has to be understood: some people sometimes take lives to understand a simple thing—that there is nothing to do. One has just to start from this moment; nothing is lacking or missing. But there is this idea that one has to prepare first.

It is just like when a child is born. He is ready to breathe—no preparation is needed, everything is ready. Just a good cry and the lungs start functioning, the breathing comes. Sometimes it is necessary that the doctor slaps the child on the bottom to give him a jerk.

That is all a master can do. He can give you a slap, a jerk, so that you start breathing. Otherwise everything is ready.

Preparation is a wrong notion that has been given by the society. If you want to appear in an examination, you have to prepare for years, but this is not an examination. Life is not an examination! It needs no preparation. Trees are living perfectly beautifully, animals also. Only man is missing because he is trying to prepare first.

Just start living, and you will suddenly see that everything is always available. There is nothing to do, nothing to prepare to become capable — you are capable. The whole effort here is to make you aware in as many ways as possible that you are ready to live, to be ecstatic, to celebrate. Good Vipassana!

Sambodhi said that she had felt some anxiety prior to doing the group. Because it was to be unstructured she felt a little uneasy, wondering if she had to be responsible in part at least for making things happen.
Bhagwan asked her how she felt during and after the group. She said she had gone to the very depths of sadness, but that she felt it had been good on the whole, and that the process had diffused a lot of things.

Mm, you are looking very calm and quiet.

In fact anxieties never come true, and we waste our lives thinking about them. Ninety percent of one's fears never actualise. That's why I asked if these anxieties were before the group or in it, because you could flow — so the whole anxiety was baseless. Let that become an integrated understanding in you, so that next time, or whenever you are moving into a new thing, don't start the anxiety again.

A RELIGIOUS MIND TRUSTS LIFE

All anxieties are useless because the future is unknown. It never comes according to your expectations or fears. It has its own way of coming, and it doesn't ask you, so why be unnecessarily worried?

Wait, and when it comes, see . . . whatsoever you can do, do. Everybody is capable of doing things when they are needed. Life sends you absolutely prepared for any situation that is possible.

You could flow, and when you flow never ask only for highs because that is patent foolishness. If you ask only for highs, then where will the depths go?

If you ask only for happiness and you are afraid of sadness, then how can you flow?

Flow means going into the depths, but going so totally that there is no resistance. Flow means going to the height, but going so totally that there is no clinging. Flow means always remaining free to move: moving with life wherever it leads, whatsoever its unknown goal. Once you start fixing your goal against life, then you are not flowing.

If life wants you to be sad, be sad—life knows more. If life wants you to weep and cry, then weep and cry—life knows more. Don't start trying to be more clever than life itself; that is the human stupidity. Just flow with it! Be like a small child who is following his father. Maybe the father is afraid of where he is going, but the child is happy and singing, because he knows the father is with him and knows where they are going.

That is the beauty of the religious mind. I call that mind religious which trusts life and says, 'Wherever it is going it knows better than me. I have just come, a late arrival, and life has been always and always and always there.' Just trust it.

That is the whole meaning of the Tao group—to flow. If you have a choice, if you say you will not move into sadness, that you want only happiness, then you cannot flow. Flow is only possible if you accept everything as it is, unconditionally.

You could have gone deeper into it if there was not this little resistance about going into depth. Go into depth and you will come up: the deeper you go, the higher you rise. It is exactly like the trees. The deeper their roots go underneath, the higher their branches rise into the sky; it is always in the same proportion. If a tree doesn't want to go deep, is afraid of the unknown earth—dark, mysterious, deathlike—then the tree cannot rise towards the sun.

This is the way all beings grow. A really mature person is always ready to move wherever life leads. This I call maturity—the understanding that life is greater than you, that you are just a tiny part of it.

So why worry? There is no reason! Move with life....

SUGEETA *I found myself... I had this feeling this morning of, just ... being.*

That's the whole point!

SUGEETA *I think I had the best meditation in my life in the group.*

That's what meditation is—just to be. Then there is no problem. If you can just be, everything is resolved, solved.

What about you?

I'M GETTING MORE THAN I COULD DREAM

PRASHANTI *I'm getting more than I could ever dream!*

Prashanti took some time to decide whether to become a sannyasin or not. Many times she expressed doubt about the value of it, and told Bhagwan her father had warned her never to follow anyone.
Finally Bhagwan told her she could drop the indecisiveness about sannyas, because he would not give it to her; she had missed the boat. Some weeks later she returned to darshan to ask for sannyas and Bhagwan relented! From that day Prashanti seemed to become an altogether different person. . . .

That's right! Life is more beautiful than any dream, and has more to give than anybody can dream, but we settle for less. We settle for nothing and we think that is life. Only when we start entering into new worlds which were always there but of which we were unaware, only then one starts feeling what a wastage, what a criminal wastage. So many people go on living in darkness, and not only that, they resist any effort to bring light to them.
Good! Much more is on the way!

DHARMA *My main sense of the group as I walked into the room was of endlessness: there seemed to be no beginning and no end. It seemed like an intensification of life.*

Very good . . . you understood. Nothing has any beginning and nothing has any end. All beginnings and all ends are arbitrary; they are human, and not really true. It is good that the group should have the feeling of being part of an ongoing process of life. It just gives you a glimpse, but that's what life is. Very good!

DHARMA

> *I come here with all sorts of questions about what to do with myself. At the same time, I usually find that it becomes clear as time goes on.*

Mm mm. Just time is needed, and patience — then things clear by themselves.

When I answer your questions, I knowingly answer them, because no answers can be given really. It is just helping you to wait a little more.

The questions are yours, so how can my answers help? Your answer has to come — but you are in a hurry and you cannot wait — so I give you toys to play with, mm? Time passes, you do this and that, until by and by you become aware that those questions have dissolved, are no longer there. When a question leaves without an answer, it leaves no trace behind. An answer can suppress a question but it cannot resolve it. I can silence you and your question, but it will remain there underneath, and it will try ways and means to come up again. It will try to assert itself in different forms, in different terminology.

So all my answers are just to help you so that you don't become desperate, so that you wait. Life gives answers, only life gives answers. Good!

NAYANA

> *I didn't flow much with the group. I feel very stuck with*

ACCEPT YOURSELF AS YOU ARE

myself, and feel a resistance to opening up.

Remain as you are . . . that very effort is creating more resistance. Accept yourself as you are: accept that you are closed, stuck, full stop. There is no need to do anything.

Participate in the groups, just sit silently, and tell the group that you are allowed to be as you are. One day, suddenly you will find that everything has collapsed—and then you will come out of it. You will not come out of it by effort, because effort is always partial: on one hand you make the effort to come out, on the other you are pulling yourself in. You take one step forward, and the other foot is ready to withdraw. It becomes futile, meaningless, and you are unnecessarily miserable.

I was waiting until this day, and I was watching what to do. Now this is my message to you: accept yourself as you are; there is no need to be anybody else. God must be trying to do something by your being stuck. There must be some purpose behind your being closed.

Drop the fighting, and instantly you drop it the resistance will disappear—because there is no point in being resistant. You will not open gradually, but suddenly.

There are flowers that open gradually and flowers that open suddenly with a noise. You will open suddenly, so don't be worried!

WEDNESDAY JANUARY 7th

VIMAL KIRTI (the father of Tanya, the five year old German sannyasin) *I am to tell you that she loves you, and to ask whether you got her picture, and whether you get strength and love from it.*

Shantidharma asked Bhagwan if the religious movement he was involved in in America was doing anything generally positive for the spiritual development of the world, and whether he should remain in it.

He said that on the positive side he felt the people involved in it were really interested in bringing God to people, but on the negative side he felt they were rather moralistic and had rigid and fixed characters.

Bhagwan said that these were not in fact two different things...

BHAGWAN People who are interested in bringing God to others are always narrow-minded, always moralistic, puritans.

In fact they are not concerned with God at all, God is just an excuse. They want to condemn, to torture people. These God-loving, so-called God-loving people, have created hell. They are sadists, and their morality has nothing to do with morality. It is an ego-trip.

A REAL SAINT LOOKS ORDINARY

You cannot hide negative things if you don't have something positive to hide behind, so real positivity has to be understood—whether it is pure, whether it is not hiding something behind it.

It is very simple and easy to watch a person who is really religious. If he is religious he will never have a narrow mind, or a moralistic mind. This is one of the basic qualities of the religious mind—that he will not have a condemnatory attitude. He will love so deeply that he cannot condemn, he cannot call anybody a sinner; that is impossible for a really religious person.

But religious people have been calling the whole world a world of sinners, and have been very inventive about how to torture people.

If you can give freedom to the other, only then can you love. If you can accept the being of the other as it is, only then you have love. If you can accept the divinity of the other without forcing anything on top of it, then only you are in love—otherwise not.

Love needs no theology, and knows no ideology. These are tricks, and the mind has been playing tricks for so long and you don't understand even now. . . .

Just watch the people whom you call religious. They may develop a certain character, they may even try to be moral, but the whole thing is an ego-trip. It is just to condemn others, to feel higher than others, better than others, superior. In their eyes you can see a tremendous condemnation. They will go on becoming holier and holier —and if you look at their holiness only, you will miss the whole point.

A real saint may not look like a saint at all, because he will be so ordinary. He will not have any programme of how to reform the world. All those programmes are political, they are nothing to do with religion. All the churches and temples and so-called prophets create more politics and more war and more violence. But these are the seeds—and the trouble is they are altruistic. They are great God-lovers, and so concerned with the welfare of the world that anyone can become a victim.

This has always been so. Mohammedans have killed so many people, and so have Christians. They are all trying to do good, and they are all trying to help people, but they are not aware of their own unconscious ego-trip. It is not a question of wanting to change the world and helping people—these are nonsensical things. One should understand that these games have been played long enough, and be aware of them. But human stupidity is such that again and again we fall into the same trap.

A really religious person will not in any way be forcing anything on anybody. He cannot be moralistic, cannot have any idea of sin. He will accept you on your terms. He won't have any terms, any conditions, saying that if you fulfill these then you enter heaven, and if you don't fulfill them you will be thrown into hell.

Any religious person will not be fanatical at all —because there is nothing to be fanatic about! He will be a wideness, an open sky. You cannot find any boundaries, any limitations to him.

So if these are the negatives, whatsoever you call the positives are bogus! If these positives are real, then these negatives cannot exist. So you sort it out. You may have a certain fascination for the positives, but that alone is not enough—because the path of hell is lined with good wishes.

SHANTIDHARMA

They don't seem to be authentically human, fully integrated. It seems like their spirituality is built on a weak foundation; it doesn't permeate their whole being.

In fact spirituality is not something separate from your being. It is your fullness of being. It is not something that you have to attain over and above you. It is you, a flowering. It is you, relaxed, integrated, total. Spirituality is not a goal. If it is a goal, then you will always find a superstructure of spirituality, and somewhere deep down, the crippled human being. All that sort of spirituality is just rot.

Be a total human being. When I say total I never mean perfect. A total human being can never be perfect, because he will always be growing; it is a process. Totality is a process and never comes to any perfection; or, every moment it is perfect, and goes on attaining to so many types of perfection. It becomes more and more perfect, perfecter than perfect, but it is a process. A perfect man is a dead man. A total man is an alive process, a dynamic force.

Spirituality is not something over and above humanity. It is just the fragrance of humanity. If you are really human, you are spiritual. We can drop the word spiritual—there is no need for it. There is no need to give it a special name, but the separate name helps the ego. You start fighting with your humanity, repressing your humanity, and trying to create a superstructure on top of it. It is a mere decoration and remains skin-deep.

So if you look deep into your saints, you will find very paralysed, crippled human beings; not flowering at all—stinking!

A spiritual being means an innocent being, and innocence requires that you should not be divided. So there should be no goal and no idea of becoming somebody or something else, but just a deep acceptance and a delight in whatsoever you are, and a celebration—so that you can flow, you can be. In unknown ways you become spiritual —not that you try; it is a consequence of being total.

If you see a crippled human being under a spirituality, then know that something has gone wrong. If you can find a man who is totally human, alive, dynamic, flowing—he

may not have even heard the word spirituality, may never have been to any temple, read any bible or geeta—there is the man. Bow to him, and touch his feet, because something has flowered there.

To be religious is not to impose a structure; rather, on the contrary, it is to reveal the being that you are already.

So go and think about it. It is up to you. Whatsoever I say is not meant to direct you. If you feel like being in that group, remain in it; it must be giving you something. You may need to be in it a little while longer. But if you feel that it is not worthwhile, if you feel that you have to sacrifice something—then sacrifice and get out of it. To be in anything that you start feeling is wrong is to be suicidal, because by and by you become hypocritical. Never be in any situation where you cannot be total. Escape from it; it is dangerous because it is dividing you.

I know a catholic missionary who is fed up with his work and can see the whole nonsense of it—but he cannot get out of it! He is on a good salary, has a good house to live in, a car, prestige. Now this I see as very dangerous. There can be some security, some comfort and convenience in it, but one has to gather courage to be true to oneself.

If you feel it is wrong, get out of it. But never sell your soul for any comfort whatsoever.

How are you? Something to say . . . tell me.

ANANDMURTI
Last time I was here I took sannyas. I was not sure I wanted to take it, but I took your advice. I took sannyas, and I'm glad. It's been good.

> *And tonight I start a group — Unconditional Acceptance. I think I need, Bhagwan . . . you know, I think I need to accept . . . you talk about being total, and I . . . I don't feel I'm a total sannyasin . . . because there are things. . .*

I understand.

> *. . . there are things that when I think about them logically, they just . . . I think about myself in orange,* (looks self-consciously down at his bright orange new clothes) *being a sannyasin, it just doesn't jive. I don't know . . . so I just don't think about it, and that's okay, but I don't feel it's total.*

It will become total. You have taken the first step, the other things will follow. You do this group — it will be very very helpful; it will bring many things to your consciousness. And after the group you will feel very very relaxed.

So in the group, don't be shy and don't feel embarrassed. Whatsoever is the truth, allow it and accept it. Don't condemn it and say that 'this is not good, I should not say that, I should not accept that this is true in me'.

If hate is there, accept it. If there is no love, accept that there is no love. Things that are, people go on pretending they are not, and things that are not, people go on thinking they are. That's how we become divided. Acceptance means that you will automatically become one. When you accept yourself however you are, there is no division. There is nobody standing inside you condemning you; there is no top-dog and under-dog.

These things are natural and you cannot drop them so easily. The only easy way is to hide them, to pretend that they are not. You can keep them in the background so you don't see them, and then by and by you forget them. But they remain part of you, and they go on influencing you. Your whole life, by and by, will be in the hands of the unconscious, and you will become a slave, a puppet.

Accept, so that you need not keep any dark corner, and you can move into your basement of being. You can look at everything because you don't have any condemnation. Once you accept, you become one. The constant conflict disappears, and you simply become natural.

Remember, to be natural is the only virtue. There is none other but this.

The dance group, with its fourteen members, and its leader, Neeraj, performed for Bhagwan tonight. Bhagwan had suggested last darshan that they try dancing in couples, a man with a woman, rather than in a line or a circle, as they had been doing.

He said that these dances were in a way a form of courtship, and that the dancers would get more from it if the male and female energies flowed together.

The seven couples went down to the area below the darshan porch where Bhagwan sits and demonstrated the steps of the Ethiopian dance that Neeraj had taught them. Then the music changed to a Brazilian rhythm and the dancers abandoned any structure and individually did their own thing.

One particular sannyasin almost completely lost herself in the dancing. She was like a woodland sprite—all legs and arms and black hair, skipping and hopping, whirling and crouching, jumping and zig-zagging among all the others, incredibly not bumping into anyone at all!

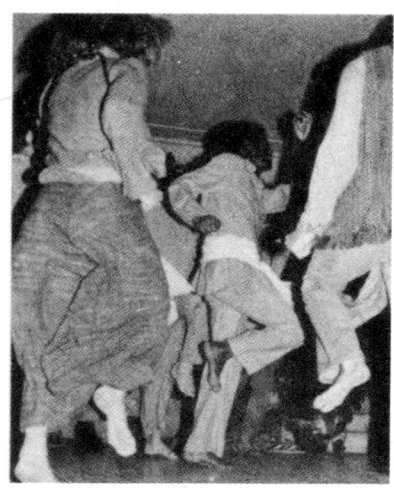

After ten minutes or so the music came to an end and the exhausted dancers came slowly back to their places. For several minutes everyone sat, some with eyes closed, others with heads bowed, dancers and those who watched—silent except for the laboured breathing of the exhausted dancers and from somewhere behind the group, the quiet sobbing of the woodland sprite. . . .

Something happened that evening, for those few seconds, to everyone present. The energy seemed to continue to vibrate, to linger on in the air a little longer, as if reluctant to leave so quickly.

THURSDAY JANUARY 8th

BHAGWAN Mm . . . something about you?

DEVA VEENA . . . I've been feeling very confused. It feels good in a way, but I just don't have any control over what happens anymore. I don't even know who I am anymore.

No need to know! That need is the trouble. There is no need to know. One should just move wherever life takes one. Trust life! This is mind interfering and trying to control; to manage and to manipulate. This is ego need.

You have come to understand a very basic thing. Now, don't forget it. Everything happens, and nobody has any power. The whole power-trip is an illusion. Nobody has any power. Everything is happening on its own. At the most you can cooperate or fight. If you fight, then too it will happen, but you will miss the bliss of it. If you cooperate, then too it will happen — but not because of your cooperation; it was going to happen anyway. You will feel blissful, ecstatic. So cooperate with life, don't create any conflict, and then everything falls in line; everything settles by itself.

So it is just that this idea is wrong, mm?—that you need to have some power. The second idea is also part of it—that you need to know. Knowledge is always a search for power. Knowledge is nothing but an enquiry to become more powerful. That's why science has become so important, because we start feeling powerful, and feeling that we have conquered nature. Nothing has been conquered, nothing can ever be conquered. Science only discovers where nature is moving, and then starts cooperating with it—then things start happening. It is not powerful.

For example, oxygen and hydrogen combined together create water. It has always been so, whether we know it or not. When nobody knew about it, then too it was happening. Science discovered that this is how water is made, so now if you follow the rule, you can make water. The water is making itself! You simply cooperate. It is not a conquering, but a deep cooperation.

And the same is true for religion. Science discovers how to cooperate with nature, and religion discovers how to cooperate with God—the ultimate nature. But in both ways, the more you know, the more you understand that knowledge is not needed.

Drop that trip, and just enjoy whatsoever you are and whatsoever is happening.

DEVA VEENA

What I feel sometimes is . . . well, when I'm in the ashram, everyone seems to be very quiet and floating. I feel like jumping about, shouting and joking, but then I feel bad when it happens. I want to try to change it.

No, no, don't try to change it. Let it happen, and don't feel bad! Silence is good, but jumping and laughing and

SILENCE AND SINGING ENRICH EACH OTHER

joking is good too. They enrich each other. If you cannot laugh and joke, your silence will be poorer for it. If you cannot be silent, then your laughter will just be superficial.

So nothing is wrong in it. Don't create any problems. Move easily from laughing to silence, from silence to laughing. Whatsoever happens, allow it. When you feel like jumping, jump! And when you feel like just sitting, and not doing anything—then just sit. Good!

MALLIKA — *... I don't know why I can't improve. Maybe I know, but it's not very nice.*

Mm mm, tell me what you know.

MALLIKA — *Such a lack of confidence towards myself. I don't know ... there is always a part of me that is against the other, always! I'm so fed up.* (looking very doleful)

(chuckling) Not really!

MALLIKA — (eyes widening) *Not really?*

Otherwise there would be no problem!

MALLIKA: *But why does it keep on going?*

Because you are not yet fed up. If you are really fed up, then nothing is needed; just being fed up is enough. If you are really fed up you drop it; there is nothing else to it! Even the effort to drop shows that you still want to cling. One goes on talking about change, but one doesn't really want to change.

MALLIKA: *It's funny, because I remember about myself that I was quite a wise person—many years ago. I don't remember when I became like this. I mean, what sort of choice did I make to become such a masochistic being?*

By and by, slowly, one chooses. It is not a jump, but something very slow, so you never really understand what you are choosing. By and by, one goes on choosing, and choosing wrongly, and then it accumulates one day. You see, one day, that you have chosen a wrong path, and now you have travelled on it for so long it has become almost habitual.

But one can go back; there is no problem in it. The only problem is that you have to be really fed up, and I don't think that is the case. You are still enjoying it!

MALLIKA: *I've learned how to find gratification in it through a cowardly attitude. But I wasn't always a coward. When I remember back....*

Your remembrance cannot be relied on, mm? That again may be a trick, because whatsoever you remember is always a choice; you never remember the whole. You remember only beautiful things about yourself, and you drop the ugly things. That's why everybody thinks that in childhood he was almost divine. You remember only happy moments, and those too, you go on magnifying.

That helps you, and gives you a little consolation that this situation is not your real nature, mm? You were beautiful and good and wise—this is just like an accident, and it will pass. Another way you console yourself is by saying that in the future you will become wise, you will become enlightened; you will become this and that. These are the tricks of the mind—either to look at the past or the future, to avoid the present. But the present has to be dealt with. It has to be transformed.

So drop this thinking about the past, and drop thinking about the future. Just see the whole mess that you have created!

Nobody else is responsible either. That too is a trick. You go on thinking that your mother is responsible, that some man who goes on haunting you and influencing you from far-away Europe and who puts things in your mind, is responsible. These are tricks. Nobody can do that, nobody has that power. You are absolutely on your own.

These are ways to avoid responsibility—thinking the whole world is responsible except you. Suddenly you start feeling helpless—because you are not responsible, so what can you do?

You are responsible, and everything can be done. Nobody has destroyed you. You have made a wrong choice, a misjudgement, that's all. Nothing like a sin; it has just been a misjudgement. Nobody knows beforehand where one is moving. It is just like a puzzle, a riddle. . . .

MALLIKA *But I always knew I was making a mistake, a wrong choice, but I thought it would make me more extraordinary.*

Mm mm, so if one wants to be extraordinary one becomes mad, because only mad people are extraordinary. Sane people are just ordinary.

If you are fed up, just become ordinary. Relax, and become just an ordinary human being. It is beautiful to be ordinary. It is very ugly to be extraordinary, it is a sort of disease, an illness, and you can never relax in it.

What I see is that you may be fed up with the misery this trip to be extraordinary is bringing you, but you don't want to change the goal. You would like all the benefits that an extraordinary person has, but you would like all the blessings that only an ordinary person can have. These two cannot go together. With extraordinariness, with ego, there are miseries. If you choose to be extraordinary, then accept those miseries. Madness will follow you like a shadow, and

JUST BEING IS TO BE HAPPY

sooner or later it will crush you completely. Only the shadow will remain, you will disappear...

MALLIKA *That's what's happening.*

...or, if you understand, drop this whole nonsense of being extraordinary. Become ordinary, and enjoy ordinary things. Let ordinariness be your religion. Eating, sleeping, sunshine, flowers, people, the marketplace—just be ordinary and enjoy these things. Then you will see that the shadow disappears.

But this is for you to decide. So for three days just think about it. You can be extraordinary...

MALLIKA *I haven't the qualities to be.*

No question of qualities. Those people who have qualities don't bother to be extraordinary. They are fully joyful in being ordinary. Only those people who don't have qualities try to become extraordinary. The very idea shows that something is lacking. So drop the idea!

To be happy, no qualities are needed. You need not be a great painter or a great poet to be happy. An ordinary man with nothing special about him can be happy. Happiness has something else, some other base. Just being is to be happy.

MALLIKA *I always tell you about myself with the possibility of being wrong, but you can see what is really the problem.*

Nothing is the problem! You are still not seeing the point of how you are creating your misery. You have to see it. You can go on fooling around and avoiding it, but see it! If you are really fed up with it, this very moment it disappears. There is no need for any postponement.

Drop it! There is no method to it. You simply understand and just laugh, because the nonsense is finished, the nightmare over!

Mallika nods silently and returns thoughtfully to her place.

DHARMANANDA

Over the past weeks my breathing has started to seize up; it just stops. I find that I become afraid, because it feels as if I am suffocating. It feels good—as if something is coming up that I should get into—but I'd just like reassurance that it's normal.

Nothing is wrong, it is beautiful. Once you start enjoying it, you will see the beauty of it. It is a deep calmness. When the breath stops, everything stops; time and thinking too. But if you become afraid then everything starts again. So when the breath stops, remain silent and watch the gap that has come to you; the interval where no breath moves. In that interval, you will have the first glimpse of what meditation is.

But ordinarily everybody becomes scared and frightened, because we associate breath with life, and no breath with death. Because of that association, suddenly the fear of death arises; a fear that you are going to die.

FEEL BLISSFUL AND THANKFUL

You are going to die. In a greater life your small ripple is going to dissolve into the ocean, but that is not death—that is real life.

There are two types of life. One life, that is very superficial, depends on breath: it is the life of the body and the mind. Then there is another type which doesn't depend on breath. It is deeper than breath and can exist without it. That life is spiritual—call it divine or whatsoever you like.

So it is natural to be afraid in the beginning, but by and by allow it. Enjoy the gap and the silence that falls all over existence when the breath stops. Nothing moves, because all movement is the movement of your mind. When your mind is not moving, nothing moves. In that no movement, a door opens. But if you become afraid you will miss, mm? Then you become so concerned about breath that you miss the door that is opening inside. So next time it happens, feel blissful and thankful. Feel grateful that a great opportunity has been given to you, and don't be worried about breath.

Just look inside—a door is opening. When you have a glimpse of it, the whole gestalt changes. Your emphasis is not on the breath, it is on the door. You simply move from the door into another world.

DHARMANANDA   *Should I try to be brave and just? . . .*

No, never try to be brave, mm? Because that is part of cowardice, and you will miss the whole thing. Just relax and accept it. If you try to be brave you start a fight, and then you will again cling to the same point.

Just relax into it. If it feels like death, say, 'Okay, I accept it. I am ready to die.' That much will do. Being brave is going to the opposite extreme and it won't help.

You are somewhere in between, where there is neither cowardice nor bravery.

DHARMANANDA — *There's one other thing. I've found that I can concentrate with my eyes on objects. I started in the morning lecture, just looking at you and phew! ... I'm enjoying now looking at the moon and the flowers, but my body starts ...* (he started swaying to demonstrate)

Mm, it is good, it will move.

DHARMANANDA — *I should let it move and not sit still?*

No, let it move. Let your enjoyment be like a dance, mm? It is a subtle dance coming to you, so when you see a flower and the body moves, move. Let it be graceful and enjoy it. This is how your whole body is trying to enjoy the beauty of the flower. When you look and your body starts moving, it means that it is allowing the moon's rays to enter you and create a new dance that you have not known before.

It is just as when the ocean comes in tide when the moon rises. Your body starts moving, and a subtle movement which has been asleep, becomes awake. Don't try to force it, allow it. Then you will be enjoying the flowers, not only with the mind and intellect, but with your total being, your body included. Unless you enjoy it totally it is just a mind thing and nothing much.

'YOU' MEANS THE MIND

DHARMANANDA

> *If I do it for three hours a day, looking at these things, is it going to give me some unnatural sort of energy that is going to flaw me? Can I do it for just as long as I want?—because I feel as though I'm settled afterwards.*
>
> *I was tremendously greedy, but over the past week that has eased off. At the same time I feel like, maybe I'm draining myself by pushing it.*

No, no, don't push. Don't push too far, because greed can take over and it will become a tiring thing. If you overdo it, the whole beauty will disappear; it will stop. So never overdo — and that means, never do on your own. 'You' means the mind, the greed.

So when it happens allow it. It will never be too much because the body takes care of itself. If you listen to the body it never goes to any extreme. The body is always true to reality.

When you have eaten and the stomach is full, the appetite no longer there, the body says, 'Stop!' The mind says, 'Just a little more ice-cream will be alright.'

If you listen to the body, everything settles. The body should be listened to, it should be the teacher. But things are happening, good!

FRIDAY JANUARY 9th

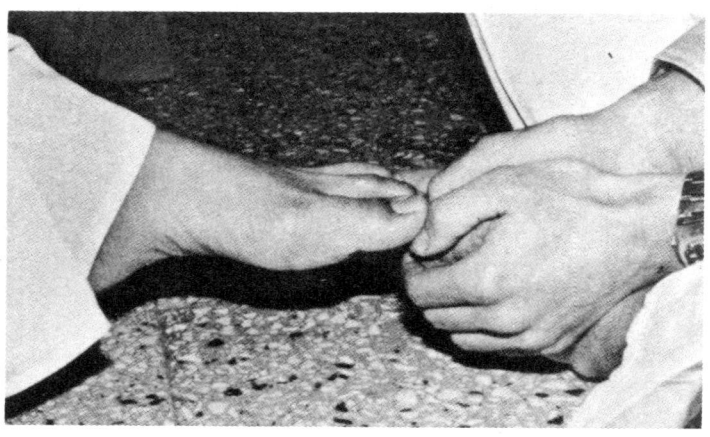

ANAND HEEREN I have difficulty accepting other people's looks of disapproval, particularly now that I'm wearing orange. I seem very sensitive to it. I was wondering if you could suggest something I could do.

BHAGWAN   That's the whole purpose of orange—so that you cannot hide yourself, and so that you stand out. You have to come to terms with every look that crosses your path.

Ordinarily we are hiding in conformity. When you conform with society you become part of the crowd, and nobody is looking at you in particular. You live an anonymous existence—that's why people live in a crowd, in society, sects, groups, parties.

WE HIDE IN CONFORMITY

To stand alone, and to become a focus of others' looks, is one of the most courageous acts. The basic thing to be understood is that you are to forget what others say. You have to ignore and become indifferent about them. It is none of their business. You become disturbed because you still pay attention to their attentions. It is not their opinion that is disturbing you; it is your expectation that they should be favourable to you, that their opinion should not go against you. Because this expectation is not being fulfilled, you are disturbed.

That's the whole purpose of why I give you orange: to make you so separate that either you will go crazy, or you will have to drop the whole wrong expectation. Why should you expect that the other should approve of you? You are perfectly good as you are; nobody's approval is needed. If you live on approval, then you live an inauthentic life. You never live your life; you only live a life that they will approve of. Then life becomes false, pseudo, and you become miserable, phoney. You feel frustrated, that life has no meaning. Life can have meaning only when it is real, and a real life means that you are not worried about what others say. You are simply working out what you can be, not what they expect or will approve of.

Simply forget others, as if you are alone. Move in the crowd, but never become part of it. Why should they be concerned about you? They are neurotic, and your being concerned about them is again a neurosis, a reflected neurosis. A healthy person is not worried about others; he has no judgement about them. If they want to be creative, good. If they want to be crazy, that too is good. That is their life, and finally they are responsible for it. So a healthy man never judges anybody, and never asks anybody's opinion. The very asking shows that you are wavering inside, that you don't have a hold on your being and you need props.

Just today I was reading an anecdote. A man enters a train which has written on it that it is going to London, but he asks a person in his carriage, 'Is this train going to London?' The person says that it is, but he is interested in reading his newspaper, so the answer sounds rather indifferent, not certain, so the man is not convinced. He asks again of the same person, 'Sir, is it really going to London?' The other man replies, 'Yes, it is really going to London,' but now he is angry because he has been disturbed.

Another person asks the questioner if he can read or not, because it is written everywhere that the train is going to London! Finally the questioner is convinced. Just then they stop at a station, and another passenger enters the compartment and asks the first man, 'Is this train going to London?' He replies, 'My God, you have made me uncertain again!'

This is what you are doing with yourself, mm? Anybody can make you uncertain whether you are good or beautiful. This is not a true being; it is a false one that you have gathered from other people's opinion.

The whole purpose of sannyas is to drop it, to be on your own; good, bad, or whatever, but to be on your own, to live a true life out of your own source. Soon you will see who you are, and once you do, by and by you forget what others say. It simply shows that they are approving or disapproving of you because they are living in the same approval/disapproval world.

Maybe, just looking at your orange, your difference, your nonconformity, they become afraid. Here is a man who can make them uncertain. You create a suspicion in people. They start thinking that perhaps there is another way of life; maybe they are not living and leading a right life. So to defend themselves they criticize you. You have brought a new window to their world. They don't want to see from this window because they have investments in their way of life, have lived a certain life according to certain rules. Now you come with a different world, and different rules. That means there was an alternative, and the alternative may have been better. Maybe they have missed the real thing. . . .

They have been missing the real thing, that's why the uncertainty. So they are simply trying to defend their own way of life. If they can make you miserable they will be happy, and again certain about themselves. Then they know the train is going to London!

But if you remain laughing and are not disturbed by their opinions, sooner or later they will start asking you what you have gained. If you persist in your way of life, they will start asking you how they should live their own lives; and that if you have found a way not to be miserable, then show them. First they will laugh and mock at you, criticize you, but if you persist, if you have the courage and the strength, by and by they will start following you.

But that is not the point—whether they criticize or follow. The point is, are you going to live your life, or are you going to follow others and their idea of what life is? And it is simple. There is nothing to be done, only an understanding is needed. Try, from this moment! Good!

KABIR   *I was wondering, that if you feel we are ready, could we have a name for the music group?*

I will give you a name . . . Nadam. It means the ultimate sound.

If every sound, every noise stops, then we start hearing the sound of that soundlessness, the sound of silence itself. That is nad.

Nad means the basic sound out of which everything is made. In yoga, it is an hypothesis that everything is made of sound, sound particles. In a way, both science and yoga agree, because science says that sound is made of electrical particles, and yoga says that electricity is nothing but a certain combination of sound particles. So they have come to the same reality. But because yoga came through silence, through dropping the thoughts and noise of the mind and heard the innermost silence, yoga says that everything is made of sound.

So I will call it Nadam Music Meditation Group, mm? Good!

A sannyasin told Bhagwan that she was living with Pujari, the Tathata groupleader, and that the previous night she had assisted him in the group.

Bhagwan felt this was not a good idea — to be together so much.

Love is killed by too much togetherness, so I don't suggest you help Pujari. You have your work to do, Pujari his. You can live together . . . but your being together should not become a twenty-four hour affair.

You will be a hindrance to Pujari too, in the group, because the group needs a certain freedom, and lovers don't give each other freedom. You will destroy Pujari's group and his freedom — and you will finally destroy your love. But it is up to you.

It is always good to be separate for a few hours each day so that when you meet again, you are ready for each other. It is a simple law of life. It is just as when you eat, and then for six or eight hours you forget about eating. Then again you are hungry, you have an appetite. You will never have an appetite if you go on eating all day. So your working lives should not be together, because there is no possibility of escaping from each other. The freedom and the aloneness is lost, and everybody needs a space of his own.

Pujari, do you have something to say?

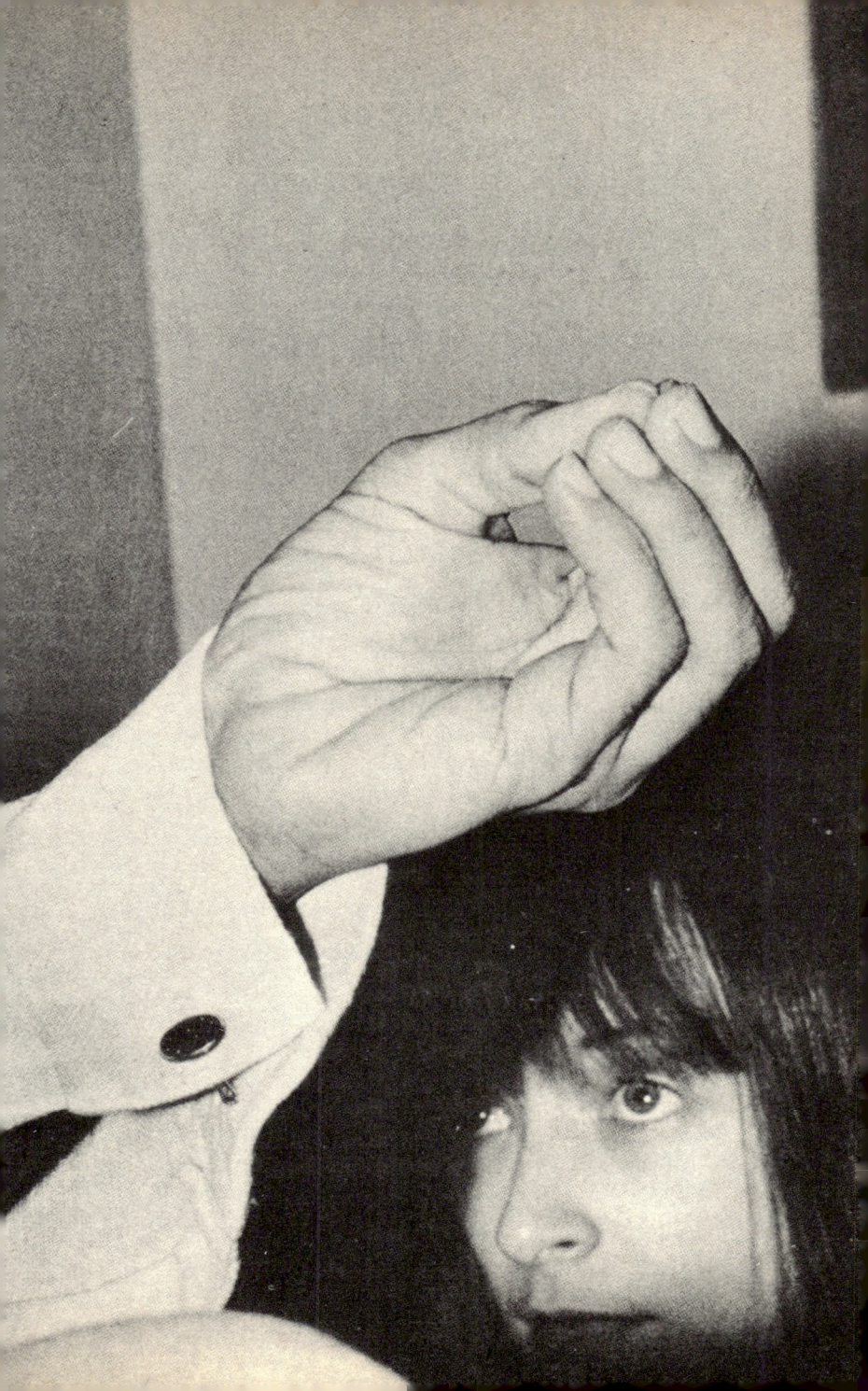

PUJARI   *I really felt a balance having her in the group.*

Every lover feels like that in the beginning; and that is the foolishness of all lovers! Every lover feels perfectly in tune, that you were made for each other. Just within a week, things start changing.

But if you want to try as an experiment, work together. . . .

PUJARI   *I've done that before—it didn't work. Lots of things came up in the group for me, though, and I like exposing different parts of myself to her.*

Love should never become part of any technique. It should have a different world of its own, a shrine. It should not become part of the work-world, never. It should remain a poetry, and not be brought into the marketplace.

PUJARI   *I'm very excited to think that we can come to you with problems that come up between us. We are ready to do whatsoever you say. . . .*

Mm mm, you can always come, but you have to listen to me! If you listen to yourself it is useless. So this is the beginning of the listening: you have to work separately.

LIFE IS TREMENDOUSLY LUXURIOUS

Bhagwan went on to talk about using one's energy creatively...

Use the energy, and more is always given to you. Life believes in affluence. The whole of life is tremendously luxurious. Flowers are not needed, and there is no particular need for butterflies, for birds and songs, for peacocks dancing and cuckoos singing. It all seems superfluous.

But in a thousand and one ways, existence goes on blooming. Life believes in being abundant, in overflowing, and those who want to move with life should remain overflowing, spendthrift. Never be miserly, be a spendthrift!

PUJARI *One more question. I was wondering if we could have a week off to go to Goa.*

No need. Never go on a honeymoon, because that finishes everything. (laughter from the group)

In India we have the wisdom of ages. Divorce was not known, because there was a trick to marriage, and it was this: there was no honeymoon in the beginning, and no possibility of husband and wife being together in the day. People lived in joint families, and it was disrespectful for the husband and wife to be together in front of the elderly people.

There are cases of the husband not having seen the wife's face for years, because in the night, only in the dark, they would meet, and that too like thieves. Their love always remained a stolen love, and it carried a thrill. Whenever love is stolen it has a tremendous beauty.

In the West, marriage has been destroyed because the joint family disappeared, and the husband and wife are left together. Nobody else to fight with, they start fighting with each other, and sooner or later they get fed up with each other. Once you know each other then everything becomes old, a repetition and routine. Then the mind starts moving to another woman, another man — because the mind is always seeking something new, something novel.

My understanding is that sooner or later, if love is to be saved, the eastern wisdom has to be listened to again.

So leave it to me. Earn the honeymoon first, mm? When I see that you have earned it, I will send you. A honeymoon should not be the beginning of marriage, otherwise it becomes the end! It should be the climax of marriage, not the beginning. My feeling is that only old couples should be allowed to go on honeymoons, because they have earned it! Good!

DHARMA CHETNA   *I feel as though I am very old and set in my ways, and it is difficult to change.*

No, it is not difficult to change, but if you have the idea that it is, then it will become difficult. This idea can create trouble — nothing else. You can drop the old as easily as you drop your old clothes; nothing much is involved in it.

Nobody is set. Your being always remains free — because freedom is your inner nature, nothing can imprison you. This very moment you are totally free, because you are the doer, and you are greater than your doing, bigger

FREEDOM IS YOUR INNER NATURE

than your act. Whatsoever you have been doing you are free, already free!

If you have been angry, when the anger has gone you are free. There is no need to bother that you have been angry, so how can you be free of it? — you are already free, the anger has gone. It was a momentary thing that you have passed, you have overcome. If you want to repeat it you can, but that will be a fresh decision to be angry. Don't say that you are angry because you have been angry so many times before. You are not a machine. It is a fresh decision, a fresh commitment to be angry. You are always free to break with the past; nobody is holding you, nobody can ever hold you. Consciousness is absolute freedom. Once you understand this, you stop putting these wrong suggestions to yourself.

Tomorrow morning when you get up, get up new, and start behaving as though you are new. Make a new decision that you will cancel all old ones, and you will start living afresh. There is no barrier. I tell you this from my own experience, and working with thousands of people — that nothing is a barrier.

People are deceptive, and go on deceiving themselves saying, 'How can I drop it now? I have had this habit for thirty years; it will take thirty more years to drop it!' Then they will say, 'Now it has been sixty years, so how can I drop it right now? — it will take sixty years to drop. Then they say one hundred and twenty years. . . .

They will never be able to drop it. Just think of the mathematics. Either you drop it right now, or you cannot drop it. It is your decision; nobody is forcing you. But remember, if you want to repeat a habit, then it is through your decision to, again and again. Any moment that you want to break the contract with the habit, you are free to do so. The habit is a dead thing — you are alive! How can a dead thing hold your aliveness? No, nothing can hold it.

Contemplate, mm? meditate on it. Good Chetna.

PRABHU PRIYA

(face aglow) *I would like to tell you what happened to me in the group.*

Mm, tell me!

It was the most ecstatic thing that has ever happened to me in my life!
I've been living in a very dingy, dark prison cell, for about thirty years. I wondered who put me there, and who had the key; how I could get out. Since I've been in Poona, I realised that I was close to the key.
When I did this group with all these people, and had all of their energy and love, and especially him, (indicating Gopur, a former assistant leader, who led this group for the first time) *I realised that I had the key in my pocket.*

Very good!

Then I put it in the door and opened it — and then I got scared, because that's the only place I've ever been. Then your presence and love came through and it said, 'Don't postpone!' — and I walked outside into the sunshine!

I REALISED I WAS NEAR THE KEY

Very good! You still look ecstatic! It has been good —
now remember it, and make it a constant awareness;
otherwise one can go back into the cell.

PRIYA *The thing is, I think it's dissolved because...*

No, it is dissolved.

PRIYA *...it is my imagination.*

Yes, it is your imagination. The problem is that as you imagined it was dissolved, you can also imagine it is there! So don't forget.

I see many people many times coming to an insight, and then again they forget it. The sleepiness of the human mind is tremendous. Many times you can come to realise that you are out of it, and then you forget. So just for a few days, constantly remember that you are out. Nothing else needs to be done — just remain ecstatic, mm? Whenever you feel that again you are losing the grip, give a jerk to your energy, and become alert and ecstatic again. Do it just for a few days so that it becomes a constant feeling, a constant flow, then one day you forget about it.

It has been very very beautiful .... and I am always there!

ANAND GEET

My thing is about the key that Gopur offered — just, acceptance. I used to put myself in front of my eyes so that I couldn't see or feel what was going on around me. I've stopped that.

I became aware in the group of how I was doing that with my body, and how I felt about my body, and about people in general. I still feel that in the deepest emotions, particularly in relating to other people and accepting others, I'm putting up a wall.

Good.

I'd just like to mention one other thing that isn't to do with the group, but which happened this afternoon.

I realised that I've been here for one and a half months now, and I'd built up a nice neat little house of cards, and that I had a fixed image of everything, including you. I thought 'Well, I'll just do a few groups, and Bhagwan will take care of it all. Everything is going to be nice and easy...'

Then the whole thing fell down, and I felt very afraid at the openness of life....

(a little chuckle) Mm mm...

...seeing that you can't rely on things.

YOU ARE THE PRISONER AND THE GAOLER

It has been good, mm? The first thing is, that if you have become aware that you have been keeping a wall around you, then drop that wall! It is not only that it is there, you have to create it constantly — otherwise it disappears by itself. So, know that not only is the wall there, but that you are cooperating with it, creating it.

This is an imprisonment in which you are the prisoner, and you are also the gaoler — because only you are there! These divisions are just your game. So watch, and drop cooperating with the wall, and neither be a gaoler nor a prisoner. Then there is freedom. It is very easy to move from being a prisoner to being a gaoler; then one is very happy because it is an egoistic thing. But the wall remains, and you are still divided. Neither the prisoner nor the gaoler are needed — then the wall disappears by itself. So don't divide yourself. Accept your totality, as you are.

Because of the first insight the second insight happened. People who live in closed walls, in imprisonments, always go on creating more and more mental securities because they don't have a real life. They are always looking for a more peaceful life; a life of comfort and convenience mm? In fact they are asking for death, because life is troublesome, a struggle — and a beautiful struggle. It is a storm, but a beautiful one — wild. . . .

ANAND GEET   *I stopped judging.*

Yes, you stop judging and creating false securities around you, because they are all part of your imprisonment. Just live an open life!

Of course, I know there is fear with an open life. You live as if under an open sky. Nobody knows when the rains will come, and you have no umbrella, nothing with which to protect yourself. One lives always open to the hazards of the elemental forces. But that is what life is, and one grows through the storms.

By and by you don't ask for a comfortable life, because you understand that even in the greatest storm, there is a point within you that remains absolutely untouched — the centre of the cyclone. Once you have realised that the storm is all around, and just in the middle of it is the centre, absolutely peaceful, then you have understood.

Then there is no problem, and no fear. Then there is no death — because your life has become so tremendously alive that death is dissolved in it. Now even death is beautiful. So don't be afraid. Just a few steps and the fear will go by itself. Good!

Bhagwan turned lastly to Gopur, who had led the group and was feeling apprehensive about taking groups in the States. In reply Bhagwan said that by the time he was ready to go, he would prepare him. . . .

Always remember that you are a vehicle to me. So don't be worried; simply allow me to function through you, and then things will happen of their own accord. Just allow.

If you take it as a burden on your own, you become self-conscious, and that creates a worry. One hesitates, and that hesitation always creates a bad vibration, mm? When you are leading a group, if you hesitate the whole group will hesitate. But it is natural — if you are carrying the whole burden on your shoulders. So just leave it to me!

ALLOW ME TO FUNCTION THROUGH YOU

Whenever you feel that there is some problem that you cannot solve, tell the group to be silent for a few minutes, close your eyes, and remember me. Then open your eyes and start working, and immediately you will feel a change of energy, mm? Good!

Pujari, would you like to say something about Gopur's group?

PUJARI   *I thought it was the best one!*

Very good! Help him to be ready!

SATURDAY JANUARY 10th

BHAGWAN   How are things going?

PREM ANAND   Well, it's my fault if they're not going well. I'm isolating myself — and I feel I should be

IN ALONENESS YOU ARE INFINITE

> *doing something else. At first I felt good alone, but now it's changed.*

Then move out of it! One should always be watchful, because if one is not feeling happy in any situation, in any mood, then one should come out of it. Otherwise that becomes your habit, and by and by you lose sensitivity. You will go on being miserable and living in it, which simply shows a very deep insensitivity.

There is no need! If you are not feeling good in isolation, then come out of it. Meet with people, enjoy company, talk and laugh—but when you feel you are fed up with it, move into isolation again.

Always remember to judge everything by your inner feeling of bliss. If you are feeling blissful, everything is alright. If you are not feeling blissful, then whatsoever you are doing—something somewhere is wrong. The longer you remain in it, the more it becomes just an unaware thing, and you completely forget that it is through your cooperation that the miserable feeling continues. It needs your cooperation; it cannot exist by itself.

Human growth requires that one moves from one polarity to another. Sometimes being alone is perfectly good: one needs one's own space, one needs to forget the whole world, and to be oneself. The other is absent so you have no boundary to yourself—the other creates your boundary, otherwise you are infinite.

Living with people, moving in the world, in society, by and by one begins to feel confined, limited, as if there are walls all around. It becomes a subtle imprisonment, and one needs to move. One needs sometimes to be perfectly alone so that all boundaries disappear—as if the other does not exist at all, and the whole universe and the whole sky exists only for you. In that moment of aloneness one realises for the first time what infinity is.

But then if you live in it too much, by and by the the infinity bores you, it becomes tasteless. There is purity and silence—but there is no ecstasy in it. Ecstasy always comes through the other. One then starts feeling hungry for love, and wants to escape from this aloneness, this vast expanse of space. One wants a cosy place surrounded by others, so that one can forget oneself.

This is the basic polarity of life—love and meditation. People who try to live by love alone, by and by become very limited. They lose infinity and purity, and they become superficial. Always living in relationships means always living on the boundary where you can meet the other. So you are always standing at the gate, and you can never move into your palace, because only at the gate is the meeting-point where the other passes by. So people who only live in love, by and by become superficial. Their life loses depth. And people who live only in meditation will become very deep, but their life loses colour, loses the ecstatic dance, the orgasmic quality of being.

In the East people have tried to live by meditation alone, and they have become very very bored. Now in the West they are trying the other polarity: just trying to live by love. Life has become very superficial; just boundaries meeting, centres have completely disappeared.

Real humanity, the humanity of the future, will live by both the polarities together, and that's my whole effort. That's what I mean by sannyas—to live by both the polarities together: love and meditation. One should be free to move from one to another, neither polarity becoming a confinement. You should not be afraid of the marketplace, nor too much afraid of the monastery. You should be free to move from the marketplace to the monastery, and from the monastery to the marketplace

This freedom, this flexibility of movement, I call

sannyas. The bigger the swing, the richer your life. There are attractions to remain with just one of the polarities because then life is more simple. If you just remain with people, in the crowd, it is simple. Complexity comes with the contradictory, the opposite pole. If you become a monk or you go to the Himalayas and just live there, life is very simple. But a simple life which has no complexity in it loses much richness.

Life should be both complex and simple. One has to seek this harmony continuously, otherwise life becomes of one note, a single note. You can go on repeating it, but no orchestra can be created out of it.

So whenever you feel that something is now becoming troublesome, immediately move before you become unaware. Never make anywhere your home—neither relationships nor aloneness. Remain flowing and homeless, and don't abide at any polarity. Enjoy it, delight in it, but when it is finished move to the other—make it a rhythm.

You work in the day, by night you rest, so that again by the next day you are ready to work, energy regained. Just think of a man who goes on working all day and all night, or who goes on sleeping day and night—what kind of a life will that be? One will be a madness, the other a coma. Between the two there is a balance, a harmony. Work hard so that you can relax. Relax deeply so that you become capable of working, of being more creative. Good! Mm?

Many seekers may just 'happen' across Bhagwan on their search for a guide on their path. Some are mature people who have delved into many different techniques and paths alone; who have had a rich and varied experience of life and what it has to offer, but remain discontent on the road. . . .

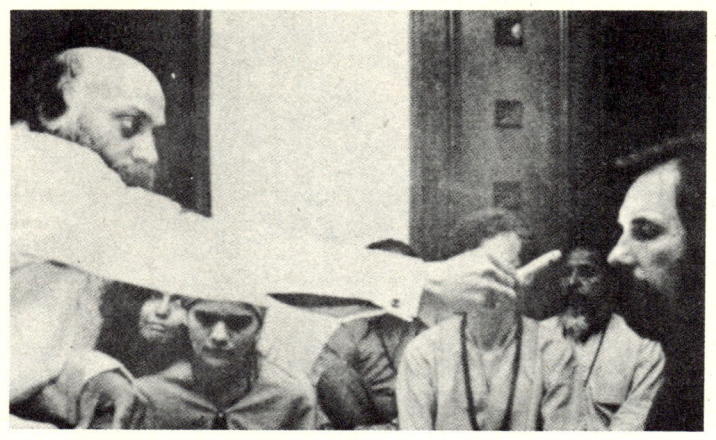

John had been in Poona for just two days before he met Bhagwan. He had been travelling for twenty years, and had had extensive experience in the theatre, writing, acting, producing and directing, and is a trained architect and engineer.

He had studied Zen for ten years in the States and prior to that had had some contact with Trungpa Rinpoche. More recently he has been leading encounter groups in Holland.

His curiosity and interest in Bhagwan became reinforced when he saw an old friend here, a sannyasin, whom he found to be incredibly changed. He made an appointment for darshan, for this evening. . . .

When did you arrive?

JOHN *Two days ago, Bhagwan.*

And you will be here for a few days or a few weeks?

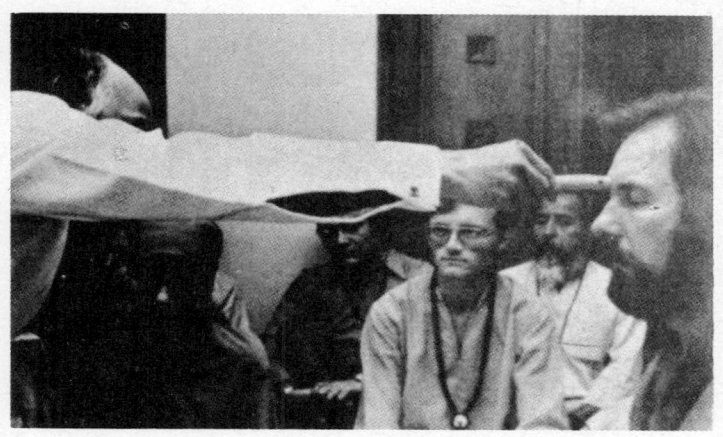

JOHN   *That depends on you! I came to India to give myself to a teacher. . . .*

That's very good!

JOHN   *I want to ask, are you my teacher?*

(smiling) Close your eyes, and if something happens in the body, allow it; if any movement, any energy flow comes, allow it.

    John started almost immediately to breathe deeply. Bhagwan shone his torch on John's forehead, on the third eye. Then John slowly lowered his head to the ground in a position as though he were going to do a headstand. Instead, he slowly rolled over into a loose foetal posture, then slowly lay on his back, sprawled out at Bhagwan's feet.
    Bhagwan, who had closed his eyes for a few moments, opened them. . .

Good! Come on, I am your teacher!
(much laughter)

Come on. . . and change to orange! I am going to change your name, so now you are a totally different man. John has died!

JOHN *Good!*

Mm, much is going to happen, this is just the beginning! This will be your new name: Swami Satprem. Sat means being — prem means love.

SATPREM *That's what I need!*

That's what you need . . . and much is going to happen. Just leave it to me and. . .

SATPREM *. . . just be!*

. . . just be! Good!

One of the newest therapies to begin in the ashram recently is Hypnotherapy.
The idea behind this technique is to help people to unlock unpleasant memories that have been pushed back into the inaccessible parts of their minds. When these feelings surface, the individual is encouraged to face and experience them and the old situation, in the light of his present growth.

DISCONTENT BRINGS CREATIVITY

Bhagwan talked recently in the morning discourse about Hypnotherapy, saying that it could be helpful in gaining insights and glimpses of one's past lives.

The implications of this are very important for one's growth, because once one sees that one is repeating a pattern of many lives past, patterns instantly change. . . .

It is because you have forgotten that you have lived lives before that you go on repeating the same nonsense again and again. We suppress that which is painful into our unconscious. This has to be brought up, because otherwise it goes on influencing your life, though you are unaware of it.

Bhagwan turned to the groupleader and asked how the group had been. . . .

SANTOSH *Well I'm never really content, but I'm happy.*

That's good! Leaders should never be content, but should always be happy! If you become content you cannot help people, because only discontent brings creativity.

Everybody is such an infinite possibility that at the most we touch only the boundary. Whatsoever is done is never satisfactory, because more was always possible. If you are not happy yourself, if you are in the same plight as others, you cannot help them; so you cannot become a leader if you are happy and contented.

In Buddhism there are two schools, one of which is mahayana, which means the great vehicle. The other school is hinayana, the small vehicle; a small boat that only one person can sit in. The school of the small vehicle used to say that it is not possible to help anybody, because the moment you become happy, you become contented—then who bothers? The Hinayanists have remained absolutely barren, because no creativity is possible—the moment you have achieved, it is the end! Your boat is ready and you go.

Mahayanists say that the vehicle is a big ship, and that one person can take many with him. But they say that before you become happy, you must have sown seeds of compassion; because if happiness comes before compassion then you will become contented. Compassion means discontent about others. Happiness means to be so contented with yourself that you can help others.

Buddha used to say to his disciples before each meditation, that whatsoever they achieved, they had to give to the people, offer to the world, and that the fruit of meditation should not become personal. Once you achieve it, you should distribute it immediately. Then you remain happy, tremendously happy, and at the same time tremendously discontent. That's the beautiful rhythm. One of the most beautiful things is to be happy and discontent together.

Otherwise a person who is happy becomes uncreative, and a person who is unhappy can create, but his creation is going to be like a catharsis, a diseased creation. He can only throw his disease and illness into his creativity, but that is not going to help; rather it will hinder.

So go on finding more ways to help people. And infinite possibilities are there. Each human being is just an opening of a space with no end. There comes no point where you can say that now the work is finished. The work of compassion is never finished.

A visitor who was leaving asked Bhagwan if there was anything he could say to help her in her meditation.

MEDITATION IS LIKE A SEED

Make it a regular habit. Just as one brushes the teeth and takes a bath, meditation should become just a part of your daily life; not something special and religious, but just ordinary. Once something is regarded as religious one starts feeling burdened.

If sometimes you miss meditation, it is nothing to worry about; but if one meditation can be started, after three months you will start reaping tremendous experiences. It takes at least three months for something to settle in your being so that you start welling up from it. It is just like a seed: it takes time to lose itself in the earth, and then it sprouts. So for a few weeks meditation brings no results; it simply sinks in, mm? One should not look for results but simply enjoy it.

After three months you suddenly become aware that something is sprouting which you have never known in you. A new facet of your being, something, starts flowering — you can almost touch it.

And not only you will become aware, but others will notice, without you saying, that you have changed, that something has happened to you.

PREM PRABHU

I'm feeling that I'm very false sometimes... and I also have this polarity between being alone, and not knowing whether I'm lonely or trying to seek aloneness. All these are mixed together.

Start doing one thing, and that is — don't try to change it. Be consciously false, exaggerate it....

Bhagwan went on to say that unconsciousness is the only problem in life, and that all other problems are just by-products of being unconscious. He said that consciousness is the only transformation, the only revolution, and that nothing else is needed.

About your loneliness and aloneness: it is always very difficult to see the distinction because it is very subtle, but you can feel it.

There are a few things. Firstly: if you are alone, a tremendous happiness is around you. If you are lonely, you are miserable, because loneliness means that you are missing the other. Aloneness means you are enjoying yourself, so it has a glow to it. Just being oneself is a tremendous delight. But when you are lonely you are depressed. Deep down you are still seeking and thinking of the other — friends, society, the club; somewhere to go, somewhere to get lost, be absorbed, so that you can forget yourself.

The taste is different. Loneliness is low energy, while aloneness is overflowing energy. Loneliness is something that you never want, it is as if you are a victim; but aloneness is something that you have desired, longed for — and now it is there. It is a deep achievement. Through it one can grow, but through loneliness one falls. Through loneliness one starts seeking others and uses them. Through aloneness, if it happens that others are around, one shares, but never uses them. But these distinctions will come by and by. . . .

First you have to watch whether you are feeling miserable or blissful. If it is misery, it is loneliness, so throw it! If it is aloneness, then close all the doors of the room and enjoy it. Dance, dance it! Let it be a profound experience of ecstasy. Or just sit silently as if you are the king of the whole world. Aloneness has to be cherished and nourished, and loneliness has to be avoided because it is like a disease, like a worm that goes on eating you from within.

ALONENESS SHOULD BE CHERISHED

PRABHU

> That's the problem. If you are in loneliness you will create a circle around you that is hard to come out of, because all the things you are doing are in some way neurotic — because you are seeking something — and so you go into people narrow-minded.

Mm mm, I understand. Ordinarily when people feel lonely they seek company; but that's not right, it is not going to help.

When you are lonely seek nature, not company. Go to the tree and talk to it. Go to the rock, touch it, feel it. Go for a long walk and feel your body against the wind. Do something with nature, because it is not company in the same sense that human beings are. In nature the company is there, but you are still alone — that's the difference.

Nature simply gives you silent company — unobtrusive, non-interfering; it doesn't force anything on you. Go to nature, and suddenly you will feel your loneliness changing into aloneness.

When you are alone, don't even go to nature, go into yourself. Try this, mm? Good!

SATYADAS

> ...the group was a very good experience for me, but I feel it can't help me completely. While I was in the group I was helped, but I don't believe that it can help me all my life.

No, this group will be helpful, but no group can become your life. A group is just an insight. It helps to give you an insight about yourself, shows you certain possibilities about yourself. It opens a window.

It is not a pilgrimage. It just opens a window and shows you a path. Then you have to follow the path — only then you reach the goal. So whatever glimpse you have attained from the group was for the time being, and can never become permanent.

It is like a seed. Let it sink into you. You can work it, help it to grow, and protect it. The world is against all inner insights, so protect it against the world. Let it become a little stronger so that it can protect itself. Then by and by it will change your whole life-style.

You will need a few more groups so that the same insight comes from different paths; so again and again a window opens, and you can see the path.

It is just like lightning on a dark night. You are lost and the night is dark; there seems to be no possibility of any morning. This is how the human situation is. Then suddenly there is thunder and lightning and everything becomes clear — just for a moment. In that moment darkness disappears. You can see the path ahead, you can even see the temples far away, but then it is gone.

Again there is darkness, and it is darker than before, but now you know that the path exists, that there is a goal. Now it may be difficult to reach, but it is not a hopeless quest. Now if you fail, it is your responsibility. Before, you could have said that there was no goal, nowhere to go, but now there is a responsibility. Deep down you know that if you seek and search, you will find it there somewhere.

So all groups are just like lightning in your confused state of mind. Don't expect more than that — and even that is too much! Don't expect that they will change you completely, because nothing can change you except

A GROUP IS JUST AN INSIGHT

yourself. But they can show the way, give you a glimpse, so that one feels confident and goes on moving, searching.

When you are thirsty, a group can simply show that water exists. It cannot give you water, but it shows you that it exists, so you know that to quench the thirst is not just a mad quest, something impossible. It is there waiting; one just has to make a little effort. So you do a few other groups, mm?

DHEERENDRA

I felt split by the group. While I was doing it I kept feeling that I didn't want to be there. But then I decided to commit myself, and to do all the structures as well as I could. Every time there's a structure I feel like I'm in a prison, especially after the Tao group. I just didn't want any more structures at all.

What happened in meditation was a freedom, I felt free. Here I felt I'd suppressed myself. Now I feel split. Like, if I shut my eyes, there's an energy, and a stillness too; so there's a split and I feel uncomfortable.

It happens to people because they don't understand the nature of freedom. A free person is one who, if he wills, can remain at ease in a prison; if he wants, can accept any discipline. Only prisoners are afraid of structure, and slaves are afraid of discipline.

A free person is never afraid of anything. As I see it, you have always remained structured, and you have become afraid of it, mm? If somebody brings alcohol near a person who is an addict, the person will at first become afraid of it, because if alcohol is there it is dangerous for him. But for one who is not an addict, there is no problem.

It is your fear, a fear of freedom. Your fear that you know you can cling to a structure has created the split. Try it next time in some other group, because it is only for three or four days, mm? You accept out of your freedom, nobody is forcing you.

Freedom is not licence, and does not mean no structure. It simply means flexibility, that one can move from one structure to another easily — from no-structure to structure, from structure to no-structure. If your freedom is afraid of being in a structure, then it is not freedom at all.

Just try to understand this, and the split will disappear. It is not there in your being, but just in your mind, just an idea. Drop the idea and enjoy freedom, and sometimes discipline.

Discipline has its own beauty, it is not all slavery. And freedom has its own dangers and is not all beautiful. A real person is always capable of infinite discipline and infinite freedom — he is not a slave or an addict to anything.

SUNDAY JANUARY 11th

An Indian sannyasin had come to darshan earlier to talk to Bhagwan about a frightening experience he had had recently while meditating.
As we entered, Bhagwan was saying:

... one gets really scared. Really, it came too early and you weren't yet ready. It can happen that suddenly a key fits, and then the experience of deep meditation is exactly like death.

The problem is created because one gets scared. Meditation leads you deep into yourself. Beyond a certain point it is felt like drowning, sinking, suffocating. If you accept it and cooperate with it and simply say that you are ready to die, then you don't create the opposite process of trying to come out of it. Then there comes a peak where all disturbance disappears. Something has happened — but you are still there. In fact for the first time you are there — and everything becomes blissful.

Before it comes to the peak there is pain and anguish, and it is natural that one starts thinking about how to get out of it somehow. In the getting out, that cooperation is broken, so you are moving now in two ways. Something you have done in meditation is taking you deep, while you are trying to cling to the surface. In that confusion and conflict, the whole body can feel in turmoil. It was not really because of the experience, but because you created the conflict.

This phenomenon has to be faced one day by anyone who is moving into meditation; there is no way to avoid it. When it happens one naturally becomes afraid to meditate again. So, don't do this method for a few days; do

something else. Humming is good. It is very slow, and will subdue the energy.

Do a camp, and if something happens then I am here, so you rely on me more easily. You could rely on me there too . . . but it was for the first time, so you were not aware of what was happening.

Next time it happens simply take the locket in your hand, and leave it to me. Simply say that you are ready to die, and relax; sink, and allow it. Once you allow it, the whole of the energy is moving in one direction so there is no inner conflict; and because there is no conflict there is no anxiety. The whole body will feel rejuvenated. Otherwise you create a disturbance.

It is just as when you are driving a car. You go on pushing the accelerator, and at the same time you brake: the whole engine feels the shock because you are doing two contradictory things—racing and braking simultaneously. That's what you have done. The meditation turned the energy inwards—and it is a tremendous experience, deeper than any death.

We are accustomed to live on the surface, and we think that that is life. We have forgotten our own depths completely. So when we encounter death for the first time, it is like an abyss, and fear takes over—because if one falls . . . it is bottomless.

This is the point where a master is needed. He is not needed in the beginning because one can start on one's own, but when this experience comes then someone is needed who can give assurance, who can give you confidence again, who can put you back on the path.

In a way it has been a blessing. It is rare, because usually people work for years before it happens. If you have worked for years there is not so much fear, because by and by you are gradually being prepared. Little glimpses of it come and go, so you know something of it and that it is going to happen.

WE HAVE FORGOTTEN OUR OWN DEPTHS

When it happens so suddenly, then either the body suffers or the mind — which is worse; some people can go mad. So both are possible. But you have to understand that it happened not because of the meditation but because you started fighting; you started to come up, to surface.

If you are in the river and you are caught in a whirlpool, the natural tendency is to somehow fight it. But this is wrong. Masters of swimming will tell you that if you are caught in a whirlpool, you should cooperate with it. If you go with it, if you give all your energy to it, there is no conflict, so no energy is wasted. At the rock-bottom of the whirlpool it is so small that it cannot hold you, so there is no need even to come out of it; you will be simply out of it. But if you start fighting it on the surface you are wasting your energy, and you will lose it before you get to the bottom; you will be gone.

Bhagwan gave the sannyasin a box, instructing him to place it in front of himself when meditating. He added that he would take care of him, but that he should avoid that particular meditation for a month or so. The sannyasin said that it was just like an explosion....

Yes, it was an explosion! People long for it all their lives! The opportunity was very close, mm?... but it will come again. That method is your method, and you have found the key!

MAHESH

I did the Gourishankar meditation, and with the very first breath I knew something was going to happen, and I got very frightened. Something physically happened ... I got very cold, and ... (crying)

I understand. Allow it. Close your eyes, and allow it, cooperate with it.

Mahesh cried for a few minutes and then went on to describe what had happened. . . .

MAHESH *Something cold was rising up, and something was happening here.* (indicating his third eye) *I took hold of the mala, because you had told me to when I get frightened. I was screaming for thoughts to come because there were no thoughts at all. But they wouldn't come!*

(chuckling) They won't come if you hold the mala!

MAHESH *I got very frightened.*

Yes, it happens, but it has been very good.

MAHESH *It gave me a feeling of being . . . cut. After it was over I was very ashamed that I didn't go through it.*

Yes, that too is right. It was good, mm?
It is such an unknown state when thoughts stop. We have always lived with thoughts—that is the known, the familiar; we are moving on a well-trodden path. When

you stop thinking for the first time, then the wildness of existence opens its door. It is chaotic. The greatest fear that can come to a man is to not be able to think. When you cannot think, you cannot be, for without thinking you disappear.

The father of modern western philosophy was René Descartes. His whole philosophy was based on three words: Cogito ergo sum—I think, therefore I am. If this is the mind: 'I think, therefore I am'—and it is—then when thoughts stop, you are not. One simply looks crazy, as if in an insane world, because what is happening is beyond control. You cannot even think—which was always so easy!

In fact it was difficult to stop thinking! But when it does stop, fear takes over. It is bound to happen the first time. The next time it will be easier. Don't try to do anything when it happens again. Just remain in it.

MAHESH *The fear was not leaving me this time when I held on to the mala.*

I was helping, but not in the way you wanted! But I will be helping, so don't be worried.

The Vipassana group came to darshan for the first time, all aglow and eager for more. The group runs for ten days, at least this first group did, but as things transpired during the evening, it may be extended.

Vipassana is described as 'the backbone of all southern buddhist meditation. Closely related to the Japanese zazen, it was referred to by Buddha as 'the only way'.

The groupleader explained the format as: 'a ten day experiment in mindfulness, without interruption or distraction of any kind. The technique of Vipassana, or insight meditation, is very simple. It includes one hour of sitting and watching the rising and falling of the abdomen, in inspiration and expiration. This is alternated with half an hour's slow meditative walking. The course is fully residential, and allows for no reading or writing for its entire duration. Silence will be maintained throughout.'

Bhagwan said in darshan several nights ago, that after everything has been brought up—through encountering and other techniques—Vipassana gives one 'a resettlement, a new pattern to one's being'.

Paritosh, (the leader) come here! Do you have something to say about the group, about your people?

PARITOSH (breathlessly) *It was fantastically steady, Bhagwan. I seemed to find it extraordinarily easy. I have done groups like this before with Buddhists who have been meditating a long time, and they were so much more restless, and fidgety. I don't understand it at all!*
(much laughter)

I am here! (laughing)

PARITOSH *...quite extraordinary, so still....*

Everything has been good.
Buddhist monks have made something ugly out of it.
No meditation should be a strain, because then it isn't going to help. It should be a play.

LEARN TO BE MORE ECSTATIC

PARITOSH
> *You said something about it being like a lizard basking in the sun ... and because I'd always found it very very voluptuous, I felt guilty about it, as though. ... It was such* a *pleasant meditation!*

Old religions depend on guilt, and they create it. Once they have created guilt in you, you are caught, and then you need their help. First they make you ill, so then you need their help.

But this is my whole point — that you are to learn how to be happy, how to be more playful. You are to learn how to be more ecstatic — and ecstatic in very ordinary ways. Life should be absolutely ordinary, and silent, and playful. All pressure should be removed from life so that the fountain flows freely.

We will create a totally different thing out of Vipassana. So many people want to go into it, so we can have another group. ...

Has anybody else from the group something to say?

RISHI
> *I enjoyed it very much. I would have liked to do it for three weeks instead of ten days. It was like sitting down to a fast in a very good restaurant — ninety percent eating, one percent fast.*
>
> *It was very good. I can't really say what has happened, but I feel I can sit now!*

You look more centred, more rooted. Good! That's how meditation should be — a celebration. Very good!

What about you?

PREM GEETA — *I loved it! I wanted to do it longer, because I think it started changing after seven days.*

Mm, it takes at least seven days to settle, then another seven days to feel the new dimension, then another seven to be completely at home. Twenty-one days is exactly the time the mind takes to change completely, to move into another direction.

For the first seven days it simply goes on struggling with the old; the old mind goes on interfering a little. After seven days that old is gone and the new is there, but you are unfamiliar with it, so it is a little strange.

After seven days again you become familiar with this. Now it is no longer new and you are settling in it. So we will make it twenty-one days.

GEETA — *And I just wanted to tell you that I am in love with Devesh.*

Very good! Out of meditation love should come!

Bhagwan turned to the sannyasin who had assisted in the group by being on the watch continuously for anyone who began to doze off. To help them return to a fully alert state, Venu had to gently but firmly hit them with a stick on the top of their head! (in the old zen tradition)

FROM MEDITATION COMES LOVE

What about you? Did you enjoy hitting people?
(to Paritosh) Was she good at hitting?

VENU — *I didn't have to hit very much!*

Not at all?

VENU — *Well I had to hit, but not very much. Gopal (her boyfriend) I hit the most! I found I got a lot of energy from it....*

Mm mm, it is very good. Who were the people who got hit? (Bhagwan glanced around the group) Doctor ... Asanga! How did you feel when you got hit?

ASANGA — *Very good when I got hit.*

Yes it is beautiful. In Zen, they wait, they pray for it. By and by you will wait and pray for it....

When you are starting to sleep, or dozing, then your energy is moving into another gear—from waking to sleeping. It is moving, changing. You are just at the door, neither alert enough nor asleep enough, and then—a hit on the head, suddenly an awakening inside, a lightning. You have been caught on the door! And that door, and the realisation of your being caught on the door, is something very beautiful.

By and by one starts praying for it. Who else was hit?

BUDDHA PREM — *I was hit several times, but for the first three times I thought something was happening inside my head! I was not aware that someone else did it.*

(laughing) It happens that way. The energy suddenly comes up. It can be a feeling of something inside happening.

Do you have something to say Gopal?

GOPAL — *Well sometimes I think I have a lot to say, but really there's nothing. It feels like there isn't anything to say.*

There is nothing—and that is something, mm? When you have nothing to say that means something has happened. Otherwise one has a lot to say, and it is meaningless; the chattering mind goes on, and to chatter is very cheap. It is a trick of the mind to avoid real problems. The mind goes on creating false problems, and you go on talking about them.

People ordinarily think that when they talk they are communicating. But the reverse is the case—they are avoiding communication, they are creating a wall of words around them. Watch yourself, and whenever you talk too much with someone immediately remember what you are doing. You are creating a wall so that you can hide behind it, so that the other cannot reach you and you become unavailable. It is not communication. It is isolating yourself through language and through words.

When you have nothing to say there is subtle communication. You say something without saying it, and your whole being becomes assertive.

SAYING NOTHING YOU SAY MUCH

Good! Whenever anybody says he has nothing to say, he has said something.

Members of the Enlightenment Intensive talked to Bhagwan next. . . .

MADHURI

In the group I found I was searching for fear. I was trying to find it, because I thought that I had to experience it in order to make it go away, but I was just looking for it all the time.

I found I'm really unaware all the time...

Mm mm, so what happened when you were looking for fear?

MADHURI

I have these thoughts all the time that I have to do this, I have to do that — that I have to go looking for fear and experience it, and wring everything out of it.

I feel almost ready to trust. . . . In the group, when a piece of fear came, if I didn't do anything, if I was conscious at the point of doing, it would go away, and that would happen all by itself.

You have a habit, and a very deep-rooted habit, of being a doer — something has to be done. Nothing has to be done! Life is a given thing, and nothing has to be done.

(Madhuri starts weeping)

All that you need is already given. One has just to enjoy it, to delight in it. You are wasting time in doing things.

MADHURI — *But the doing is so minute.*

It is. I understand.
Drop it, and when I say drop it, don't start doing!

MADHURI — (laughing) *I think I'll practically have to become enlightened before I stop doing!*

No, it is going to happen any day. All that is needed is a small understanding — that everything is given, and nothing is lacking. You just have to start delighting in it, and the more you delight, the more possibilities start opening, the more capacity arises. There is nothing else to do.

In the West the mind is constantly trained to do something, to be active, because if you don't do anything you will not achieve anything. So a mind to achieve has been conditioned. In the East we have been thinking in totally different terms. We say not to be a doer; you already have everything.

MADHURI — *In the group the fear came and went by me like a comet.*

THERE IS NOTHING TO DO

Mm, everything comes and goes. You are just a witness, and nothing really happens to you. You just remain untouched.

It is just like a bird that comes into a room. He flies around in the room, afraid, then he goes out a window. A little fluttering, then he is gone. Your mind is just like that: a small window through which thoughts and emotions come and go. If you simply remain a witness, doing nothing, they go.

Have you sometimes tried to help a bird to go out if he has entered your room? You make him more confused. He may become so afraid that he hits himself, wounds himself. Never try to help a bird if he has entered your room. Just sit quietly, and he will go of his own accord. Your compassion is not needed; it can be dangerous, mm? murderous.

So don't do anything about what happens in the mind. Just watch. But don't make it a serious affair; just watch deeply relaxed, because there is nothing to do, so why be tense?

BODHIDHARMA
I still have this — I don't know whether it's resistance to groups. Like, I feel more attracted to the deeper silent meditations, but I always have the uncertainty about whether there's something I'm suppressing and should go into. There's always a doubt.

I think an Encounter group will be helpful. There is not much there, but even if a little is there, it can become a problem in Vipassana. Vipassana should be done only when you have finished with catharsis, otherwise it will become a struggle.

That's what is happening in buddhist monasteries. They don't have cathartic methods, they simply teach Vipassana, and then it becomes suppressive. When you try to suppress something it becomes a fight.

That was the difference here — because these people are doing dynamic meditation and cathartic methods; Encounter groups and Primal Therapy. Their minds are clean, and they have nothing to suppress, so they could enjoy it tremendously. So I suggest you do Encounter first, and then do Vipassana.

All the methods that are being used in the West are cathartic, and all that have been used in the East are non-cathartic. My effort is to bring a new synthesis to them. The western methods should be used in the beginning so that one is clean and has thrown out all repressions. Then the eastern methods should be used, because then they go to the very core of your being. You enjoy them then, and there is no effort involved; they are almost effortless. Things settle by themselves while you simply sit and watch. But right now, if many things are there and you try to sit, they will bubble up, and you will go on thinking and thinking and thinking about them.

Always remember the difference between isolation and solitude. This is the difference. Isolation is a sort of suppression — forcing yourself to be still, being alone, cutting yourself off from other people. Solitude is not isolation. You are not cutting anything, because there is nothing to cut. You are not trying to be alone; you are simply alone, and there is no effort involved.

Vipassana in buddhist monasteries has become isolation, and I would like it to become a solitude. Isolation is negative, because one wants to break all communication with the world. One is fed up with all relationships and with love. One simply wants to withdraw into oneself.

DIP INTO YOUR OWN BEING

The whole thing is negative. You are left in a negative emptiness, a sort of darkness.

Solitude is very positive. It is not going away from society, or cutting relationships. On the contrary, it is not a withdrawal but a dipping into your own being; it is an in-going. In withdrawal the focus is on the other, you are going away from the other. In solitude the focus is no longer on the other, you are simply sinking into your own being. Before you can communicate, you have to enter into your own shrine to bring something to share.

It is just like a well from which you draw water. If you draw continuously and don't leave any gap for the well to renew itself, to refill, it will become dry. So for a few hours you leave it alone so it is again overflowing.

Solitude is like that. One becomes depleted leading the ordinary life — with the thousand and one problems and anxieties and worries. Solitude is like moving into your own world to become revitalised, to be rejuvenated, refreshed and overflowing, so that you can come back to the world again and share.

Vipassana becomes isolation if you are suppressing something. It is a withdrawal and a fear-oriented thing; basically ill. Vipassana can be very healthy and wholesome if you are not withdrawing but just going in to come back again. It is not a renunciation, a rejection of the world — it is just a rest into oneself.

What was your experience of the group?

BODHIDHARMA *I had found when I first came here that my mind slowed down, and it felt good, but I found it difficult to keep talking.*

I understand. That's a good sign — you are getting ready for Vipassana!

BODHIDHARMA
Well it must have been a good sign, because this morning when I woke up, I never felt more asleep in my life. I'd done no work whatsoever, and I felt totally asleep! I think that's because I was more aware of my sleep.

It can happen, it is possible. In fact if you are not really aware, your sleep becomes superficial. When things deepen, everything deepens, so when you become more aware your sleep also becomes deeper.

It is not the other way around. The higher the awareness, the deeper the sleep. If your awareness is just dim it means that already a little sleep is there, so there is no need for your sleep to be so deep. They are always in proportion. It is just like when you work hard in the day you can rest deeply in the night. If you rest in the day, then in the night there is insomnia.

One person used to be with me for a few years. I had given him a method to work out — a very intense method of awareness. For three months he worked hard, the effort was really hard, and after that he fell into a coma. A coma! —for four days. His family became very afraid and wanted to call a doctor, but I said not to disturb him, otherwise his whole life would be disturbed.

He came out of it as if coming out of death, totally renewed. He had not had a single dream in those four days. The sleep was absolute, as if everything had stopped. He relaxed as if he had not been asleep for many years, many lives.

DEEP LOVE BECOMES MEDITATION

So it is possible, and there is nothing to worry about. The opposite polarity always happens. If you meditate very deeply, suddenly one day you will find you have fallen in love. If you love very deeply, one day or other, suddenly you will become aware of a new dimension which is opening its door — the dimension of meditation.

If you love deeply, one day or other you will become meditative, and if you meditate deeply, you are going to become a lover. So if somebody is trying to be meditative without being in love, he is just trying to fool existence, and existence cannot be fooled! If anybody is trying to live just a life of love without being bothered about meditation, he is trying the impossible.

ANAND DEVA *I thought much would come up from my past but nothing came up, but I did not feel I was hiding. . . .*

I understand your situation. This was your first group, so Primal will help you — it goes into the past.

ANAND DEVA *I think I can just forget about the past. It never bothers me, and I never think about it.*

Then you come here! (sounding fierce) It never bothers you?

(more laughter)

ANAND DEVA (hesitant) *Well, I was just going to say something more that bothers me...*

(chuckling) It has already started! From tomorrow it will start bothering you!

It is there, and you cannot just forget it. It has to be consciously removed, and consciously dropped. You do the Primal, mm? You can forget about the past, but it will go on hanging in the shadow, manipulating you in millions of ways, but you never become aware; you remain a puppet....

VIMAL KIRTI (looking intense and serious) *Please give me a new name.*

(chuckling) What is the matter?

KIRTI *It doesn't feel right anymore. This morning I woke up and it felt old, like a skin hanging around me.*

Mm, that's very good, it has been a good experience.

You are not the name. Every name is just a utility, a label to be used — otherwise you are nameless. So I can give you another name, but after two days it will become old. Once it is given, it is already old. It has been a very good experience, because now you know that you are not the name.

YOU ARE NAMELESS

KIRTI *I feel young now, I...*

I understand. You will feel younger and younger. But it will become difficult to change the name again and again. Others will start coming, and I'm already short of names!

(gales of laughter)

MONDAY JANUARY 12th

The sannyasins who had done the Aum marathon had darshan this evening. The marathon is, 'a forty-eight hour intensive, ego-awareness, and ego-reducing, encounter group. Within the structure given by Bhagwan, situations will be created, the emphasis being on awareness, exposure of blocked and reflex emotions, and avoidance mechanisms.

Techniques from the various therapies, including bio-energetics, gestalt, synanon, energy awareness, and meditations, will be used — but mostly the moment will determine what happens.

There are short breaks for eating and sleeping, but the group stays together for the entire duration of the marathon. No physical violence is permitted.'

Bhagwan read a letter that the groupleader had sent in to him prior to darshan. He then turned to Veeresh and asked him if he had anything else to add.

BE RESPONSIBLE AND FREE

VEERESH *I realise that a lot is myself ...I've been a leader in the West, and I've been looking into myself about what throws me off a bit about doing a marathon here.*

It's almost like I'm ... I've never had anyone to account to. I started to look at what I'm doing, and I realise that a lot is wanting to please you, to get your approval. I think that was important for me.

The marathon seemed to be turning out better for the leaders than for the participants, from my point of view.

BHAGWAN Mm mm, I understand. I was thinking that it was going to happen that way, because you have been working on your own. Of course you could have more freedom that way, and there was no one you were accountable to. So it was easier; you could do things more spontaneously. I am here, and that was constantly in the background. That became a problem for your leadership. You could have dropped it — and then it would have been a great maturity for you.

To be free in the sense of being irresponsible is not really freedom. Being responsible and free has something of tremendous value in it. Responsibility becomes a growth for you too, so not only the participants, but the leader too is part of the whole group. If you are working on your own you don't grow through it — you can't, because you remain outside. So you help people — you push and pull and manipulate and force, and you create an urgency in them — but you remain an outsider.

That's what I have been feeling, not only about you, but about all the groupleaders who have come here — and many more will be coming. They have been helpful to other people, but they have not been helpful to themselves. In fact they are in a mess. When I say that, I don't mean that they have not been helpful; they have been tremendously helpful, but they have become divided. Their own personality is just standing outside the group, and they have become technicians. So they use a technique, and they help others, but they have a dual personality. When they are dealing with others' problems they are very true to the point; they know exactly what should be done. But when it comes to their own problems they completely forget their own advice, their own wisdom.

I wanted it this way so you become aware that you still have to grow. Sometimes helping others can become an escape, because you forget your own problems. There is no time or space to think about them; so many people, so many problems that you have to solve. You always have to be the wise guy, so you remain outside. How can you bring up your own problems? If you do, it will be difficult to help others, because they become unconfident about you. So you have to pretend that you are absolutely certain about what you are doing. The act helps others, it certainly helps, but for your own growth it is poisonous.

By and by you will forget completely that you were acting. Your problems will remain in the unconscious, waiting, but by and by you will stop looking at them. In fact you will avoid them whenever they come up.

This is not only for you, but for all groupleaders. This is so for Divya (the Primal Therapy leader, who was also present). She is perfect in helping others; then her technical knowledge functions. But when it comes to her own problems all technical knowledge flops.

I wanted it to become difficult for you because only then can you become aware that helping is good, and being of service to people is good, but you should not be

lost in it. It is your growth, finally, for which you have to do something.

In this group suddenly you were not a leader but a participant too, because I was waiting outside the group. I was forcing you into the group, and that became the problem, and because of that you were not so certain about yourself. That's why you thought that the group was average, below average, but it wasn't. The leader wasn't perfectly a leader. I was pulling your leg. The group was perfectly good, but you were missing your confidence, so your problems were coming in.

That's how I managed the whole thing. I had forced Sudha to be in it, with Asha there too, and you were in trouble. One woman is enough to create trouble, but your beloved and your ex-wife were both there. They created much trouble; not that they created it, but their presence was there—watching you, watching where you were going, and what you were doing. And on top of it, I was watching continuously! So I know it was difficult, but it can become a very very valuable insight to you.

Next time simply relax. You need not be worried

about my approval. What you do is not the point, but what you are. Whether you do or not, succeed or fail, is irrelevant. My approval is unconditional, and you can rely on it. You can be a failure and rely on it; you need not bother about being successful.

So next group, rather than working on your own, allow me to work through you, and then you will see the difference. Just work as a vehicle. Whenever you feel hesitant or uncertain, close your eyes and remember me. Suddenly you will feel a bridge between you and the sannyasins.

You have been working with other types of groups, and this was totally different. You belong to me, and they all belong to me. Other groups were all individuals. They were crowds, because each individual existed separately. This, for the first time, was a group, because the sannyasins are not a crowd. They belong to me, and are my family. They have a certain affinity with each other.

That also created trouble — the group was bigger than the leader. You could have tackled each individual easily, but it was not simply a group, mm? This time you made it a problem, and that was your mistake. You could have used it. This time you thought I was coming in between, because they repeated my words, hid behind them. So it became a problem for you — but next time you can use it.

In fact anything that can become a hindrance can become a help. The same stone or rock on the path can become an obstacle or a stepping stone. If you can struggle a little and climb the rock, you can reach a higher point of vision — and through using the rock. Next time use me, and then you will see that they are not hiding behind my words. You also try to become my vehicle, and then suddenly you will see there is a bridge, and you will never again find such a beautiful group.

MY APPROVAL IS UNCONDITIONAL

When you go on working with groups, with people, a certain subtle ego goes on being strengthened. Drop that ego! Next time work as my vehicle, my medium, and just be instrumental. Don't let Veeresh be there, but just my sannyasin helping other sannyasins. You need not be a leader really, but at the most, a catalytic agent. Then you will see a totally different phenomenon arising.

But it was going to be like this for the first group. Next time relax, mm? and work totally differently, and much will happen. Much has happened in this group too. I will ask people now individually, and you will realise that much has happened, but you were so worried you could not see it. Wait here...

(addressing a sannyasin from the group) Were you in the group? Come here and contradict Veeresh!

VIPASSANA — *Where to start? I have one important question. Once you said that if your meditation is going right, then there is no need to go back into the past. I don't know whether I should go back into the past more, or if my meditation is going right and I should go on with that.*

Mm mm, I will tell you later on. First tell me about the group and how it was for you.

VIPASSANA — *Well, all the emotional things, catharting things, seemed to be superficial on the one*

> *side, yet on the other seemed to be true, as I feel them. I don't know if it is because of my knowing it or.... It's not acting or theatre, because I feel it. Perhaps it's because I'm aware of it, and that's why I see the difference, that's why I see myself doing it.*

If you become aware, then everything becomes superficial, outside you. When a moment of awareness is there, then nothing is deep; everything is outer and superficial because you are standing at the innermost core of your being. From that vantage point everything is superficial. For example we are sitting here in the porch. It is not on the outer or superficial, but from inside the house it will be just on the boundary, on the surface.

The more aware you become, the more things will become superficial. One can become scared sometimes, because even love will look superficial. If you watch and are alert, then whatsoever you do will look like acting, because you are no longer identified with it. It is no longer an act, but acting.

So a really aware person becomes an actor on the great stage of the world. He is never in anything deeply. He cannot be, because something transcendental is always there. Whatsoever he is doing he is always far away. Not that he is not authentic. He is, but he is so deep himself that nothing can be deeper; anything relative is superficial.

This is a good insight. Nourish and enjoy it more, and don't start condemning because then you will miss the whole point. Don't start saying that this is superficial and that nothing deeper is coming—there is nothing deeper.

YOUR CONSCIOUSNESS IS DEPTH ITSELF

When consciousness is there, that is the most profound and the deepest thing there is. Even if God is standing there He will be superficial, because He cannot be deeper than your awareness. He will be an object of awareness, just like any other object. Your consciousness is depth itself, abysmal. So it has been a good insight.

Now try to live it twenty-four hours a day. Accept it, and don't condemn it. It is beautiful, and everything will look superficial and like acting.

VIPASSANA   *It's very strange . . . like a dream.*

Yes, it looks like a dream. It is! That's why in India, people who have attained to higher consciousness have called the world maya, illusion. It is not that it is unreal, but their depth is such that from there everything looks unreal in comparison. So enjoy it, and don't be puzzled by it, because in the beginning it is confusing.

You need not go into the past, but just remain more and more alert. The need to go into the past is because you are not aware. Veeresh, this has to be understood. In the West, going into the past has become very very prevalent. Since Freud, to go into the past, into one's memories and dreams, has become very important, and now even more important because of Primal Therapy. It seems that it is the only way to get rid of the past; but there is another way which the East has tried.

Whatsoever you call your past is present right now, in this moment. When you go into your childhood you go in the present tense, because you can never go in the past. You can remember it, but that childhood, and the concept and the memories, are all present herenow.

As we move, the whole past moves with us, and it goes on growing in us. We are carrying it, containing it.

In the East we have tried a more simple method which is quicker and more valid. It is just to become aware of the present moment. There is no need to go anywhere, past or future, but just to be totally aware of the content of the mind, whatever it is. Suddenly the bridge is broken, and you are no longer concerned with it. It is as if it is somebody else's life, and no longer your autobiography. You are just the watcher, and the watcher has no autobiography, because in that depth nothing ever happens, there are no events. It is simply pure and uncorrupted.

So you can go into the past and try to clean your mind of all memories. But it is almost impossible to finish if you do this, because the moment you have finished with this life, another one immediately starts. When you have finished with that one, another life. . . . Buddha tried it, but it is non-ending.

When you have finished with your lives as a human being, you have still to go into your lives as animals and trees and rocks, and you can go on and on. In fact, (turning to Divya) you never really come to the primal. To come to the primal means to come to the very beginning of existence, and that's not possible! There has never been any beginning, because existence is without a beginning; it has always been there. If you go on cleaning, it is non-ending. You can clean a little spot, that's all, but you cannot clean your whole being.

Then isn't it possible to reach to the purest point in you? It is possible, directly, now, with no need to go into the past. You can take a jump directly from the present moment, and become alert and aware. Suddenly everything is just on the surface, just ripples on the surface, and you are not bothered. In fact you don't belong to it, nor it to you. A great distance exists between you and all that has happened to you. It is good to try, mm? then one becomes more aware — but there is no need for you to. Just become more and more aware.

That's why I have given you the name Vipassana — it means awareness!

Just remain alert, and happily alert. Don't make it a serious thing; be happily, joyfully alert! Good Vipassana!

Who else was in the group? If anybody has something to say, they can come.

VIYOGI

> *I feel that my heart is opening. I don't know what exactly has happened in this group, but I can feel it.*

Very good. There are things that you can only feel but never say, and they are the real things. Things that you can relate and describe are worthless. When something really happens it is indescribable. You cannot say it but you can feel it; it permeates your whole being.

Try to live from the heart more and more. Whenever it happens that your heart is feeling a little open, don't miss that opportunity, because the door to the divine is open in that moment. Catch hold of it and taste it as much as you can, so by and by it becomes part of your life.

Feel more — because you had a closed heart — and if a little opening has come to it, help it to become more and more open. Otherwise you will fall again and again into the old pattern and your heart will close again. Then it will remain a memory; then by and by you start forgetting, wondering if it really happened or not.

It is real, but make it more real. Wherever you can find a situation in which you find you can feel — listening to the birds, or singing to the sky, or just sitting silently doing nothing — use it, so that your heart can open more easily, all the petals open.

After such groups you are very sensitive for a few days. If you don't use that sensitivity then you will become closed again and dull, and things will go back into the old pattern.

DAYAL   *I feel a similar dropping from here* (indicating his head) *to here* (indicating his heart).

Dayal has changed tremendously since first taking sannyas several months ago.

When he had his first darshan he seemed ill at ease, pale and tense, and had a nervous habit of rolling his eyes, of which he was quite unaware. There was an awkwardness in his movements, and a sense of hesitation about him.

Now he no longer suffers from the asthma that had been with him for much of his life. Tonight he sat at ease in front of Bhagwan, talking freely, laughing and smiling spontaneously and often. His whole being seemed grounded, as though he was more connected with the outside world, and more in touch with his inner one. . . . .

Very good! Close your eyes, and just feel your heart dropping so I can see. Whatsoever happens, allow.

Dayal sits with his spine erect and hands, palms down, on his knees. He begins to breathe deeply, the ingoing breaths becoming increasingly deeper and deeper. Bhagwan shines his torch on Dayal's face, on the place of his third eye. After a few moments, Bhagwan lowers his torch. . . .

DEATH NEVER HAPPENS TO YOU

Good Dayal! Come back, slowly. Very good. No need to say anything!

A member of the group said that he had told the group that he felt he wanted to make a breakthrough, so the group had formulated a structure in which Asutosh was made to lie down, and be as if dead.

They covered him with a blanket, and said that now he was dead and that he felt cold so he really must be dead, etc.

Asutosh told Bhagwan that he had not felt dead at all, and that when he heard them talking, he had felt it wasn't true at all.

The same is going to happen when you really die. Then too it is false, because nobody ever dies. It has been a good insight. So remember on the day you die that it is just like when you 'died' in Veeresh's group! It is just as false as this, because death is a drama. Real death is not real, so how can a dramatic death be real! It was just to give you an insight, and it has been good.

Nobody ever dies; it is just a belief of yours and of other people. Death is always outside, it never happens to you. So just do one thing...

Every night before you go to sleep, lie on the bed for five minutes and think that you are dying; enact the whole drama. Remember the group surrounding you, talking about you as if you are dead, but you knowing you are not. But go on thinking you are dying. And thinking . . . thinking . . . fall into sleep.

Soon you will become aware that when you think you are dying, something in you—your body and your mind—lose their grip, but you become more and more alert. You feel more and more deathless.

It is one of the old meditations. Buddha used to send his disciples to the hindu cemetery, shmashan, to watch dead bodies being burned. Every disciple had to go, and had to remain there for at least three months, day and night. Many people would come to burn bodies and the disciples just had to sit and watch. The meditation was to think that it was their body that was being burned, that was in among the flames.

One day, suddenly they would understand the whole thing and start to laugh — because they would understand that it is only the body that dies and nothing else!

Bhagwan spoke next with the sannyasin to whom, last darshan, he had said to simply be herself; that she was not to try to do anything against her resistance to changing, but was to attend all the groups — even if she just sat in the corner and watched.

Nayana said she hadn't been a good group member, and had felt tired and disinterested. At the same time she had felt guilty when the group confronted her about her attitude.

No, I only send you into the groups to create trouble! You do it perfectly well, because now all the groupleaders are afraid of you! (much laughter from the group; pained expressions from the groupleaders!) A trouble-maker is needed, otherwise things become too easy for the groupleaders. So you remain the way you are. Now which group are you going to do?

(more laughter)

Nayana counted off on her fingers all the groups she had done, which were all those available except Vipassana. Bhagwan said she could rest for a few days, and then do the Vipassana, adding:

MIND IS RUBBISH

But you are not to defeat anyone there because there is nobody to defeat, no groupleader, nothing, mm? It is going to succeed because in this group you are alone, so if you defeat anyone you defeat yourself.

It is up to you whether you do it or not. It may suit you perfectly because there are no enforcements, nothing. And it is not cathartic, there is nothing you have to bring out. You simply have to sit silently and move within.

There is nothing wrong. All these groups have been helpful because you have become more aware of things that are within you: your ego, your resistance and fight, your non-cooperation. It is as if the whole world is at stake if you change. You are clinging to something that is not worth clinging to. But it is perfectly natural, there are people like that. There is nothing to feel guilty or condemned about.

As far as I am concerned, you have been very helpful! Even if you change later on, I will send you to a few groups just to create problems! You are my representative there!

ARCHANA
> *. . . for me it was more an experience of seeing the conditions I put on my growth. And as he (Veeresh) says, I have so much rubbish—but I can't find it, I can't find it. . . .*

Mind is rubbish! It is not that you have rubbish and somebody else hasn't. It is rubbish, and if you go on bringing rubbish out, you can go on and on; you can never bring it to a point where it ends. It is self-perpetuating rubbish, so it is not dead, it is dynamic. It grows and has a life of its own. So if you cut it, leaves will sprout again.

Bringing it out doesn't mean that you will become empty. It will only make you aware that this mind that you thought is you, with which you have been identified up to now, is not you. By bringing it up, you will become aware of the separation, the gulf, between you and it. The rubbish remains but you are not identified with it, that's all. You become separate, you know you are separate.

So you have only to do one thing for seven days: don't try to fight with the rubbish, and don't try to change it. Simply watch, and just remember one thing, 'I am not this.' Let this be the mantra: 'I am not this.' Remember it, and become alert and see what happens.

There is a change immediately. The rubbish will be there, but it is no longer a part of you. That remembrance becomes a renunciation of it.

Try it, mm, and after seven days tell me how things are going.

KAVITA

> *I didn't do the whole group. All of a sudden I felt, 'Now it's enough!' I...*

(laughing) Good! So just in the middle you?...

KAVITA

> *I did it up to as far as I felt I had not finished things. All of a sudden I started to feel finished with it. The thought came, and my body was feeling really calm. Then I thought that it was an escape, that I should stay there, but then at one o'clock in the night something happened, and I thought, 'No! Now I'm going. Enough!'*

LISTEN TO YOUR INNER VOICE

(still chuckling) Very good! And how have you been feeling since?

KAVITA *Really good . . . I've got certain habits, but I'm not aware how to change them I guess.*

No, there is no need to change anything. Just awareness is enough—things change on their own.

KAVITA *Well that's what I thought when I left.*

You have not done anything wrong. When your inner being says that that is enough, it is enough.

You have to listen to your own inner voice. Even if it leads you into error, takes you astray, you have to listen to it then too. One has to learn to listen to one's inner voice, and to interpret it. You will commit mistakes a few times, but by and by they will become less, till the time it becomes absolutely clear. So always listen to it.

KAVITA *Grown-up people from my childhood have tried to condemn me. They have always said it is wrong.*

Yes, grownups have that habit. (laughter) They enjoy condemning people. But don't be worried. They are not grownups, mm? They have remained a little childish. When they were children, grownups tried this trick with them, so now they are repeating the same with others.

This is how diseases go on perpetuating themselves for centuries. You cop out of it! Don't condemn anybody. Even if you feel that the other is absolutely wrong, don't condemn him. Condemnation is more wrong than any wrong.

Never condemn anybody — that is the quality of a religious person, who accepts and doesn't interfere. Good Kavita.

ASHA (who helped assist the group) *I felt that what I learnt from the marathon is that I have an incredible need to control. I just don't understand what you are saying right now. I understand it, but I don't. I understand the words, I hear them, but. . . .*

I became really aware that I have a huge ego, really huge, and I don't feel that it's healthy. The more I'm hearing, the more I feel that it isn't healthy for people in the groups. I'm probably causing more damage than. . .

(almost sadly) It causes damage. It causes damage to you, and to others. It is poison, but you are not yet fed up with it.

That too, you are just saying. You are still nourishing and feeding it. In fact you are afraid that if it leaves, you will be left in a ditch or a vacuum. You are safe-guarding and protecting it in every way, so that it can remain.

We can become addicted to our misery, and rather than becoming empty, we would rather go on being miserable. Rather than being nobody, one would prefer

SUFFERING IS THE ONLY TEACHER

to be the most miserable man in the world. At least one is the most miserable!

This is stupid, but ego is stupid; not your ego, but ego as such, and one has to understand this some day. The understanding cannot be forced, so you have to live it, to suffer a little more. But you will suffer, and then by and by. . . .

There is no other teacher than suffering. You have suffered a lot, and you are suffering now, but you go on hiding it. That's why you seem to listen, seem to understand, and yet no understanding happens.

Bhagwan broke off to address another leader who was apprehensive about taking future marathons alone when Veeresh returned to England in several months.

Bhagwan reassured her saying that she could drop the fear because she was going to take them! That was settled so now she need not be worried!

NEERJA

> *I became aware in this group how much I cop out of everything. It has been obsessing me a lot since the group finished. I've been feeling that nothing's ever finished.* (close to tears)

Accept it, there's no need to. . . .

NEERJA

> *And there's so much. Every time I touch on something I think it's out — but there's so much more. It seems like I should never have touched one block — because now I've got hundreds of blocks.*

No, nothing to worry about. Just don't create a problem out of this. Accept it. This is your way, this is how you are.

I call this maturity—to accept oneself as one is. Don't create an ideal that you should not be like this, that you should not cop out, that you should finish everything.

'Shoulds' have to be dropped. Be natural! Whatsoever happens naturally is good, and all shoulds are repressive. If you are feeling like copping out, cop out! It will be wrong and you will be going against nature if you force yourself and remain in it.

Everyone should feel their own spontaneity. When you feel you want to withdraw, withdraw; when you want to be with someone, be. If you only want to half do something, only half do it. There is no urgency to complete it.

NEERJA *But I've always done that! I always do things half.*

There is nothing wrong in it, nothing wrong in it. You have an idea that one should do things completely. That idea is creating the trouble. There is nothing wrong in it! You half do things—why be worried about it? That worry is your own creation.

One should start loving oneself, accepting oneself, because there is no other way for you than to be yourself. Just accept, otherwise you will create misery.

All 'shoulds' are dangerous, and all ideals and perfectionist ideas are very very dangerous. There is no need for them! Whatsoever you can do, do, and enjoy it. When you feel that you want to get out of it, simply get out—with no grudge, no grumble or guilt, so you remain clean and pure.

ALL 'SHOULDS' ARE DANGEROUS

NEERJA (still distressed and seemingly unplacated) *I've got so much guilt!*

It is you who create it, nobody else.

NEERJA *It came out in the group. When I came to see you about Siddharth,* (her son) *you said, 'Don't have any more guilt.' Then I was talking to Sudha,* (one of the groupleaders) *and suddenly I realised that on a conscious level I was saying to myself 'Bhagwan says you should have no more guilt', so I thought I had none. But I still have some, deep inside!*

So accept it! That is what the problem is! If you have guilt, accept that too. Now you will create another should—that one should not have guilt—and then you feel guilty about that!

I am saying that whatsoever you are, relax and accept it. That's the way God wants you to be, otherwise why should He make Neerja? He should have made a second Veeresh!

So don't be worried — there is no need.

A sannyasin said that since he had been in India he had been receiving letters from his wife, which were becoming increasingly demanding. At first he had felt disturbed, but he said that he now no longer felt guilty; he felt she could cope without him for some time more.

Bhagwan said that it was good that he no longer felt guilty because if ne did feel guilty and acted out of that guilt, resuming responsibilities for her, he would finally take revenge on her.

Bhagwan pointed out that it was irrelevant whether she could in fact manage alone or not; the main thing was that Visuddah should not feel guilty. . . .

. . . and thinking that she can take care of herself may again be just a trick so you don't feel guilty.

Simply don't feel guilty, and don't find any reasons for it. Just enjoy your non-guilt, and if out of that a responsibility arises, that is beautiful. If out of your non-guilt you feel that she needs you, it is beautiful. If you feel she doesn't need you, then it is perfectly good, and there is nothing wrong in it.

Never fulfill any responsibility out of guilt, because then it becomes ugly and an imprisonment. Out of non-guilt, responsibility is a sharing and it is beautiful.

TUESDAY JANUARY 13th

AMITABH *I wrote you a letter, and I feel clearer, but I'm still in it. My mind is doing a beautiful job of driving me crazy! But I feel that mostly I'm witnessing, rather than doing anything about it. . . .*

BHAGWAN   Just be a witness. Don't do anything about it, because anything that you do can never be very deep.

DROP DOING AND PROBLEMS DISAPPEAR

It can be at the most a temporary arrangement. All that man can do is going to be on the surface. So if a problem arises and you do something, temporarily it is solved, but the same problem will arise again in some other way. If there is an indecision, you can patch it up by doing something, but somewhere else the division will bubble up. And this goes on and on. Problems change but the problem goes on and on.

The basic thing is that the problem should dissolve, and that only happens when you simply don't do anything. By just watching it, a distance is created, and the distance goes on becoming bigger and bigger and bigger. One day the distance is so great that suddenly you realise that the problem does not belong to you; it is as if it has never belonged to you. Just distance is needed, and that comes only through witnessing.

All else that man can do is, in a way, self-defeating. For example, if you are feeling a certain doubt or an indecisiveness, in that indecisiveness you try to create a decision. How can decision be born out of indecision? You can only decide that yes, a decision has been reached, but deep underneath a current of indecision goes on growing. There is just a thin layer of deception, a very thin layer, which can be broken any moment by any situation.

In the East this has been one of the basic things—that no problem can be solved by doing anything. In fact the problems arise because man has become a doer. If man can remain with the being only and can drop the doing, problems disappear. In a witnessing consciousness there are no problems. Only in a doer's consciousness do problems arise. So the whole thing is to change the emphasis from doing to just being.

So just watch. Sit aloof and go on seeing the games that the mind goes on playing. One day suddenly, when the distance is right—and you cannot manage it, it just happens—and the perspective is clear, you and the problem are far apart. And there is no bridge: the problem is there and you are here. In fact in that moment you cannot even comprehend how it was bridged before, or how it was that you were so worried about it. It is somewhere in some other world, belonging to somebody else, and it has not even left a scratch on you. The truth of this experience becomes the key to dissolve all problems. So whenever a problem arises, just watch.

It is difficult because the whole western training is to analyse. (Amitabh was a psychotherapist in the West.) Witnessing is a totally different dimension. It is not analysis. The western training is to analyse, to understand it, to find out the cause of it — but you can never come to any end. You can find a cause for one problem, and then you try to find out another cause for that, and it goes on ad infinitum. Every cause in its own turn is an effect. You can go on and on, just like peeling an onion, layer upon layer. An onion is finished sooner or later but the onion that is the human mind is never finished; it is non-ending. It goes on creating its own layers continuously.

In the East we have never tried analysis, because one of the profoundest insights has been that analysis is not going to end it. At the most it can force it backwards, it can put it away, but it can never end it. It is going to be there somewhere, and just forcing it away cannot help.

In the West you try to force the problem, you reduce it to the cause. In the East we try to put consciousness back to its source, and we don't touch the problem at all. You try to force the problem away, and we try to bring consciousness home. We don't touch the problem, but rather remove ourselves from it.

For example, you are there, and you are the problem. In the West, I become interested in you, and I try to force you to go away from my consciousness, and that's how the unconscious is born. In the East, you are the problem, I am the consciousness. I leave you where you are and simply move myself away; then no unconscious is created, no repressions. I move; I don't touch the problem. Just by moving myself into my own core, the necessary distance is created.

The West is also trying to create a distance — by forcing the problem away — but then it creates more problems, because they can never be forced away. In the very effort, in the fight with it, you remain close to it. When you analyse, the same mind that is creating the problem is also analysing it. It is trying to pull you by the shoe strings. You can jump a little, but it is not going to help much. You will be back on the earth again. It is like trying to catch your own tail.

So just watch, and by and by a deep unconcern arises. In that unconcern, everything dissolves. Nothing needs to be done. Simply sit, enjoy, be, and just watch. By and by when the problem understands that Amitabh is not interested in it, it will go.

When a guest is uninvited, unwelcome, and the host does not bother about him, doesn't even say hello, how long will the guest go on knocking at the door? One day he simply goes. Each thought, each problem, is a guest. Don't do anything with them, but remain a host — unconcerned, indifferent, and centred.

How are things going with Anupama?

AMITABH *Beautiful.*

Anupama. Come here!

Several weeks ago Bhagwan had talked to Anupama about the beauty of a love that was given time to mature, about the need to nourish love, and not allow one's affections and energies to be distracted by vague attraction to others.

He told her to set aside a time each day in which she could fantasise whatsoever she wanted to do in reality. He asked her tonight how this was going. She said the feelings still persisted, off and on. . . .

Let it come and go, but don't be worried about it. When it comes, take note, that's all, and in a very indifferent way.

In Buddhism they have a particular method which they call taking notice thrice. If a problem arises — for example, if somebody suddenly feels a sexual urge, or greed, or anger — they have to note three times that it is there. If anger is there, the disciple has to say inwardly three times: anger, anger, anger. Just to take complete note of it so that it doesn't miss the consciousness, that's all. Then he goes on with whatsoever he was doing, mm? He doesn't do anything with the anger but simply notes it thrice.

It is tremendously beautiful. Immediately you become aware of it, take note of it, it is gone. It cannot take grip of you because that can only happen when you are unconscious. This calling thrice makes you so aware inside, that you are separate from the anger. You can objectify it, because it is there and you are here. Buddha told his disciples to do this with everything.

Just try it, and there is nothing to worry about. It is human, and there is nothing to feel guilty about. It is good that you know it comes — don't repress it. Ordinarily, all the cultures and civilizations have been teaching us to repress problems, so that by and by you become unconscious of them — so much so that you forget them, you think that they don't exist.

Just the opposite is the right way. Make them absolutely conscious, and in becoming conscious and focusing on them, they melt. So try this, and don't miss a single moment. Just repeat three times 'again, again, again.' You have to repeat

LIFE CAN BE A SONG, A DANCE

it inside, and if you feel it is helpful, you can repeat it out loud, so Amitabh will also know — 'again, again, again!'

It is going to go, and when it does you will feel really relieved. You already look better! When one is unburdened by these vagrant desires and ideas, one feels more innocent and pure. That fragrance surrounds you, and by and by life becomes a totally different song, a totally different dance. So now start this!

Tonight, two sannyasins asked Bhagwan about problems connected with their work. The first sannyasin's problem was about her work in the ashram.

Many sannyasins work in the ashram — transcribing and editing the daily discourse, caring for the ashram's gardens, house cleaning, cooking, making malas, leading groups, doing library and general office work.

Bhagwan allocates work to people for varying reasons it seems. Some who have had much experience in a particular field may be put to work where their accumulated skills can best be used. Others may be given just the opposite kind of work to what they have been accustomed.

The usual frustrations of a working routine and the problems that come up in relating to other people, are encountered here of course, for the ashram is both marketplace and monastery. Those that live and work here do not live a cloistered and protected life, but are constantly being put into situations which can be used for their growth and maturity.

But work and its related problems take on an entirely different perspective in the knowledge of Bhagwan's being so close by, and the feeling of him being always present in whatsoever one is doing.

The whole concept of work in the ashram is totally different. Whatever the occupation, it seems more like love, or play, or meditation.

If one works with love, then work happens rather than being done as a result of one's effort. The less you are in your work, the more room there is for Bhagwan to work through you, to use you as a medium, a channel.

To work playfully is to be non-serious, yet sincere, in whatever one is doing. There exists a feeling, and it grows stronger and stronger each day now, of a deep rapport, a kinship among those who are involved here in Bhagwan's work. Somehow connected with this is a constant sense of adventure and light-heartedness. People tend not to become overly engrossed or absorbed in their work; it is almost as if it is understood that it is all really just an excuse to be near Bhagwan, to allow him to work on you through the work.

And to be meditative is to be total. One's effort may not be perfect, but if it is total it is enough, more than enough.

The sannyasin who is working in the ashram said she was finding it difficult to enjoy her work of typing. She said she knew it should not matter what she was doing, but nevertheless she found herself fighting against herself all day, telling herself that the work had to be done and was useful.

She said she worked without enthusiasm, without passion, and asked that she be helped to find a more positive attitude.

There is no need to find any attitude. There is no problem if you feel surrendered to me: if I have said to do it, you do. Then it is not a question of your attitude, because that is not going to help. You can find some positive attitude, but within a week it will be gone because you cannot remain in one attitude continuously.

Only a no-mind can remain in one attitude, and in fact it is no-attitude, that is why he remains in one state. Attitudes are bound to change. So if you are trying to make your attitude about it positive, you may be able to by much effort, by suffering and forcing yourself, but then again you will slip back.

Simply surrender to me. Don't think that Purna belongs to Purna. Purna belongs to Bhagwan, and Bhagwan says to type, so type!

Do you understand me? And whenever I see that you are happily typing I will change it! I will give you something more difficult, so don't be worried, mm?

Everything is, in a certain way, going to help you. If you are really interested in changing yourself, then don't

DON'T CLING TO YOURSELF

cling to yourself; otherwise, how are you going to change? If your mind is to be fulfilled then it will become more and more strengthened. If your mind says that you don't like typing, that you prefer something else, and you do that, then it becomes strengthened.

Precisely because you don't like it I say that you are to go on doing it — precisely because of that. It is so that you can have a feeling that you are not a mind, or a slave to the mind; that the mind has no business to dictate, that you can by-pass it and be on your own. This is a great learning and a great discipline.

So there is no need to create any positive attitude. Simply drop all attitudes and just function as a vehicle, a passage, that's all, and you will see everything change.

And when everything is flowing and you are feeling perfectly beautiful, tell me, mm? Good!

DEVAMURTI

What do you want to do with me? Perhaps I shouldn't ask, but I'm very curious, and constantly thinking about possibilities.

Just tell me what possibilities you have been thinking about.

DEVAMURTI

Well, doing something for you in Ireland; doing something about changing my profession into a vocation — which I have difficulties with at the moment — or coming back here to type and do the things that I don't like doing! (Bhagwan laughs)

What type of profession do you have?

DEVAMURTI *I'm a lecturer in psychology.*

And you like it, or not?

DEVAMURTI *I like the teaching, and I see myself as a teacher rather than anything else. But it's difficult to find an aspect within the discipline that I can give my heart to. I've been very proud of being professional for years and that's got to stop . . . . But I like teaching.*

Then continue, because if you like it, it is very creative, and if you really like it you can find ways of being more and more creative in it.

To be a teacher is one of the most creative things in the world, if you have a call for it, an inner quality, mm? It is an art, and teachers, like poets, are born. In a hundred teachers there are rarely one or two real teachers.

As I feel it, you have an inborn quality, so I will not suggest that you drop out of it. This is your vocation, so drop all other alternatives because they are disturbing. Go deep into it, and really become a teacher.

Later I will call you, and you will become a teacher for me. Soon I will need teachers to travel all around the world for me, because I am not going outside this porch!

But be creative, and don't regard it as a profession. Let it become a calling, an inspiration. Don't do it just as a job; love it. There is nothing like it. A painter works with

TO BE A MOTHER IS A REVOLUTION

colours and canvas, a sculptor with marble and stone, but a teacher works with human consciousness, and that is the greatest thing there is.

So you go on working. I am not going to make you a typist! I will make you a teacher soon, but you have to get ready! So go back, continue teaching in the university, and start spreading my message. . . .

PRAFULLA *I'm going to be a mother.*

Mm mm . . . and you want it?

PRAFULLA *Yes, I want it.*

Do you understand what it means? If you want it, it is okay, mm? But one should be more conscious about it. To be a mother means a great revolution, and a radical change.

To be a woman is one thing, and to be a mother is totally another. You are entering into a commitment with somebody you don't know, and you will have to plan your life accordingly. Then your freedom is gone . . . so just think about it.

If you take the responsibility of the whole perspective clearly, you will not be able to be as free as you have been. The responsibility of the child will be on you — and not as a duty. If it is a duty, it will become a burden, and then one starts to take revenge on the child.

Right now you don't know, so everything is good, but when the child comes there are responsibilities. Your freedom is cut completely. You have to think about the child first, and then yourself. The child becomes more important than you who will be secondary. Now you can go on changing lovers and doing whatsoever you like, but once the child is there, things will become different. So think about it because it is a great decision.

If you take it consciously, it is perfectly okay, but don't move into motherhood unconsciously — becoming pregnant by just drifting into it. Before, it was okay, because there were no methods available and pregnancy was always an accident, but now it need not be.

PRAFULLA *It wasn't.*

Then it is okay. If you have taken the step decisively, it is okay and there is no problem. You go into it!

The Nadam Music Meditation group performed for Bhagwan tonight.

The group, consisting of twelve or so sannyasins, formed a semicircle at Bhagwan's feet. Their leader, Kabir, told those who were not in the group about what they usually did. . . .

. . . what we've been doing mostly, these last few weeks in the group, is that we do music from anywhere between thirty seconds and five minutes, just allowing something to come up.

Then somewhere we just keep on listening very carefully. Really, that's the primary thing we're doing, just listening. When

we hear a silence coming, we just stop and allow it.

Allow me to break the silence, and each time there is a silence, feel yourself drop. Feel your consciousness drop lower each time; each time let it go deeper, deeper, deeper . . . and we usually hold hands.

Come close everybody, and participate with them!

The music group formed an inner circle, while other sannyasins sat with hands linked. For several minutes everyone was silent, heads bowed, eyes closed.

Slowly, out of the silence, voices began to rise, tentative at first then becoming bolder. Voices rose and fell, now a murmur, now a rising wave, a crescendo, the singers becoming lost in their vibrations.

Bhagwan sat for much of the time with his eyes closed, his hands clasped gracefully under his chin.

Somehow the silences were richer, more loaded than the sound. It was not an empty, passive silence, but was pregnant with feeling, with energy. It seemed that it was the overflowing of the energy that called every so often for release in song.

Sound rose between silences, rather than silences falling between sound.

After fifteen minutes or so the music came to a peak, lingered there a little, then faded away. After Bhagwan had left, people began to move silently from their places, arms around each other....

Bhagwan said recently in a discourse that music and meditation are not two different and separate things. Meditation is music that has melted into the dimensionless, and music is meditation crystallised in a certain dimension.

If you love music, you love it because somewhere around it you feel meditation happening. You are absorbed in it, and you become drunk with it . . . God starts whispering, your heart starts to beat in a different pattern, one in tune with the universe. . . .

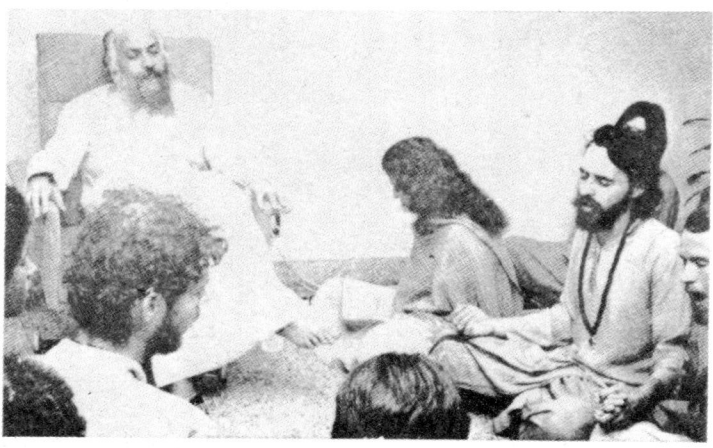

WEDNESDAY JANUARY 14th

A sannyasin said that when she meditated, many pictures would emerge which she liked to draw and become involved with.

BHAGWAN   . . . if pictures come it is a good release, so paint them; you continue it. Just go wild in it, and don't paint through reason.

Don't be worried about what you are making, because it is not a performance. It is not going to be exhibited, and you are not going to show it to anybody. It is just an outpouring.

Paint just like small children. If you give them colour and crayons, they will paint, not even knowing what they are doing. It will be a natural thing: just as grass grows, and birds sing, children paint.

That is the beauty of modern painting. It is more child-like and more primitive than painting has ever been before. The classical painters were very much concerned with the form, with the geometry and mathematics of it, but the modern painter has forgotten everything and all technology has been dropped.

Modern painting is just like a child painting, and tremendously beautiful things have come up. They are meaningless, remember — beautiful, but meaningless. In fact all beauty is meaningless. Wherever meaning enters, mean-ness enters. Wherever there is reason, things become limited.

ALL BEAUTY IS MEANINGLESS

So just paint, mm? And next time you come, bring some paintings! But don't paint with the idea that you are going to show them to me! Only bring those that you have painted without any idea, just irrationally.

Just the other day I was reading about a man, a very rich man, who asked Picasso to paint his portrait. So Picasso painted it.

When the man came to see it, he said that it was good except that he didn't like the nose — so Picasso said he would change it, and the man should return in a few days time.

Picasso became very worried, and the woman who was living with him in those days asked him what he was worrying about. He said, 'I am worried because I don't know where I have painted the nose.'

So like that, mm? Good!

ANAM

After I wrote to you yesterday, I realised that the problem wasn't with Gopi (his girlfriend) but with me.

I've got a real sense of self-disgust. I realise that all my life I've been trying to make myself respectable, and to give myself some kind of esteem.

I've been going after every substitute for love — and for me love just means manipulation. I can't take it because I've got this tremendous fear of being manipulated.

To seek respectability is a substitute, and a worthless substitute, a counterfeit. Only if respect comes through love is it meaningful. If it comes through any other way, then not only is it meaningless, it is poisonous.

That is how a man becomes political. Politics is a substitute for love. When somebody loves you they care about you, they make you feel worthwhile and significant. Whatsoever you are, howsoever you are, you are accepted. But if people miss love they start playing tricks. The trick is to manipulate others' respect by doing something, having something—character, morality—something that people have to give respect to. But it is never fulfilling, and one can go on and on till you need a whole crowd. . . .

You can become a president or a prime minister of a country where millions of people pay you attention. They have to because you are powerful, and you can manipulate and become dangerous.

But even then, the love of one person is more valuable than the whole country looking up to you. One person's love is enough because that is real value.

If you are given respect, it is never for you but for something else. For example, if you are a very good man, moral, the respect is for morality, not for you. If you are very rich, you are respected for your house and your car, not for you. You know too, deep down, that if the car disappears and the house is no longer yours, if you are defeated in the elections and are no longer prime minister, all the respect will disappear, because it was never for you in the first place. So you become afraid. . . .

Respect is for something you have, not for you and what you are. Love is simply for you—whether you are rich or poor, capable of certain things or not, talented or not, it is simply for you. At least to one person you are not a stranger. Somebody has given you his or her total friendship and heart; that is fulfilling enough.

Respect is like when you are hungry and you go on reading a book on cooking. Your appetite will not be satisfied, because you need real food. You can have a

thousand and one books on cooking, but that is not going to help. Love is food—and respect is a book on cooking.

Everybody has been conditioned, taught from the very childhood, to become respectable: to come first in the class, to win the gold medal in the university—to do something so that you become precious. It has been taught that only by doing something can you become precious—while you simply are! Whether you do something or not is secondary, irrelevant.

So if you have become aware of it, drop it immediately.

It is a dangerous poison, so don't allow it to remain in you a single moment. Accept yourself; because whenever you want respect from others, it simply shows that you don't respect yourself. Otherwise what is the need?

You hate and condemn yourself, so you go on creating masks to hide behind, to deceive others with. At least you can try to deceive others, even if you cannot deceive yourself. But nobody is deceived, because those people are trying the same trick themselves! The whole world is in the same mess.

So the first thing is to respect yourself, and not to make any demands on yourself. There is no should to life. Life is as it ought to be; it already is. You just have to accept and enjoy yourself, and give yourself in love. If respect comes through love it is beautiful. And it always comes through love because there is no other way.

. . . and I don't see any problem. You have simply created them. There are people who really do have problems, and people who don't have any, but just to remain occupied they create them.

So drop them, they are simply rubbish, and start to enjoy from this very moment. Right? Give it a try!

AMRIT

> *I feel a bit without any direction. I don't quite know what to do between now and when I go back to England in March.*
>
> *. . . I feel like I ought to be doing more, working harder. I'm not doing very much in the way of actual work.*

Never go ahead, remain with the present. Today is enough unto itself, and March is far away, millions of miles away. There is no need to be worried about it. Why waste these moments?

Live now, and when March comes you will be there, so whatsoever life demands at that moment, you respond. If you plan something from here, you are creating a problem for yourself in two ways.

Firstly, you are wasting this moment which could have been lived: by planning you are wasting it. Secondly, whatsoever you plan is never going to be exactly as you plan, never, because there are millions of causes that go on working to create the future. So it will never fit with your plans, and that is going to make you frustrated.

Man thinks that he proposes and God disposes. God is not there to dispose anybody's plans. The disposition is in the very proposition. In the very planning, you are creating a structure. The future is open, and it cannot follow anybody's structure.

You waste this moment, and then you will waste those moments of the future in being frustrated. And out of frustration you will plan even harder; you will think that because you weren't accurate in your planning you missed. Again you are missing the point.

Howsoever accurate the plan, it cannot be exactly that way because you are not alone here, mm? You can go out on the street and a drunken driver hits you — and it was never in your plans. You go to Goa, and some germs enter you and give you hepatitis. It was not in your plan, but the germs were planning their life, and the drunken driver was going on his way.

Live this moment totally, and the next will come out of it. Live an unplanned life, because only then it is life. . . .

And I don't see that you are not working hard, you are doing as much as you can. That too is greed — that one should do more. That greed can never be fulfilled, because whatever you do, you can always imagine that more can be done. Greed is never satisfied.

So drop it, and whatsoever you can do you are doing. Enjoy it rather than expecting more. Bring a deeper quality to it, rather than a quantitative increase. And forget about the future!

How is your relationship going?

VEENA
> *Well, I feel good, and it's the nicest thing that has happened to me for a very long time. But what's happening is that he wants me to just be a friend— and I want more than that. He says that he cares about me, but he is not turned on by me....*

Don't insist for more, just friendship is perfectly good. There are two possibilities for every human being. One is that you fall in love, and by and by friendship grows out of that. Lovers always become friends in the end—and if they cannot, then somewhere they have missed and something has gone wrong—because by and by the passion settles.

Passion is a very very excited state of mind which you cannot live in for very long. By the time the honeymoon is over, so is the passion. Then friendship arises. So this is one possibility—that two people fall in love. There is tremendous passion; they are almost in a cyclone, lost. They move at the peaks, they have completely forgotten the valleys for a few days.

NOBODY CAN LIVE AT THE PEAK

But nobody can live at the peak; at the most you can be there for a holiday. One settles in the valley.

So by and by a love relationship settles and becomes calm and tranquil and harmonious—then friendship arises. Husband and wife become like brother and sister. But there are problems, because once the fever has gone, the woman starts thinking that the man doesn't love her enough now, and the man thinks the same of the woman.

But the other possibility is that you start as friends, without any passion. The trouble will be that the mind will be asking for passion in the beginning. If you can drop that and not be worried about it, you can grow in friendship, so that by and by without any passion or peak you will come to the valley and settle in it.

And my feeling is that if love starts by friendship, though it may be difficult in the beginning, in the end it is very very beautiful, because you never miss anything. If from the beginning a friendship can remain a friendship, it will go deeper; it will not go higher, but it will go deeper and will settle.

This type of relationship is difficult in the beginning, and the other type is easy to begin with, but difficult in the end. In fact if you look at the whole, both are the same. So don't make it a problem, or Prem (her boyfriend) will start escaping!

A sannyasin told Bhagwan that all her meditations became latihan, but sometimes there was no movement at all.

Latihan is a meditation in which one allows the body to be taken over, possessed, and to move as it will in slow and graceful movements. Bhagwan has given people this meditation to do on their own, in the past, and it is also incorporated in one of the meditations that are done during camp time—the Gourishankar meditation.

The sannyasin went on to say . . .

> ... the energy stops moving, and the muscles in the lower part of my abdomen go into contractions and then this part of my body, (indicating neck) contracts as well, for maybe minutes. Then there's like, a relaxation, a very sudden relaxation.
>
> Sometimes I feel very floating, and at other times I become very aggressive and reckless. It happens after I've done the Gourishankar, and I drive my bicycle home like a madman!

Stop the Gourishankar, but do the other meditations.

Everything is going well; it is just that this is how it happens in latihan. First there are the gross movements of the body, and then the subtle movements of the inner structure of the body, the contractions of the muscles. One day these movements will also disappear. Don't try to force them though, allow them. As the body movements have disappeared, these will too. Then you will have a really flowing body, really alive.

Otherwise many parts of the body are dead. Those muscles which are not really relaxed are contracting, and through contracting they will become flexible. So it is going well. Continue it.

Sometimes when latihan is going deep, anything concerned with eyes can be a disturbance, so don't do the Gourishankar.

The meditation that Bhagwan is referring to consists of four stages:

In the first stage, breathing is done slowly and deeply. You inhale slowly, and then hold the breath for as long as is comfortable.

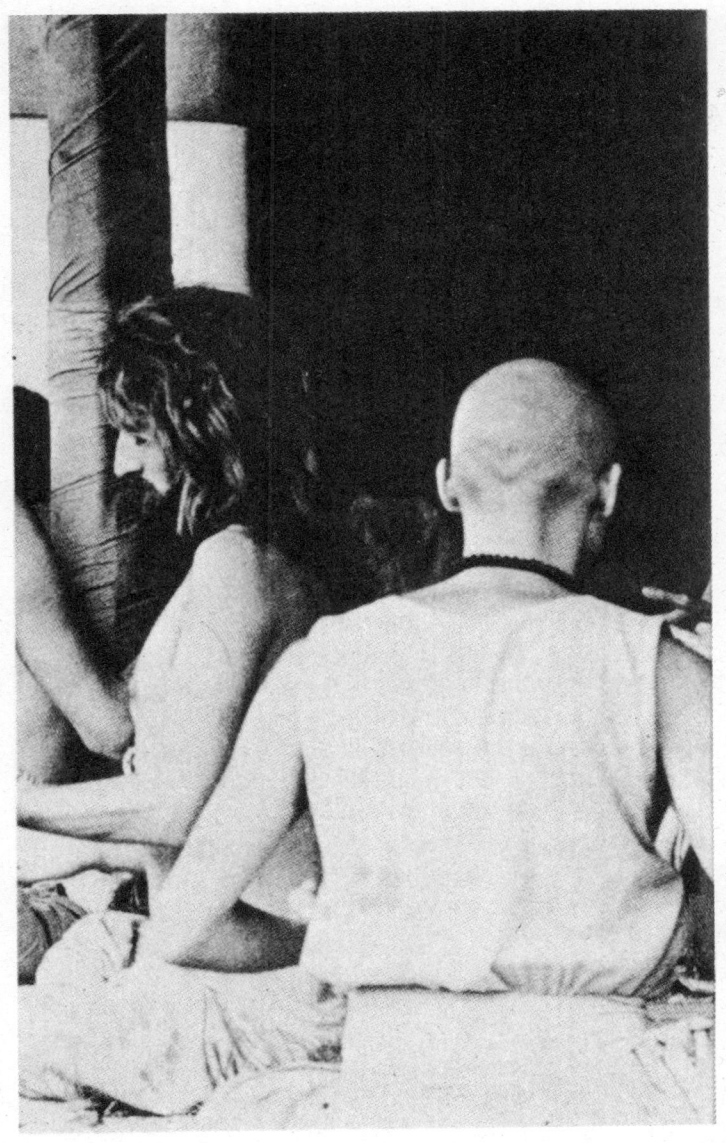

Exhalation is also slow, and when all the breath has been expired, again you pause on the out breath for as long as is comfortably possible. This is for fifteen minutes.

In the second stage you gaze at a flickering blue light—softly 'as if gazing at one's beloved'.

The third stage is fifteen minutes of latihan, described earlier, then a final fifteen minute period of just resting. This is done in the evening, when the light of the day has gone.

Bhagwan went on to ask the sannyasin how she was feeling on the whole.

PIPASA

I think I like to move really close to people, but then I become afraid that I will be rejected. But I've been able to come closer to people than ever before.

No, you will be able to move even closer. You need first to see that when somebody rejects you, he is not in fact rejecting you; he is simply saying that he doesn't fit with you. He may even like you, but somehow the energies don't fit.

So no rejection is personal—nor is any acceptance personal; deep down they are energy phenomena. If somebody falls in love with you and accepts you deeply, it doesn't mean that he has accepted you, or you, him. It simply means that these two energies are meeting on a deeper level, and you are just instrumental.

Sometimes energies don't fit, and you can't do anything about it, can't force them to meet. But from childhood we are taught that every rejection is a personal thing, and that acceptance is personal too, but they are just energy phenomena.

So don't be afraid of rejection. Otherwise how will you move closer? Move closer, because it is worth the risk of being rejected. It is good if a person can simply say that he does not want to move deeper with you, because if he moves with you, yet deep down there is a feeling of no affinity with you, then that is dangerous. Sooner or later you will be fighting and quarrelling and destroying each other.

So say if you don't feel good about moving closer with someone, but don't hurt him. Always be true, because some people who cannot say no, who are afraid of hurting the other, make their whole life a mess. . . . By and by they completely forget how to judge with whom they fit.

A sannyasin told Bhagwan that he had been being intimate with different women, and wondered if he should continue to do that.

There is nothing wrong in it, but just don't get too involved. That will be a distraction right now. Let the intimacy be more like friendship than like love, because right now that will be more helpful.

Once you change friendship into love, you are moving in troubled waters, so wait a little. When you have a really rooted and centred being, then move, and there will be no problem. But first one should become so totally oneself that you can move into love and remain undistracted. Then you can go to any depth in relationship, but somewhere deep down you remain above and beyond it. You become like a lotus flower — in the water, but untouched by it.

I am not against love, I am all for it, but to move in a love relationship one should have a certain maturity, a certain integration. Then love is really beautiful and helps you to grow; otherwise it can become very crippling and destroy you completely.

Love is destroying millions of people. In the name of love, more people are destroyed than in the name of war. We never become aware of it because it is never reported in the newspapers, but in the name of love there is such ugliness, such jealousy, anger and continuous quarrelling. The war is nothing by comparison, it is a tiny affair.

But this has to be so because people who go into love are not yet worthy of it. Before you enter the shrine of love, you have to be worthy of it. That worthiness comes only when your flame is centred and has become silent.

What I mean by this is that when you are capable of being absolutely alone, and when there is no need to move in love, then love is beautiful. When there is no need, no obsession, then there is no dependence, so when you move into love it will be a sharing. You want to share because you have so much, and you want to share it with someone with whom you feel an attunement.

But if you go into love to seek happiness, then you are wrong. Then love will only give you misery. If you go into love to share happiness, then love is tremendously beautiful, the greatest experience there is. Can you see the distinction? If you go to find happiness you will find only misery, because you were already miserable. A miserable man moving into love is going into even deeper miseries — and the other is also in the same plight. The other is also seeking somebody in search of happiness. Both are miserable, and both meet together in search of happiness. You can just see the absurdity of it! The misery will not only be doubled, it will be multiplied.

So first become happy and blissful, then move into love. Love is a function of bliss. Bliss is not an outcome of love; rather, love is an outcome of bliss. That is what Jesus means when he says that God is love. You can change it completely, and say love is God—it is perfectly true too. You can even forget the name God, love is enough. Love is God, but then that love has a different quality, a different dimension, than what is ordinarily called love.

So first become ready, worthy, and full of bliss—then move. But right now just be friendly, no more than that! Good!

Bhagwan then asked the sannyasin how he was feeling after completing the Enlightenment Intensive.

ALOK *I was very blessed to experience myself as the silent one for some time.*

Very good! You are getting more silent every day. Just enjoy it.

Silence has something in it that is very much like sadness. It is not sadness, but it is very much like it. So when you start becoming silent, you may also feel a certain type of sadness. Don't be afraid of that, or you will start trying to get out of it.

It is not sadness, but just the feeling of silence, the depth, gives you a certain sadness. It is beautiful, mm? People who go into silence have to encounter this problem, and have to understand that there are different types of sadness. There is a sadness that comes out of frustration; a sadness that comes out of being empty, and inner poverty. And there is a sadness that comes out of silence, out of total fullness, but it is also alive.

That's why, if you look at Buddha's face, you will feel a little sad. Jesus' face has been continuously misinterpreted. Christians started to think that he was a sad man, but he was simply silent. They say that he never laughed, and he may not have, because he had such a subtle smile that only very perceptive people could be able to understand it. He was so silent that a certain sadness surrounded him, but that is not the sadness we know. His sadness is totally different; its quality is different because it is not of this world. It has nothing to do with any negative emotion; it is absolute positivity.

So remember this, because soon you will start feeling silent and very alone. Don't become afraid of that aloneness either, or your mind will start thinking to move into relationships, into society, to become occupied — and that is dangerous. When you start feeling aloneness, nourish it and help it to grow. Feed it with all that you have, so that it becomes a very deep experience.

Silence will give you sadness, and aloneness. You will need a little time to become familiar with those different shades and different flavours, mm? So if you start feeling sad or alone, immediately come and tell me, mm?

THURSDAY JANUARY 15th

A sannyasin said that since his girlfriend, also a sannyasin, had been involved in a serious car accident some months ago, she had changed quite dramatically, and seemed no longer to be the woman he had known before.

Bhagwan said he felt that she was in a very deep crisis, and in need of much tolerance and care.

BHAGWAN   Sometimes it happens after such severe accidents that the whole personality changes, and may become split. Your left hand may not know what your right hand is doing. I feel this is part of her situation.

So have a little more care, and be alert. When the body suffers such a collapse, the mind is also affected, because the mind is part of the body and they are deeply related. Take care, because she may try to destroy the relationship. Don't be a party to that. If she goes on being angry and saying negative things to you, you may start drifting away.

But she needs you. She may not know it, but she needs you. You have a responsibility, now more than ever. So be loving, and don't pay too much attention to anything she says. This will be a deep meditation, and a great experience for you, because when somebody is loving, it is easy to love them, but if they are angry and continuously trying to destroy the relationship, then to be loving is something exceptional. It gives you a new integration of being.

Whenever you do something that is, in a way, supernatural, it gives you a height of being.

Only your love will be able to bridge the gap that has come to her mind, mm? If you listen to her, she may try to force you away. This may be just an effort to see if you really love her. This sort of problem arises in such situations.

There may be a deep fear of whether she will still be loved or not, of whether she will be rejected by you because now she is no longer beautiful, she is crippled, and this and that. These ideas come to a woman's mind more naturally, because for a woman, the body consciousness is very very deep.

A man never thinks about the body much, but a woman thinks about the body continuously. Woman is the body. So, because she has been in such an accident, she will be afraid that you don't love her anymore. Before you can reject her, she will play the game of rejecting you. Then she can feel happy and good, because she can tell herself that she rejected you, she was not rejected by you.

So be careful, and love her as much as you can and soon she will relax. Once she knows that you still love her, and that this accident doesn't matter, then she will withdraw all these things that she has been saying. Once she becomes certain that there is no rejection from your side, then her rejection will disappear, and you will find a completely new person arising. For the first time you will see her real self.

Whenever a woman comes to know that she is accepted as she is, that there is no condition for her acceptance, she becomes beautiful for the first time; a grace of a different world arises in her. Then the beauty is no longer of the body, it is something from the depth, and you can see and feel the glow of it. When she carries an aura of grace, even an ugly woman can become beautiful. Ordinarily even beautiful women are not graceful,

THIS CAN BECOME A TRANSFORMATION

because that aura has not come yet.

In the East we have been in deep search for that grace, but in the West, people have still not touched upon it. The eastern and western beauty, and particularly that of a woman, is totally different. In the East we call a woman beautiful if she is graceful. When something beyond the body goes on overflowing and surrounds the body, only then is she beautiful. In the West the physiological is more important than the spiritual.

She is in a deep crisis, and only you can help her to come out of it—so there is a great responsibility on you. It will be very enriching for you both. The whole accident can become a transformation. . . .

A sannyasin said that he felt he had regressed lately, because he was less happy now then he had been months ago when he had first taken sannyas. Then too he had felt clearer in his feelings, his love, for Bhagwan. Now the love fluctuated; sometimes it was present, sometimes it seemed to disappear.

It happens, mm? because the mind cannot remain in one state. It changes from positive to negative, and from negative to positive. But wait, and just watch it, because soon the positive will come again, and this time it will be greater than the first time.

But always remember that the negative turn will come again. It is just like day and night following each other. Unless you transcend both, unless you become such a pure witness that you are not bothered by either and become indifferent and unconcerned, these states come and go. And unless that state comes, things will always change — from bad to good, from good to bad. Sometimes you will be flowing and happy, and other times you will feel unhappy and frozen.

This is natural, because mind is a wheel that goes on moving. One spoke comes up, then goes down; another comes up, and then goes down—it goes on moving like a wheel. In India, we represent the word 'world' by the symbol of a wheel. The Indian word for world, 'sansar', means the wheel. Success is followed by failure, hope by hopelessness, happiness by misery.

One has to understand that this is the natural state of the mind and cannot be changed. The thing is to accept it, and not to get identified with it. When happiness comes, don't say, 'I am happy.' Say, 'Happiness has come, I am the watcher.' Remain separate and distant. When unhappiness comes, again do the same. Watch, and note the fact: 'Unhappiness has come.' Don't make any judgements, don't cling or push it away; rather, just watch.

You will see, by and by, that moods come and go and you remain undisturbed, undistracted. That's what we call awareness. All else is identification and unawareness. So try this, mm? . . . and it is natural, whatsoever is happening is natural.

The sannyasin said that in the down moments, even doubts about sannyas came up.

Mm, that's natural, and it will happen many times, because when the negative moment comes, everything becomes negative. You will doubt sannyas, you will doubt me, you will doubt yourself. You will even start doubting the previous moments of happiness; you may start thinking that it was just imagination. When one is in the dark night of negativity, one even doubts that the day that has preceded it was there; maybe it was your delusion. When doubt grips your soul, it grips from all directions. One becomes simply doubtful, it is not a question of about what.

I'M LOOKING FOR PROTECTION

When the moment of trust comes, you simply trust — not only me, you trust everybody. In that moment of moving higher and higher, who bothers to doubt?

Just remain a witness to it. That is the work to be done. Be unconcerned, and remember that everything passes. Nothing can be stable and permanent in this world, because the very nature of the world is change. Except for change, everything changes.

If you watch, suddenly you become the eternal, and you are no longer part of the changing world. The changes may be all around you, you may be surrounded by a thousand and one changes, but you remain the centre of the cyclone.

Try it, and then tell me later on. Good!

Nitya, how are you? Something to say?

NITYA

Well, I was going to ask very much the same as Muni — about just how long it goes on, the cycles of the mind. When I go through those dark moments, it's like, I don't feel I've got the strength to go through it. It's like a fear of madness. There is this incredible feeling of insecurity, of everything shaking.

In those moments I just don't have any conviction of my own strength to carry on. It's like I'm looking for protection. I've felt this desire recently just for somebody, somewhere, to protect me, to save me from something I know not what.

I mean, that moment passes, but at the time it is so intense that I almost feel suicidal and very weak.

Are you feeling like that right now?

NITYA   *Not right now. I'm just coming out of that space which I've been in for the last few days.*

Just come here, and lie down here. (Bhagwan indicates the floor in front of him) Head that side, and feet that side.
Just look at the ceiling as if you are mad, have a mad look on your face.

Bhagwan leans forward in his chair, and shines the torch on her face. Nitya lies quite still, without any obvious expression on her face.

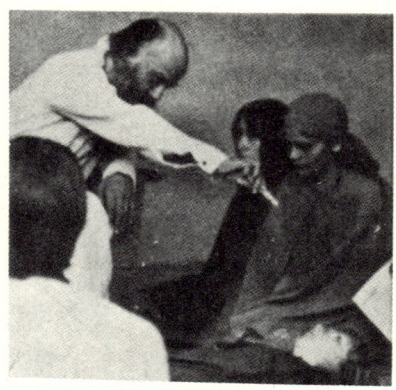

I AM HERE TO PROTECT YOU

Allow madness, just look like a madman.

NITYA   *Well, madness to me is fear.*

Let it be, let it be. Allow it to take possession so that the whole body is possessed. Where exactly do you feel the fear?

NITYA   *Now it's in my back, other times it's mostly in my head.*

Mm, very good. Is it ordinarily in the head?

NITYA   *When it comes it is like an incredible tightness here.* (she indicates her forehead)

So do one thing. Whenever it comes, lie down. If it drops from the head to the back, it is very good. Whenever you feel it, do this in three steps.

Bring the feeling of fear completely into the head, as if you are accumulating it there, concentrating it there. Imagine the fear and the anguish, death and suicide, are coming from all over the body and being collected in the head. Make your head as heavy as possible.

Then imagine that the fear is leaving your head and flowing down into the spine. Lie down on your back and let the feeling move into your backbone.

Then when you feel that the fear has moved to the

spine, dance a wild dance — just for two or three minutes — and it will disappear completely.

Do it for at least three weeks, and then tell me. There is nothing to worry about. I am here to protect you!

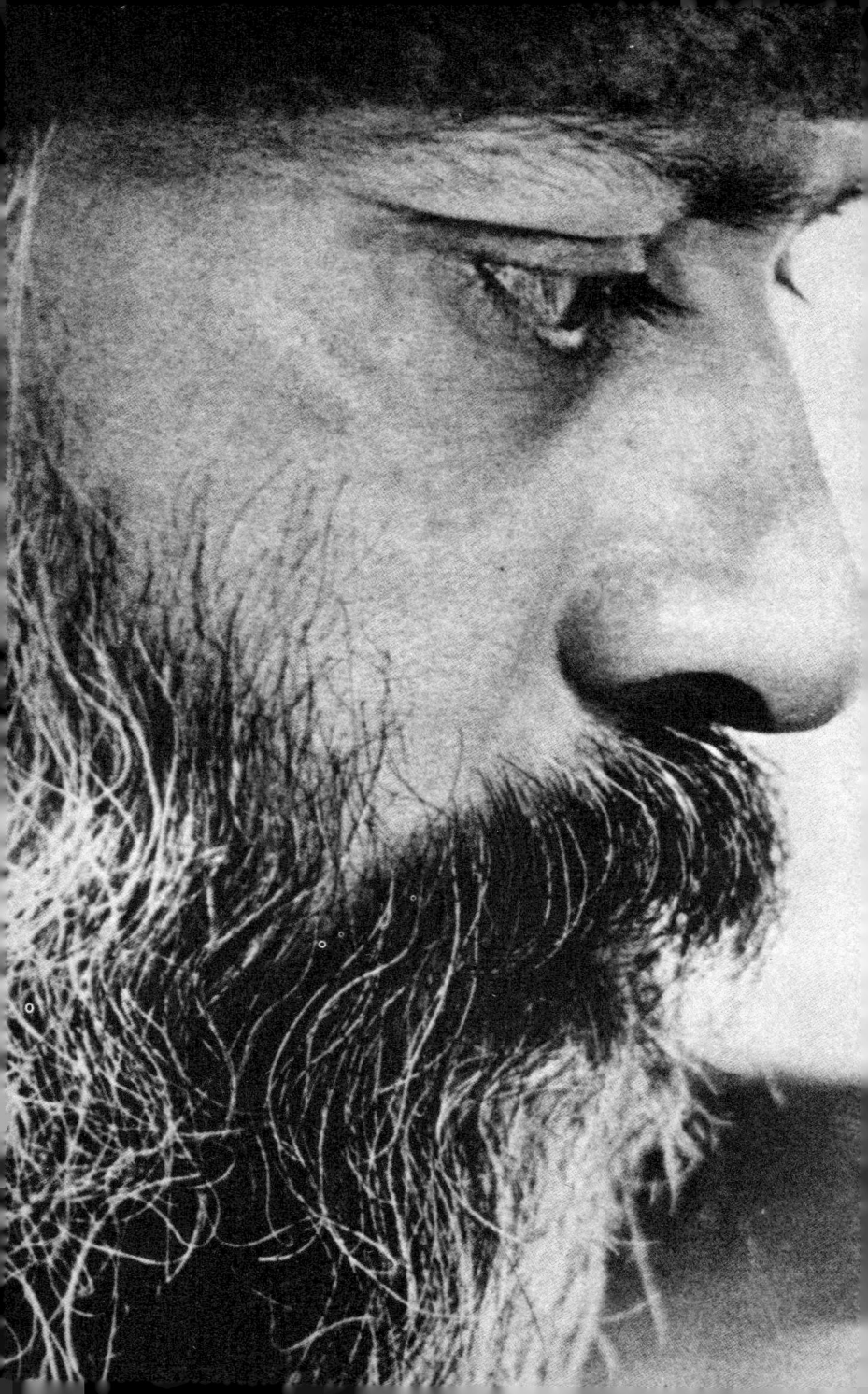

EPILOGUE

His Words . . .

Flowers and honey, knives and flames,
a hammer on the rock.

If you want to understand Bhagwan
you will have to leave your head behind.

To be with him
is to surrender your ideologies,
your preconceptions, your conditionings . . .

To be with him
is to die and be reborn . . .

To be with him
is to fall in love as never before . . .

There is an understanding that comes with love,
deeper than that of the head.

Deep enough
to encompass opposites

Subtle enough
to be conveyed without words

Trusting enough
to let go, and to flow.

For a complete list of books by Bhagwan Shree Rajneesh, please contact the Rajneesh Foundation, 17 Koregaon Park, Poona 411 001 Maharastra, India.